Social Studies
and the World

World

Teaching Global Perspectives

Merry M. Merryfield

and

Angene Wilson

NCSS
Bulletin 103

National Council for the Social Studies

8555 Sixteenth Street • Suite 500 • Silver Spring, Maryland 20910

www.**socialstudies**.org

Editorial staff on this publication: Steven S. Lapham, Michael Simpson
Design/Production: Cowan Creative, San Jose, CA. www.cowancreative.com

Library of Congress Control Number: 2005927850
ISBN: 978-0-87986-097-4

Printed in the United States of America

5 4 3 2 1

DEDICATION

We dedicate this book to our granddaughters

Candler Isabella Cate
Grace Caroline Cate
Allison Anne McElroy
Erin Suzanne McElroy

and to all the children of their generation

May their education be global

Contents

Introduction

And so, my fellow Americans, ask not what your country can do for you, ask what you can do for your country. My fellow citizens of the world, ask not what America will do for you, but what together we can do for the freedom of man.
JOHN F. KENNEDY

Why this Bulletin?

The pace of the world's economic, political, technological, population and environmental changes poses critical challenges for teachers. It is difficult to keep abreast of events in another region, let alone the whole world. Yet we know that our students need to be informed about many global issues that affect their lives—terrorism and other threats to security, the global movement of jobs and labor, immigration and refugees, pollution, and the rising costs of oil, to name only a few. They also need to understand the cultural and historical contexts of global issues. More than any previous generation, today's students will be actors on a global stage. Their lives will be shaped by events and issues around the planet, and they will influence the world through their substantial purchasing power and their political and environmental decisions.

This bulletin was developed to help teachers prepare students for citizenship in a culturally diverse and globally interconnected world. As stated in the NCSS Position Statement on Preparing Citizens for a Global Community: Students should "develop the skills, knowledge and attitudes needed for responsible participation in a democratic society and in a global community in the twenty-first century. . . A global perspective is attentive to the interconnectedness of the human and natural environment and the interrelated nature of events, problems or ideas."[1]

The NCSS statement distinguishes between global education and international studies, with the latter focused on the in-depth study of a specific area or region of the world to develop knowledge and understanding of another culture. While both of the authors come originally out of area specializations, in this bulletin we are particularly concerned with a global perspective that sees the earth as whole from space and from the multiple perspectives of its many peoples. We emphasize the perspectives and voices of people who are not always heard.

The NCSS social studies standards make an important contribution to global education, especially Theme **IX**, **GLOBAL CONNECTIONS**. We know teachers are accustomed to working with NCSS standards, discipline standards, and state standards and can include those as they develop their own plans.

Teachers we work with want to deal with the concept of globalization both historically and currently as they prepare students to participate in the world. Their wish is the context for this bulletin, and we discuss it in more detail at the end of Chapter 1, The Many Dimensions of Global Education, and in the beginning of Chapter 6, Teaching Global Issues. In both chapters we mention and quote from a number of people who have written about globalization. Chapter 1 also outlines the elements of global education, recognizes the controversial nature of global education, and looks at the relationship between multicultural and global education. Chapter 2 looks at five dimensions of the impact of international and cross-cultural experience and then translates those into attributes of global competence.

Chapter 3, Teaching for Understanding of World Cultures, includes explanations of substantive culture learning and stages in culture learning and then describes six strategies that are essential in teaching about culture.

Chapter 4, Global World History, begins with a brief history of teaching world history and then describes possible ways of organizing the course.

Chapter 5, Connecting the United States to the World, recognizes that a global perspective can be infused into U.S. History and U.S. Government courses and briefly discusses possibilities of using comparative studies and combining U.S. and world history.

Chapter 6, Teaching Global Issues, considers what issues might be taught and where in the curriculum. The chapter reiterates the importance of globalization and also suggests ways to connect problems and progress, and to identify global issues that are faced by both the United States and other countries.

Chapter 7, Teaching Current Events from a Global Perspective, describes how social studies teachers are addressing current events and how current events can be taught from a global perspective.

Although some chapters focus on discipline-based topics, each chapter provides ideas that can inform every social studies course. We integrate content to bring together cultural, political, economic, historical and geographic dimensions. We also utilize literature and media as resources to teach about other cultures and the power of people's experiences and perspectives. We value interdisciplinary social studies and the possibilities of working with teachers of language arts, foreign languages, English as a second language, art, music, technology and science.

Given the dynamic nature of our world today, infusing global perspectives into the social studies is always a work in progress. We ground students in the past as we involve them in the present and prepare them for the future.

Who Are We?

We are teacher educators who are passionate about getting young people to understand and participate in the world. Our passion comes from our experiences as secondary social studies teachers and social studies professors in the U.S. (Merry in Georgia and Ohio, Angene in Michigan and Kentucky), as Peace Corps volunteers (Merry in Sierra Leone and Angene in Liberia) and through many other cross-cultural experiences within the U.S. and other countries that have taught us much about ourselves and others across the planet. We rejoice in the increasingly multicultural and international natures of the cities that we now call home—Columbus, Ohio, and Lexington, Kentucky.

Throughout the bulletin we draw from our own experiences and those of teachers with whom we work face to face and online. We hope our ideas and illustrations will inspire teachers who read these chapters to infuse global perspectives within their teaching and learning.

We all live in the world, as well as in the United States. We are comfortable with the notion of educating our students to be citizens of their local communities, their states, our nation, and our world. We believe that our job as social studies teachers is to help students become citizens who will make our nation and our world a better place for all peoples.

As we write this introduction, Merry has recently returned from Taiwan and is teaching a course on infusing global perspectives in education to educators from Ohio, Tennessee,

Turkey, Botswana, Germany, South Korea, Peru, Suriname, and Kazakhstan. Angene has just returned from a conference in Mexico and is preparing to take teachers to Ghana in July. Merry is remembering yesterday's teacher workshop on Somali culture and history and thinking about her upcoming research study in Hong Kong. Angene is remembering standing last week on the church steps where Hidalgo spoke to begin the Mexican drive for independence. This week she has talked with students and colleagues who have returned from Botswana, China, Ireland, Kyrgyzstan, and Vietnam. She has also attended the U.S. citizenship naturalization ceremony for a Liberian friend. We are both reading and watching the news—from Iraq and from many other places.

Global education, it seems to us, begins with learners recognizing how their own experiences, beliefs, and values shape their worldviews. It is easier for students to appreciate other people's standpoints if they have identified ways in which their own cultural beliefs and norms shape their ways of making sense of events and issues. In the rest of this chapter, we suggest some ways teachers and students can begin to share their perspectives and connections to the world both individually and as a whole class.

Readers will note that this bulletin is dedicated to our four granddaughters. Between the ages of one and five, Allison, Candler, Erin, and Grace will live through the 21st century. We wonder what experiences, beliefs, and values will shape their worldviews and how they will make sense of the world and act in it. We hope their teachers will teach from a global perspective.

Getting Started

Below are some activities (Teaching Ideas 1-5) that encourage students to reflect upon their own cultures and their connections with the world and recognize how their worldviews are informed by their lived experiences and knowledge of power. These activities are often used by teachers at the beginning of a new year or a new unit to build awareness and motivate students to reflect on their own experiences and recognize global connections. Relatively simple activities are described first, followed by more complex ones. You can learn more about Merry in the "Tree of Life" activity and more about Angene in the "I Am... Poem" as below we use our own lives to illustrate these activities.

When students reflect on their own identity, their experiences with "The Other," and their global connections, they begin the journey towards global understanding.

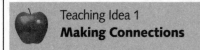

Teaching Idea 1
Making Connections

Goal: Students recognize basic economic, cultural, political, and environmental connections across countries and regions.

Procedures: Making Connections is a simple activity that is successful with children, young people, and adults as an introduction to the concept of global connections. Begin by putting a dot in the middle of a chalkboard or dry erase board to represent the place where you are. Then ask the audience to imagine that the dot is in the middle of a mental world map. Next ask people to brainstorm connections and draw lines from the dot to approximate locations in the world.

Consider the background of the audience or class when asking questions to simulate brainstorming. For children you might suggest looking at what people eat, play with and wear; students like checking labels. Make business connections such as exports and imports and multinational corporations. Ask for people connections, including "roots" and heritages, friends, the military, missionaries, pen pals, immigrants, refugees, and exchange students. See if they can think of environmental connections, energy connections (where does their gasoline originate?), or political connections.

Be sure Canada and Mexico are not taken for granted. Encourage connections to all continents and fill up the board. Consider distinguishing between incoming and outgoing connections and two-way connections. Discuss blending and mixing—in food, music, clothes, media, and people.

Debriefing the connections is crucial, and the debriefing can lead to research groups who will find out more about local/global ties. For example, in central Kentucky, students would quickly note connections with Mexico, so research might include visiting a Mexican mercado or supermarket and interviewing a police officer who spent several weeks in a training program in Mexico to learn Spanish and find out about the towns of origin for local migrant workers. In Ohio, the decision to end tariffs on steel might be raised. What does that mean for steelworkers, for car manufacturers? What are the advantages and disadvantages of free trade—in our community, and in communities elsewhere in the world?

Believing that we must develop "the capacity of our students to perceive where in the world they are," Chadwick Alger suggests a similar activity: having students record their personal world connections. "This can be followed by an evaluation of the local impact of these world connections and their likely impact abroad. And this in turn can lead to class discussion of desirable changes in world relationships and how they might be achieved."[2] He encourages students to learn what other local people are doing in organizations like Sister Cities and international exchange programs and world affairs councils, as well as for campaigns such as Adopt A Minefield or earlier opposition to apartheid.

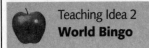

Goal: Students identify global connections in the school and community.

Procedures: The World Bingo game works well as an introductory activity. Teachers construct a bingo sheet. Each square has a connection with another part of the world such as those related to trade (I have shoes made in Asia), languages (I know someone who speaks Spanish), experiences outside the U.S. (I have traveled to Canada) or knowledge (I can name 5 African nations). The teacher passes out the Bingo sheets and instructs students to interact with each other to find people who can write their names in the boxes because they can answer 'yes' to the content of the squares. The goal is to fill out as much of the sheet as possible. No student may sign his or her name on more than two squares; the student can sign two squares on his or her own sheet. The first student to fill all squares yells "Global Bingo!"

The Bingo content can be geared to the characteristics of the students as well as the content of a course. With a group of students from many backgrounds, "born in Bosnia" or "born in El Salvador" might work. In schools without students from many national backgrounds, Bingo should include the exchange students in the school or other international connections of their community or parents. A teacher who knows the parents and the community may be able to develop squares such as "parent works for Toyota," "knows someone who has adopted a child from China," "knows someone who has gone to Haiti on a mission trip," "knows someone who is overseas with the military," "knows someone whose parents were born in India" or "knows someone who was born in Mexico." (These could all work in central Kentucky.) Knowing what students wear—and where it is made—what music they listen to, what food they eat, what cars they or family members drive will lead to other Bingo squares.

As with any activity, the discussion afterward is very important. The teacher might ask: "What surprised you?" and "In what ways has our community changed in the last ten years?" Bingo answers can also be related to a world map, and questions asked about what parts of the world the students and community are and are not related to and why and why not.

Teachers can create their own Bingo sheets to match the content of a particular unit (as an introduction to a unit on East Asia, for example). International Bingo games are published in *Passport to Learning, Teaching Social Studies to ESL Students*, NCSS Bulletin 101, and in the American Federation of Teachers curriculum, *Down the Street, Around the World: A Starter Kit for Global Awareness*. (See the Resources at the end of the chapter.) They include squares such as:

- Do you have a Spanish surname?
- Do you listen to music that comes from another country?
- English is not the first language for someone in my family
- I know how to eat with chopsticks
- I believe that medical breakthroughs could be achieved by studying the rainforests.
- My favorite professional sports team has a player from another country.

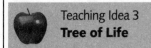

Goal: Students reflect upon their experiences and knowledge and discuss how people learn their own cultural norms and those of others.

Procedures: It is important that students identify events and people who have made a significant difference in their knowledge or understanding of people different from themselves. Trees can provoke intriguing analogies with human lives. Tree roots can signify our family's heritage, its values and beliefs. The trunk can stand for early experiences, and each limb can represent different events or people that through the years have taught us about other cultures, religions, or other ways of thinking about the world. Students enjoy deciding on which tree they are most like—some have chosen oaks, redwoods, a dogwood, "a willow blowing in the wind," a palm tree with coconuts, even a cactus.

Assignment: Choose a tree to symbolize your life and sketch it out on a large sheet of paper. In the roots, make notes on your family's "roots"; in the trunk add in values and beliefs you were taught as a young child by your family or people in your community. Each limb identifies a person or an event that taught you about people different from your own family. From the lowest limbs to the higher ones, provide a chronology of experiences on how you have learned about other cultures, religions, languages, etc. You might include how you have learned about different people through travel, readings, movies, new neighbors, school, or adventures. In the example below, Merry chose a pine tree from her native Tennessee. See the following page for an example model of the Tree of Life assignment for her classes.[3]

Commentary: As I begin to share my own Tree of Life on an overhead, I ask my students to think back to when they were growing up and how they learned about people different from themselves. I begin with the climate of the community towards diversity and the racism that was part of my childhood in the 1950s and 1960s. Since many of my students today never experienced Jim Crow, I describe the segregated schools, neighborhoods, restaurants, and buses. I share an experience I had as a young girl when some friends and I went downtown on a Saturday afternoon and found black teenagers lying on the sidewalk protesting our segregated movie theater. When my friends and I were literally led by a white usher around and across the black protesters, I explain that I began to grapple with the privilege I have because I am white.

Each limb on the tree identifies how I learned about "The Other" from different sources, including a Jewish friend I was not allowed to go home with as a child and colleagues in Botswana as an adult. As I trace my own journey up the tree limbs, I ask others to identify how people, work, travel, reading, language study, or other changes helped them learn about other people. Often students and people moving into their neighborhoods had profound effects.

When the students bring in their completed trees, they present them in small groups and then the whole class debriefs together. How have we learned about other cultures? What strategies appear to be the most effective? What else could schools do to help young people learn about others cultures? How does prejudice or privilege affect our learning?

Merry Merryfield

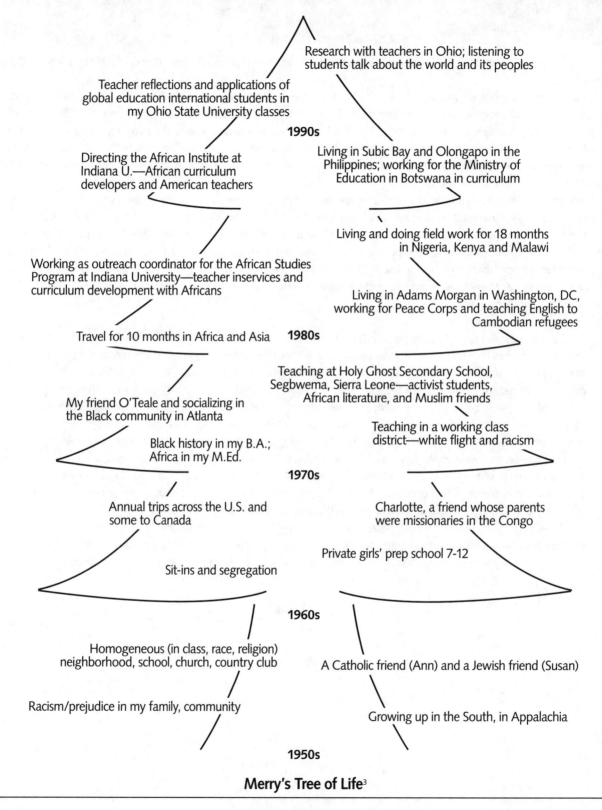

Research with teachers in Ohio; listening to students talk about the world and its peoples

Teacher reflections and applications of global education international students in my Ohio State University classes

1990s

Directing the African Institute at Indiana U.—African curriculum developers and American teachers

Living in Subic Bay and Olongapo in the Philippines; working for the Ministry of Education in Botswana in curriculum

Living and doing field work for 18 months in Nigeria, Kenya and Malawi

Working as outreach coordinator for the African Studies Program at Indiana University—teacher inservices and curriculum development with Africans

Living in Adams Morgan in Washington, DC, working for Peace Corps and teaching English to Cambodian refugees

Travel for 10 months in Africa and Asia   **1980s**

Teaching at Holy Ghost Secondary School, Segbwema, Sierra Leone—activist students, African literature, and Muslim friends

My friend O'Teale and socializing in the Black community in Atlanta

Teaching in a working class district—white flight and racism

Black history in my B.A.; Africa in my M.Ed.

1970s

Annual trips across the U.S. and some to Canada

Charlotte, a friend whose parents were missionaries in the Congo

Private girls' prep school 7-12

Sit-ins and segregation

1960s

Homogeneous (in class, race, religion) neighborhood, school, church, country club

A Catholic friend (Ann) and a Jewish friend (Susan)

Racism/prejudice in my family, community

Growing up in the South, in Appalachia

1950s

Merry's Tree of Life[3]

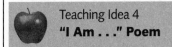

Teaching Idea 4
"I Am . . ." Poem

Goal: Students reflect on their lived experiences.

Procedures: Another personal way to think about yourself in the world is for the teacher to write and have students write an "I am From" poem. I first saw this kind of poem in Mary Pipher's *The Middle of Everywhere, Refugees Come to Our Town*. An English as a Second Language (ESL) teacher she was observing was using the poem strategy and Pipher wrote one, too, which she includes in her book.

Linda Christensen describes how she encourages students to write an "I Am From" poem in *Reading, Writing, and Rising Up: Teaching about Social Justice and the Power of the Written Word*. She begins by asking students to read aloud together George Ella Lyon's poem "Where I'm From." Before working on drafts of their poems, Christensen's students make lists of specific words, phrases, and names. She then asks them to end the poem with a line or two that ties their present to their past. Samples of student poems are in her book.

I Am From
By Angene Hopkins Wilson

I am from the Hopkins family who came over on
     the Mayflower
And Sir Francis Drake's brother.
I am from Annie Lawson's Scottish teapot
And Alonzo Drake's shoe lasts.
I am from rural and small town northern Ohio
And two blocks from "as far as you can see water"
     Lake Erie in Cleveland.
Then I sailed across the ocean on a ship and lived
     in Paris for a summer.
Then we Peace Corps volunteers flew across the ocean
     in a prop plane to Liberia,
With a live white chicken to present properly,
     ceremonially.
And then we lived in Sierra Leone and Fiji and I in Ghana.
So I am also from *les bouquinistes* on the Seine,
And from pounding drums and big-big pineapple,
From pounding waves and bright, soft kente cloth.
For 29 years I have been from Kentucky bluegrass and
     basketball and horses,
But I am also from Annie Lawson's farm 150 years later,
Through Ethel and Clayton, Dean and Harriet
To five children and our spouses and children and
     grandchildren.
I have roots and I have wings.
I am from places like Aruba and Cuba where I have been,
And from South Africa and China where I want to go.
The world is a glass I drink from.
I almost always see the glass and the world half full.

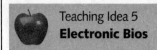

Teaching Idea 5
Electronic Bios

Goal: Students learn to recognize worldviews through interactive discussions of cultural differences, racism, prejudice, and privilege.

Rationale: It is difficult for students looking at each other in a classroom to discuss prejudice and how it is related to people's daily lives. When people interact online, often they are more willing to tackle these prickly issues, share their own experiences and respond to others. In this assignment students are graded on the substance of their bios and their ability to interact respectfully with others.

Procedures: Ask students to reflect upon experiences they have had with people different from themselves. When have you experienced prejudice or observed inequities? When did you feel "centered" within a group? When did you feel you didn't belong or were "different" from others? Choose what you want to share with people in our class so that they will begin to understand who you are. Reveal only what you feel comfortable in sharing.

Then give them directions on writing their bios. First, type in your name and list three or four words you would use to identify who you are. Write a description of what values/beliefs you have been taught as a child, how you were taught to behave and what expectations your family and community had for you. Most people include gender roles, insights into social class distinctions, what they were taught about different races, ethnicities and religions and the languages they learned. Post these online in the discussion entitled "Bios." Then read other people's bios and respond to three. Choose people different in some way from yourself. Your responses should work at building relationships and community as they address something special about each person.

Excerpts from a Bio and some excerpts from the discussion that followed it.[4]

Message no. 71
Posted by **Vladimir** on Thursday, June 20 5:21pm
Subject Vladimir

Vladimir
Russian Cossack, from Kazakhstan, Student

I grew up in the former Soviet Union where all roads led to Moscow. Growing up in Shymkent, Kazakhstan, I spent most of my summers in the Soviet "city of lights". My uncle, then a mechanical engineer, amused himself observing the culture shock I underwent during each of my visits. To him, who left Shymkent after high school, my adolescent experiences of coming to Moscow were slightly reminiscent of his own. He religiously took me around the city trying to teach me as much of its history and culture as I could absorb.

One does not comprehend nor does one really care about the political or cultural reality at the age of nine. Playing tag in the local park in the center of Shymkent, I never wondered why my best friends looked Asian, why they were circumcised by the age of 5, or why at home spoke a different language. Going to Moscow and listening to my uncle's take on life made me notice such things.

In mid 1980s, Almaty (the capital of Kazakhstan, then known as Alma Ata) saw a series of ethnic riots directed against Russian population. At the time I was staying with my aunt in Omsk, a large industrial city in Siberia, Russia. My Russian buddies gave me a warm welcome and the scent of exciting adventures in the city's allies and parks was in the air. Everything was going great – the tag, the hide and seek, the back-yard soccer – until one day I found myself all alone, boycotted by everyone I knew. Not understanding why, I tried to make a conversation only to get beat up by a local bully. Injured and humiliated, I couldn't stop hearing the words he repeated as he roughed me up: "You, damned Kazaks, will pay for everything you've done!" "Kazaks", but I was Russian!

My life has never been the same. It changed forever and also for everyone. Suddenly, I found myself in a clear and well-defined reality, where there were Kazaks and there were Russians, and no Soviet Union in between. After 1991, and the "break up" of the USSR, my family, all the Russians, and I became guests in our own country. Kazaks became our hosts. Our physical and cultural differences became more obvious than ever. Things like the color of one's skin; the shape of one's eyes; one's original culture became the main factors of social definition and separation. Pretty soon being a Russian meant a tougher job market, narrower educational opportunities, and more defined social borders. Russians started to develop a complex of inferiority in many areas of social and personal life.

My family stayed. Surprisingly, I managed to keep most of my Kazak friends. I knew all of them since early childhood and our old friendship kept us together. In fact, my friends were a ray of light in my life. My parents were not. My father, who was a dedicated communist once, took the "break up" very personally, as did my mother. All they have supported, believed, and lived for crumbled in front of their eyes. The wave of "new culture" was too strange, too drastic, and too liberal to accept. Street violence of the degrading society frightened them. Concerned about my physical and moral well-being, they became very protective. Ever since the "break up" my trips to Moscow became a way of escaping from the suffocating social environment of Shymkent.

In August of 1991, my uncle (already a street vendor with engineering degree) and me spent a night at the barricades of Kremlin. It was a life-changing experience for me. It was there that I first heard such words as "democracy", "freedom", "independence". It was then that I started to dream about changing the former USSR for the better. Vladimir

---

Message no. 192 [Branch from no. 71]
Posted by **BEN** on Monday, June 24 10:07pm
Subject Re: Vladimir
Vladimir- Your bio is fascinating. Living in the U.S. I am so conditioned to think of racial issues as being about black and white. Your life illustrates how racial issues can exist outside of this paradigm. Your observations about the artificial attempt of Soviet brotherhood to erase individual culture is very thought provoking. Ben

---

Message no. 233 [Branch from no. 192]
Posted by **Vladimir** on Tuesday, June 25 11:41am
Subject Re: Vladimir
Ben, I am glad you have noticed another perspective on racial relations. The Soviets started from "zero". To put in bluntly, they had erased all history prior to 1917. "Over night" Russians, Tartars, Kazakhs, Tajiks, Ukranians became Soviets. Suddenly, it didn't matter whether you came from the South, North, East, West, or what color skin and what shape eyes you had. It didn't matter if your family tree dated back 500 years. At a drop of a hat all that ceased to exist. From the very early age you were taught to define yourself as a Soviet person, the most fortunate title in the world! Vladimir

---

Message no. 558 [Branch from no. 71]
Posted by **Maryam** on Friday, June 28 9:31pm
Subject Re: Vladimir
I found your bio quite personal and provocative. I read your response to my bio as well, so you know my Czech background as well. I was in the Czech Republic during its break-up from Slovakia. The break-up of Czechoslovakia was relatively peaceful.

I was wondering if you feel that the ethnic strife that lies throughout the former communist bloc will ever lessen? As an undergraduate, I had a history professor who said that the only way to maintain ethnic peace in this region was to have a strong authoritative government. At the time, I vehemently disagreed with him, but today I am a little less hopeful. Maryam

---

Message no. 724 [Branch from no. 558]
Posted by **Vladimir** on Monday, July 1 12:14pm
Subject Re: Vladimir
Dear Mary, how are you? I would like to disagree with your history professor. I think that the former authoritarian governments are the reason of the today's ethnic strife in several countries of Eastern Europe. As I've said, the Soviet Union and other authoritarian states under its influence, suppressed the original cultural, religious, traditional identities of their people for many decades. The revival of these identities is currently resulting in sometimes severe conflicts and wars. Vladimir

Notes

1. See www.socialstudies.org/positions for the NCSS Position Statement on Preparing Citizens for a Global Community.
2. Charlotte C. Anderson and James H. Landman, *Globalization and Border Crossings: Examining Issues of National Identity, Citizenship, and Civic Education* (Chicago: American Bar Association Division for Public Education, 203), 20-21.
3. Merry's Tree of Life was originally published on page 29 of Merry M. Merryfield, "Reflective Practice in Global Education," *Theory into Practice* 32, no. 1 (Winter, 1993), 27-32.
4. The entire bio assignment and complete illustration are available online in Merry M. Merryfield, "Like a Veil: Cross-Cultural Experiential Learning Online." *Contemporary Issues in Technology and Teacher Education* [Online serial], 3(2). 2003. Available: www.citejournal.org/vol3/iss2/socialstudies/article1.cfm

Resources

Linda Christensen, *Reading, Writing, and Rising Up, Teaching about Social Justice and the Power of the Written Word* (Milwaukee: WI: Rethinking Schools, 2000). Contact www.rethinkingschools.org

Bárbara C. Cruz, Joyce W. Nutta, Jason O'Brien, Carine M. Feyten and Jane M. Govoni, *Passport to Learning: Teaching Social Studies to ESL Students* (Silver Spring, MD: National Council for the Social Studies, 2003).

Down the Street, Around the World: A Starter Kit for Global Awareness. Available from American Federation of Teachers, 555 New Jersey Ave. NW, Washington, DC 20001. Contact www.aft.org

Mary Pipher, *The Middle of Everywhere: Refugees Come to Our Town* (New York: Harcourt, 2002).

CHAPTER 1

The Many Dimensions of Global Education

Before you finish eating breakfast this morning, you've depended on more than half the world. This is the way our universe is structured.... We aren't going to have peace on earth until we recognize this basic fact of the interrelated structure of all reality.
                                                                    MARTIN LUTHER KING

Students today take for granted that they live in a globally interconnected world. Unlike previous generations, they have grown up watching the instantaneous broadcasts of a tennis match in London, a New Year's Day celebration in China, and American troops entering Baghdad. Many have daily interactions with immigrants or refugees who have moved to their communities from Mexico, Vietnam, Bosnia, or Somalia. These 21st century learners can examine South African websites to learn about apartheid, compare the reporting of today's news in Egyptian, Jordanian and Israeli online newspapers and communicate with environmental organizations and multinational corporations working in the Amazon basin. Most cannot imagine a world without running shoes from Indonesia, cartoons from Japan, baseballs from Haiti, MP3 players from Taiwan, or inexpensive t-shirts from Pakistan.

Young Americans are already actors on the world stage due to their enormous purchasing power, and they will affect our planet in profound ways through their choices on energy, water, land use, and wastes and their involvement (or lack of involvement) in addressing political, economic and social problems facing the planet. Within the social studies, global education aims to prepare young people for these decisions and other challenges of an increasingly complex and interconnected world.

In this chapter we review the beginnings of global education and the ways in which it has strengthened the social studies. We outline elements of global education as they are taught in social studies classrooms today. Recognizing the controversial nature of global education, we identify some issues that teachers need to consider. Since questions continue to be asked about relationships between global education and multicultural education, we discuss their different origins and their commonalities. Finally, we place global education within the contexts of the broader literature on globalization.

Out of a Changing World

Remember the first time you saw a photo of Earth taken from space? There was this beautiful blue, green, and brown planet wrapped in wisps of white and gray. As you looked for your city or country, you found only natural borders of water and landforms. This global perspective provides a view of our world as a finite system, as one interconnected world. If we examine our communities, nation, and world from a global perspective, certain realities emerge as critical to our planet's survival and the quality of life of the Earth's peoples. Some issues—such as nuclear power or gene therapy—are as new as the advanced technologies that brought us that photograph from space. Others—religious conflict, hunger, disease—were evident in ancient civilizations and have become global issues as technology has accelerated the connectedness of the world's peoples.

It is not surprising that global education grew out of the era of the space age, a time when Americans were involved globally in the Cold War and multinational organizations were expanding in new nations that had recently gained independence from colonial rule. The founders of global education recognized that the social studies had to move beyond an American-centered curriculum if young people were to understand other cultures and how their world was becoming an increasingly interconnected system. Three related conceptualizations of global education in the 1970s continue to influence the social studies:

Anthropologist Robert Hanvey's *An Attainable Global Perspective* grew out of his concern that Americans develop cultural understandings in a global context.[1] To prepare young people for their interconnected world, Hanvey set forth these elements for a global education: perspective consciousness, state of the planet awareness, cross-cultural awareness, knowledge of global dynamics, and awareness of

Global Village
If the world were a village of 100 people, how many would come from each world region?
61 from Asia
13 from Africa
12 from Europe
8 from South America, Central America (including Mexico) and the Caribbean
5 from North America
less than 1 from Oceania

See Population Connection (www.populationconnection.org/Communications/ ED2002WEB/Fd4Thought.pdf) for these and other current statistics on world population.

Teaching Idea 6
The World in the Classroom

Goal: Students visualize and discuss the distribution of the world's peoples.

Procedures: Before class begins divide up the numbers of the class by the percentages above. So in a class of 30, you will have 61% or 18 students as Asians, 13% or 3 students as Africans, and so forth. Use a different colored or shaped sticker for each region (colored stars work well) so that you have ready 18 blue stickers for the Asians, 3 red stickers for the Africans, etc. Explain to the students that you are going to do a simulation and that they are to close their eyes and you will place a sticker on their foreheads (or another place they cannot see). They are not to speak when they open their eyes or touch the stickers; they are to get in a group with people who have the same sticker that they have. Mix up the regions and go around and place a sticker on each student's face. Once the students find their groups, debrief them by asking: How did you find your group? How does it feel to be in large group? A very small group? To be the only one in a group? Then ask them if they can think of why the groups are the sizes they are. What do these groups have to do with the study of the world? Finally show them the list of regions and percentages and discuss what implications those numbers have for the study of the world.

Resources: This lesson combines statistics from the Population Connections at www.populationconnections.org with an activity called "Going Dotty" developed by Graham Pike and David Selby. See also materials from the Population Reference Bureau at www.prb.org.

human choices. Over the next 20 years, his ideas were often adapted by districts and schools.

As a political scientist, Chadwick Alger was especially interested in young people understanding local/global connections in their own communities. In *Columbus in the World/ The World in Columbus*, he worked with social studies teachers in Columbus, Ohio, to develop materials and pedagogy that enabled students to become involved in their community as they learned about real economic, political, cultural, technological and environmental connections people in Columbus had with people and places around the world.[2] His ideas led to over 50 city and state curriculum projects (such as *Indiana and the World*) around the country.

In a third conceptualization, Lee Anderson, Chadwick Alger, and James Becker worked together on global education as citizenship education for a global age.[3] Many of their ideas were adopted in the 1982 National Council for the Social Studies position statement in which global education was said to cultivate in young people a perspective of the world which emphasizes the interconnections among cultures, species, and the planet.[4] The position statement affirms that the purpose of global education is to develop in youth the knowledge, skills, and attitudes needed to live effectively in a world possessing limited natural resources and characterized by ethnic diversity, cultural pluralism, and increasing interdependence.[5] It emphasized student understanding of a changing world.

In 2001, NCSS issued a position statement on Preparing Citizens for a Global Community, which was accompanied by an analysis of global and international education. This analysis recommends that students should learn:

1. The human experience is an increasingly globalized phenomenon in which people are constantly being influenced by transnational, cross-cultural, multicultural, multiethnic interactions.

Viewing human experience only in relation to a North American or European frame of reference has been a long-standing bias of education in the United States. If students are to understand their world, they must be able to look at events and issues from a global perspective.

2. There are many actors on the world stage.

The dramatic increase in transnational interactions in recent years has produced growing numbers of individuals, groups, and agencies with international contacts and influence. The character and influence of multinational corporations, church groups, scientific and cultural organizations, United Nations agencies, and local, state, and federal agencies deserve fuller treatment in the social studies curriculum.

3. Humankind is an integral part of the world environment.

The human-natural environment should be seen as a single system. This requires an emphasis on: (a) the ultimate dependence of humankind upon natural resources; (b) the fact that natural resources are limited; (c) the nature of the planet's ecosystem; and (d) the impact of ecological laws on human culture.

4. There are linkages between present social, political, and ecological realities and alternative futures.

Students should understand relationships between past, present, and future. The use of "historical flashbacks," for example, can add to students' understanding of the relation of past to present. Greater emphasis is needed on studies designed to improve students' ability to see present choices as links to possible alternative futures.

5. There are many ways in which citizens can participate in world affairs.

World affairs have often been treated as a spectator sport in which only the "expert" can participate. The increasing globalization of the human condition has created additional opportunities and responsibilities for individuals and groups to take personal, social, and political action in the international arena. The curriculum should demonstrate that individuals and groups can influence and can be influenced by world events. Furthermore, the social studies curriculum should help to develop the understandings, skills, and attitudes needed to respond effectively and responsibly to world events.[6]

Global Education in Social Studies Today

Over the last 20 years global education has evolved to address new challenges and meet the needs of diverse schools and students. As more women, people of color, and people originally from other countries entered the field, global education expanded to include women's issues, anti-racist pedagogy, linguistic diversity, post-colonial theory, and immigrant students in American classrooms. A new generation of scholars—Helen Benitez, Roland Case, Rudy Chavez Chavez, Bárbara Cruz, Ken Cushner, Carlos Diaz, Bill Gaudelli, Toni Kirkwood, Binaya Subedi, Omiunota Ukpokodu, Guichun Zong and others—has strengthened the field. Global education has also benefited from the scholarly work of classroom teachers, such as Khadar Bashir-Ali, Tim Dove, Jana Eaton, Jim Norris, Steve Shapiro, and Connie White. Global educators have worked with area studies specialists and colleagues in intercultural and multicultural education to develop materials integrating prejudice reduction, intercultural competence, and environmental and development education into the social studies curriculum.[7]

Many educators working in culturally and linguistically diverse classrooms have recognized the need to "move the center" of American social studies to give voice and agency to people in other parts of the world whose beliefs, experiences, and worldviews have rarely been heard in American classrooms. Others want young Americans to recognize how the center of the world is constructed differently by people around the world. See the sidebar "The Banana" on page 18 for one such construction.

The World History Association has provided leadership in rethinking the teaching of history from a global perspective. Its work in the development of standards and curricula offers teachers ideas and resources that can profoundly affect the ways in which young people come to understand the past. As global education has been adopted across the country, researchers have observed that it is often shaped by the cultural, geographic, economic, environmental or political issues of the state or district in which it is taught. For example, in teaching local/global connections, teachers in Miami may focus on South Florida's cultural and economic connections with Latin America and the Caribbean while teachers in Columbus, Ohio, may want their students to understand the decisions of local multinationals to move their plants to China and Mexico or examine how Ohio's coal-fueled electricity affects Canada's forests. Many teachers we work with relish teaching global education because it allows them to bring in local issues, events,

The Banana

Several North Americans were traveling in a vintage truck on a remote road in the Andes. Midway in the journey, steam suddenly rose from the hood and the truck came to a halt. The travelers made an effort to rummage through their toolbox, but none of them knew a thing about repairing vehicles. As they considered their options, three local people came walking down the road. The villagers were very sympathetic to the plight of the travelers. They kicked tires, examined the engine, and shook their heads. Yes, indeed, this radiator was overheated. And it was just about 20 kilometers to a town in either direction – too far for North Americans to walk.

But, "No problem," said the youngest villager. "Just make a paste of banana and smear it over the radiator. You'll be able to get to the town up ahead."

"Hmmm," one of the travelers nodded with a certain skepticism.

"You are very lucky to have broken down here," the oldest villager said, "This is the center of the earth."

As the villagers walked off, the travelers rolled their eyes in disbelief.

There was nothing to do but wait for someone to pick them up or take a message for help. The day passed but no vehicles. Just as they were giving up hope of being rescued before dark, a farmer came out of the forest carrying a stalk of bananas. The travelers looked at one another. "Why not?" said one. They bought the stalk of bananas, ate a few and hurriedly (they were North Americans after all) mashed and spread the remainder on the radiator. The truck coughed and sputtered, but it did start.

"You will have a safe journey," called the farmer. "This is a very lucky place. It is the center of the earth."

By the time the travelers reached the next town it was well after dark. Nevertheless, a crowd gathered to welcome them.

"You are very lucky," an old woman smiled at them, "do you know what this place is?"

"Of course," proclaimed the North Americans, "it is the center of the earth."

From the foreword of *From the Center of the Earth: Stories Out of the Peace Corps*, 1991, edited by Geraldine Kennedy.

and knowledge to teach about global interconnectedness and multiple perspectives.

Global educators also incorporate current events into their instruction of the mandated curriculum. Events that change our world are powerful teachable moments. When Poland rejected communism and the Soviet Union broke apart, educators helped their students understand the ramifications of those events for the U.S. and the world. The oil spill in Prince William Sound in 1989, the Gulf War of 1991, and the North American Free Trade Agreement (NAFTA) that took effect in 1994, provided powerful connections between real-life and mandated social studies content. Current events motivate students because they are immediate and tangible. No students asked "Why do we have to learn this?" when their U.S. Government class examined multiple perspectives on American foreign policy and responses to terrorism after the events of September 11, 2001.

From research studies we know these elements characterize globally-oriented social studies today:

- **Local/Global Connections**
  Students come to understand their own connections to the larger world. They learn how the actions and beliefs of people around the planet have an economic, political, technological and cultural influence on American students, their communities, and their nation, who in turn have an influence on the rest of the world. Teachers organize their teaching of history, economics, geography, world cultures, and politics so that students learn how people and ideas across the planet interact with and affect each other.

- **Perspective Consciousness and Multiple Perspectives**
  Students develop skills in perspective consciousness. This is the ability to recognize how people different from oneself construct events and issues through their own histories, cultural lenses, knowledge bases, and experiences. Students study cultures, issues, and events from diverse people's points of view. They use primary sources, media, first-hand experiences, and literature written by people in many cultures to understand their lives and actions.

- **The World as a System**
  Students are asked to examine and think about the world as a system. Teachers situate current and historical events and issues (such as land use, movement of people, national security, or labor markets) within a world context. Students come to understand global political systems, global economic systems, and global environmental systems.

- **Global Issues**
  From terrorism to fishing rights, many issues cannot be understood without knowledge of many countries, the global commons, or the planet. Educators integrate global content into their instruction on topics such as energy prices, loss of manufacturing jobs, biodiversity, and new immigrants in the community so that their students see local issues through global perspectives and recognize that global issues are often significant within their own community, state, or region.

- **Power in a Global Context**
  Students come to understand power in a global context. Students learn how governments, non-governmental organizations, multinational corporations, individuals, and other groups have acquired and used global economic, cultural, technological, political, and military power and how nations, organizations, communities, and individuals have resisted or challenged the power exerted by others.

- **Non-State Actors**
  Students learn about non-state actors. Globally-oriented social studies curricula strengthen the teaching of American foreign policy and other topics by having students examine how non-state actors such as individuals, multinational corporations, and non-governmental organizations (as diverse as CARE [Cooperative for Assistance and Relief Everywhere], the International Monetary Fund, the Grameen Bank, Greenpeace, the World Council of Churches, and the Palestinian Liberation Organization) interact on the world stage and influence local, national, and global events and issues.

- **Attention to Prejudice Reduction**
  Teachers work to reduce chauvinism and prejudice. Students learn to recognize and reduce their own parochialism, resist stereotyping, and develop the ability to empathize. Teachers work at opening students' minds so that they can see their local community and nation from a global perspective. In their teaching of history, teachers help students see connections between prejudice and inequities across time and space.

- **Cross-Cultural Competence**
  Students develop skills in communicating and interacting with people different from themselves. Through cross-cultural experiential learning, students learn skills and cultural knowledge that help them understand and collaborate with people from different cultures.

- **Research and Thinking Skills**
  Students acquire skills in research and evaluation of materials from diverse sources with conflicting points of view. Students need to be able to find information, evaluate its merit and worth, and detect bias and unstated assumptions in order to acquire the decision-making skills they need as citizens in a democracy.

- **Participation in Local and Global Communities**
  Teachers recognize the need to foster participation in local and global communities through service learning projects or other collaboration. Participation may be part of a required assignment or a voluntary extracurricular activity. It may be local, such as work with neighborhood groups concerned with land use, racism, or poverty, or more global, such as online work with Amnesty International.

- **Use of Electronic Technologies**
  New electronic technologies have revolutionized global education in the last decade. The Internet not only gives teachers and students instant access to documents, media, and other print and visual resources across the planet, it also allows interaction with people and organizations in every world region. Many global educators use online newspapers in other regions to provide their students with primary source material on a daily basis. Others organize collaborative online or

video-conferencing relationships with schools, organizations, or experts so their students can talk with people in Japan, Mexico, or Germany about their histories, literature, issues, or current events. Where once global educators had problems finding materials needed to teach the topics noted above, now they are faced with such a plethora of online resources that they can become overwhelmed by the possibilities. Even without classroom access to the Internet, we believe all social studies teachers can use the Web to improve the way students learn about the world. Throughout this book we recommend websites, and we provide examples of how these new technologies can create global teachers and global learners.

The Controversial Nature of Global Education

Elements of global education have been challenged by people who disagree with its ideas or have found problems with specific content or some instructional materials. Some critics are opposed to the basic assumptions of global education, because they believe schools should focus on American content and mainstream American worldviews. Some see the study of global topics and diverse cultures through multiple perspectives as a threat to American values and patriotism. As Steve Lamy points out in "Conflict of Images," Americans hold different views on what students need to know about their world.[8]

Critics have attacked specific curriculum documents, instructional materials, books, or other resources that they perceive as global education. Some criticisms of instructional materials in the 1980s undoubtedly strengthened the field by improving its knowledge base and its balance of different points of view.

Critics have based their judgments on texts or other written documents instead of spending time in classrooms, talking to teachers, or examining research on how teachers actually teach about the world. Table 1 presents some of the accusations against global education along with our perspectives.

It is important for teachers to recognize how these criticisms may relate to strongly-felt issues in their local communities. A community with many Cuban families who fled Castro will be very sensitive to any teaching that could be perceived as teaching students pro-Castro points of view. A community with a large defense contractor will be sensitive to how issues of war and weapons are taught. A huge uproar resulted in a Midwestern farm state when one lesson out of hundreds in a new global education curriculum focused on whether it was better to eat grain or feed grain to animals in order to feed the world. Suddenly global education was accused of promoting vegetarianism and subverting the economy in a beef-exporting state![9]

Global education needs to be adapted to the contexts of one's school, mandated curriculum, and community as it should be responsive to local concerns and issues as well as global ones. And most importantly, teachers need to provide balance so that students learn from many points of view.

Global Education and Multicultural Education

Multicultural education and global education had very different origins. Emerging from the Civil Rights Movement in the 1960s, multicultural education was initiated by African Americans and others to bring about educational equity, social justice, and academic success for children of color. As global education developed in the 1970s and 1980s, tensions developed between these fields as they competed for resources and the attention of the education community. Some multicultural educators perceived global education as elitist because it pays attention to world systems and world cultures, but, in their view, ignores racism, injustice, and inequities in American communities. They did not see evidence that global education prepared students to understand diversity and equity or that it improved the quality of schooling for children of color.

For their part, some global educators in the 1970s and 1980s viewed multicultural education as narrowly focusing on a few selected groups of Americans while ignoring other cultures and economic, political, environmental, and social inequities around the world. However, by the 1990s there were educators in both fields who began to build bridges as it became clear that shared goals did exist and K-12 teachers needed to integrate the best of both fields in their classrooms.[10]

Multicultural and global education have many commonalities. They both:

- Teach historical antecedents of structural and institutional inequities
- Teach about people's efforts to overcome oppression and gain self-determination
- Work to improve intergroup relations and cross-cultural skills

Table 1

Criticisms of Global Education[11]	Our Perspectives
Detracts from the study of Western civilization and the US; places US within world history; de-exceptionalizes American history—Buehrer, Burack, Schlafly	We agree. Courses have finite time constraints. If teachers teach all world regions instead of just Western Europe and the US, world history or world cultures courses will spend less time on Western civilization and the United States.
Teaches cultural or moral relativism —Buehrer, Burack, Schlafly	We disagree. Global education teaches students that they need to understand other people from multiple perspectives, but it does not teach cultural or moral relativism.
Teaches students to divide the world between oppressors and the oppressed—Burack	We disagree. Global education is against dichotomies of rich/poor, first world/third world, oppressors/oppressed, etc.
Is unpatriotic—Buehrer, Schlafly	We disagree. Love of country and patriotism are taught as a cultural universal. People can think globally and love their country at the same time.
Promotes one-worldism, one-world government, a new world order, renders the nation-state obsolete —Buehrer, Burack, Cunningham	We disagree. We know of no educators who teach one-world government or a new world order or teach that nation-states are obsolete.
Is hostile to capitalism —Cunningham	We disagree. Global education teaches students to understand global economic systems, local/global economic connections, and global economic issues such child labor, comparative advantage, the global assembly line, the environmental impact of industries, trade practices and agreements, and the roles of multinationals and labor organizations, etc., from the perspectives of different people in different countries. Many of these viewpoints are supportive of capitalism.
Teaches activism, students taking action— Cunningham	We agree. Global education teaches students to be active participants in the world around them.
Teaches nuclear issues such as a nuclear freeze, nuclear war —Cunningham	We agree. As one of many global issues, a global education curriculum may include issues related to nuclear power, nuclear weapons, nuclear wastes, etc.
Teaches pacifism, non-violence— Cunningham, Kersten	We agree that a global education includes the study of pacifism and non-violence along with the study of war, military issues, ethnic cleansing, peace, peacekeeping, genocide, land mines, etc.
Teaches against ethnocentrism, stereotyping— Buehrer	We agree.

- Reduce stereotyping, prejudice, and the use of pejorative language
- Teach understanding of both cultural universals and cultural differences
- Help students reflect on their own culture and what it means to be an American
- Provide access to multiple perspectives through the use of literature and other primary sources
- Develop an understanding of power and its role in the process of knowledge construction

Multicultural education and global education promote environments of mutual respect and understanding of others guided by democratic principles. They value skills in communicating and working with people of different cultures. They share a commitment to replacing stereotypes, pejorative language inherited from colonialism, "us and them" dichotomies, and a "food and festivals" superficiality with in-depth knowledge and cross-cultural competence.

The two fields have traditionally differed when it comes to scope. Multicultural education has focused primarily on

Multicultural and Global Education Together

Middle School Interdisciplinary Curriculum
Beginning with the assumption that multicultural and global education are connected, a middle school team of teachers could choose a major international sports event as a theme. An ideal example would be the Summer or Winter Olympic Games. For the social studies part of the program, teachers would ask individual students—on the basis of ethnic heritage or interest or randomly—to become researchers of participating nations, including the United States. The students could learn greetings in other languages, read news stories, figure exchange rates, study trade connections, and compare political systems. Students could send suggestions about Olympic coverage to the television networks and then evaluate the television commentary on their individual nations during the actual opening parade of athletes. They should also research backgrounds of athletes representing "their" countries and create world maps for each nation that show heritages of the athletes.

Cultural Diversity Class at High School
A multicultural course usually includes units on the variety of ethnic groups in the United States. First the teacher might decide to include historical and current information on the origin country of each group so students would learn a little about the Philippines as well as about Filipino Americans and a little about Mexico as well as about Mexican Americans. Second, the teacher could choose several ethnically diverse countries to compare with the United States, asking questions such: What is the ethnic diversity within Brazil and Russia? How have Brazil and Russia dealt with diversity historically? How do they deal with diversity currently? Finally, students should discuss the question: How can we make the world safe for and safe from ethnicity?

Global Issues Class at High School
A teacher uses case studies of South Africa and the United States to study how change can happen in race relations, focusing especially on the concepts of racism and leadership. Students could research how education in both countries once contributed to and now tries to ameliorate racism. They should learn about people in both countries who have been leaders for equality and change, from Nelson Mandela and Martin Luther King Jr. to Albertina Sisulu and Septima Clark. Finally, the teacher could organize a project through the iEARN network or otherwise to link schools in South Africa and in the United States online to discuss race relations and racism and leadership today and plan for prejudice-reduction workshops in their schools.

---

content within the U.S. For example, in the study of migrations, global educators may look at the history of migrations across the world while multicultural educators might focus on migrations of African Americans from the South to the North after the Civil War. But what about the Bosnian refugee who wants to share her culture and history, bringing "them" here from there? Is that kind of sharing global or multicultural? Learning from the teachers with whom we work, we have come to believe that our time and efforts are better spent on improving teaching rather than debating differences between the two fields. The box on this page suggests some ways of combining multicultural and global themes.

Globalization and Global Education
Scholarship on globalization has expanded significantly in the last decade in concert with the tidal waves of public debate and popular protest about the meaning and effects of globalization. The literature is multi-disciplinary across the social science disciplines of economics, political science, sociology, and geography, as well as the humanities and education. Some people are concerned with globalization's dilution of cultural identity, as discussed in Huntington's *The Clash of Civilizations and the Remaking of the World Order* and Meyer and Geschiere's *Globalization and Identity*. Others express fears that people and countries are losing political or economic control as seen in such work as in Martin and Schumann's *The Global Trap: Globalization and the Assault on Democracy and Prosperity*, Sassen's *Sovereignty in an Age of Globalization*, and Stiglitz's *Globalization and Its Discontents*.[12]

Other scholars have focused on concerns that globalization is increasing political polarization, economic and technological inequities, and cultural conflicts. This debate has created best-sellers such as Friedman's *The Lexus and the Olive Tree* and Barber's *Jihad vs. McWorld: How Globalism and Tribalism are Reshaping Our World.*

Other writers, such as Kaplan in *The Coming Anarchy*, McCarthy in *The Uses of Culture*, and Cvetkovich and Kellner in *Articulating the Global and the Local*, have addressed the paradoxes of divergent, even conflicting local and global forces that are occurring at the same time, even in the same places, and the resulting hybridity of ideas, experiences, and cultures that increasingly characterize the human experience.

In the last few years people engaged in electronic technologies have begun to ask how the internet and World Wide Web are affecting people's world views and the felt realities of globalization. Scholars have raised critical issues about the power of electronic media and communication in globalization and changes in culture, community, work, politics, education and identity in such works as Chen and Starosta's *Communication and Global Society*, Warschauer's *Electronic Literacies*, Kiesler's *Culture of the Internet*, Fabos and Young's "Telecommunication in the Classroom: Rhetoric Versus Reality," and Harcourt's *women@internet: Creating New Cultures in Cyberspace.*[13]

Educators such as Nelly Stromquist and Karen Monkman in *Globalization and Education*, have joined the debate by raising questions about the effects of globalization on schooling. Social studies educators have asked if globalization means countries should move from national to global curricula. Parker, Ninomiya, and Cogan's "Educating World Citizens: Multinational Curriculum Development" and Pike and Selby's *Reconnecting from National to Global Curriculum* have examined the implications of this question for developing curricula for world citizenship.[14]

Scholars with backgrounds in history and the social sciences have conceptualized global education within the contexts of globalization. These are the topics they suggest should be taught within the social studies curriculum.

1. Human values
   - Cultural universals
   - Diverse human values and beliefs within and across nations and world regions
   - The relationships among peoples' values, patterns of thinking, and behavior
   - Recognition of the effects of one's own values, culture, and worldview in learning about and interacting with people different from oneself
   - Cultural blending and borrowing and culture change

2. Global Systems
   - Economic, political, ecological, technological systems
   - Knowledge of global dynamics
   - Local/global interconnectedness
   - Procedures and mechanisms in global systems
   - Transactions among people around the world
   - State of the planet awareness
   - Global organizations, such as the United Nations, multinational companies

3. Global Issues and Problems
   - Development issues
   - Human rights issues
   - Environmental/natural resource issues
   - Issues related to power, distribution of wealth, technology and information, resources
   - Population issues, including immigration, refugees, displaced persons
   - Terrorism, peace and security issues

4. Global History
   - Acceleration of interdependence over time
   - Antecedents to current issues
   - Origins and development of cultures
   - Contact and borrowing among cultures
   - Evolution of globalization
   - Changes in global systems over time

5. Cross-Cultural Understanding
   - Skills and experiences in seeing one's own culture and country from others' perspectives
   - Experiences in learning about other cultures and the world from another culture's values and world views
   - Extended experiences with/in other cultures

6. Awareness of Human Choices
   - Awareness of choices by individuals, organizations, local communities, nations, regions, economic or political alliances
   - Past and present actions and future alternatives
   - Recognition of the complexity of human behavior and decision-making

CONTINUED ON PAGE 26

"Magic" Pablo
by Mark Brazaitis
Guatemala 1991-93

Pablo and I liked to play "Let's imagine." We'd be walking down the street, a basketball under one of our arms. Clouds would be gathering in the east, as they tended to do in early evening. A light rain – chipi-chipi is what everyone in town called it – might even be falling.

"Let's imagine," Pablo would say, "that Michael Jordan is walking with us."

He would smile. "What would these people say?" he would ask, pointing to the women in dark blue cortes and white huipiles, the native dress in this town in the northern mountains of Guatemala. "What would they do?"

"They'd be amazed," I'd say. "They wouldn't know what to do."

Pablo would agree. "They'd probably run. But we'd just keep walking down the street, the three of us, to the basketball court."

Then Pablo would ask, "And how would we divide the teams?"

"Michael Jordan versus the two of us."

Pablo would consider this. "No," he'd say, "it'd be you and Michael Jordan versus me."

Pablo was sixteen when I met him, another indistinguishable face in my English class of forty-five students.

I was twenty-five when I arrived as a Peace Corps Volunteer in Santa Cruz Verapaz, a town of 4,000 people. I was prepared to be alone during my entire two-year service. I figured this was the way my life was supposed to be: silent sacrifice. I wasn't, at any rate, expecting to make a friend my first night in town.

But the night after my first English class, Pablo knocked on my front door.

I invited him in, and he entered, looking around shyly. On a table in my dining room, he saw a copy of Sports Illustrated that my stepfather had sent from home. He pointed to the cover photo.

"Robert Parish," he said. "The Chief."

Pablo, it turned out, knew as much about basketball and the NBA as I did, and I was a former sportswriter.

I don't know where he got his information. El Grafico, the only newspaper from the capital sold daily in our town, rarely had stories about American basketball. A Mexican TV station that reached Santa Cruz showed NBA games on Saturday mornings, but the town's electricity was so unpredictable—occasionally it would be off for three or four days in a row—that I wondered how many of these games he could have seen. Pablo just seemed to know, and he was familiar not just with Robert Parish and other All-Stars; he could talk about obscure players like Chris Dudley and Jerome Kersey as if he were an NBA beat reporter.

Pablo would come to my house at night and we would draft imaginary lineups. Pablo liked non-American players. Hakeem Olajuwon was his favorite. He liked Mark Aguirre because he'd heard that Aguirre's father was born in Mexico. Dikembe Mutombo. Manute Bol. Drazen Petrovic. Selecting our imaginary teams, he'd always draft these players first.

I didn't get it. Why would he pick Vlade Divac instead of Charles Barkley? But the longer I lived in Guatemala, the better I understood.

The American presence in Guatemala is about as subtle as a Shaquille O'Neal slam dunk. Pepsi covers entire storefronts with its logo. In Santa Cruz, the town basketball court is painted with a Coca-Cola motif, right down to

the backboards. In remote villages, children wear "Ninja Turtles" T-shirts.

We had long arguments about who was the best player in the NBA. Hakeem Olajuwom versus Michael Jordan. Hakeem versus Patrick Ewing. Hakeem versus Magic Johnson.

Pablo stuck by his man.

Pablo and I played basketball on the court next to the cow pasture. Pablo was taller than Muggsy Bogues but shorter than Spud Webb, both of whom played in the NBA. When we first began playing, I could move him around with my body, backing him close to the basket. If I missed, I was tall enough to get the rebound. In games to twenty-one, I would beat him by nine, eleven, thirteen points.

Pablo was the first to tell me about Magic Johnson. He came over to my house one night, late.

"What is it?" I asked.

His head was bowed.

"What is it?"

He looked up. He wasn't crying, but he looked like he might need to. He said, "Magic Johnson has the AIDS virus."

We mourned together. Feeling sentimental, Pablo admitted, "Magic might be better than Hakeem."

Pablo's dream was to dunk a basketball. We calculated how many feet he would have to jump—about four.

Pablo drew up a training plan. He would jump rope two hours a day to build his leg strength. Every other day, Pablo would ask his younger brother to crouch, and he would leap over him, back and forth, for half an hour.

Two weeks later, Pablo came to my house and asked me to set up a hurdle in my courtyard. I stacked two chairs on top of each other, then another two chairs a few feet away. I placed a broom across the top chairs and measured: the broom was four feet off the ground.

"I'm going to jump it," Pablo said.

"You sure?" I asked.

"Yes, I'm sure."

We stood there, gazing at the broom.

"You sure?" I asked again.

"I'm sure."

Then he backed up, took a few quick steps, and jumped. His knees shot into his chest. He leapt over the broom like a frog.

"You did it!" I yelled.

"I can dunk now," he said, grinning.

The next morning, we went to the basketball court. Pablo dribbled from half court and leapt. The ball clanked off the rim. He tried it again. Same result.

"I don't understand," he said.

I didn't have the heart to admit I'd misled him: to dunk, he'd have to jump four feet without bending his knees.

As a player, though, Pablo was getting better. He couldn't dunk, but he'd learned to use his quickness to drive by me and score. He had grown stronger. I could not back into him as easily.

"Let's imagine," Pablo would say, "that David Robinson came to visit us."

"All right," I'd say.

"Where would he stay?"

"I don't know. At a hotel, probably."

"No," Pablo would say, "he'd stay at your house. You'd let him sleep in your bed."

"Yeah, that would be better."

"And you'd make him dinner."

"Sure."

"And at night," Pablo would say, "we'd sit around and talk about basketball."

Pablo was not my best student. He was more interested in basketball than books. But he knew how to make his teacher laugh.

When he missed a quiz, I allowed him to make it up by writing five sentences—any five sentences of his choice—in English.

He wrote:

1. Charles Barkley sang a song in my house.
2. I beat Patrick Ewing in slam dunk.
3. I beat David Robinson in block.
4. Hakeem Olajuwon is my brother.
5. Magic and Pablo are the best friends of Mark.

Despite his interest in basketball, Pablo's best sport was soccer. He played for San Pedro Carcha, a nearby town. Pablo was known as a good player. Quick dribbler. Good passer. Soccer's equivalent of a point-guard, not a power forward.

I'd seen several of Pablo's games and had watched him make gorgeous passes, beautiful sky-touching passes that his teammates batted into the net for goals.

My last week in Guatemala as a Peace Corps Volunteer, I attended a game Pablo's team played against San Critobal, a town nine kilometers west of Santa Cruz. The game was tied 1-1 going into the final minutes. Pablo's team had a corner kick. The crowd, about a thousand strong, was silent.

The ball soared into the air. A mass of players, including Pablo, gathered to receive it. Pablo jumped, his body shooting up like a rocket off a launcher. His timing was perfect. His head met the ball and the ball flew past the goalie.

Pablo's teammates paraded him around the field on their shoulders. People from the crowd, per custom, handed him money.

When I talked to him later, I didn't need to point out why he'd been able to jump that high. He said it himself: "It's basketball. I learned that from basketball. From trying to dunk."

We played our last game the day before I left Guatemala. We played in the evening, as a light rain—a *chipi-chipi*—fell.

He had learned to play defense. I tried to back him toward the basket, but he held his ground. I was forced to use my unreliable jump shot. I could no longer get every rebound because he'd learned to block out. And, of course, he could jump now.

I got lucky and hit two straight jumpers to pull ahead by four. But he countered with a reverse lay-up. He scored again on a long jump shot, a shot he never would have made when we first played.

The rain fell harder now. Puddles were beginning to form on the court. Pablo and I were both panting. It was getting dark; we could hardly see the basket.

"Let's quit," I said. "Let's leave it like this."

"If you want," he said.

"Yeah, let's leave it like this. A tie."

"All right," he said. "A tie. Good. Let's leave it."

We hugged each other.

"Let's imagine," Pablo said, as we walked to my house for the last time, "that you and I played against Michael Jordan. Who would win?"

"Jordan," I said.

"No," Pablo said. "We would. Believe me, we would."

Mark Brazaitis, "Magic Pablo," in *Voices From the Field* (Washington D.C.: Peace Corps, no date), 23-27.

7. Development of Analytical and Evaluative Skills
- Abilities to find, collect, analyze, and use information
- Critical thinking skills (e.g., ability to detect bias, identify underlying assumptions, etc.)
- Recognition of the role of values in inquiry and the creation of knowledge[15]

In this book, we recognize the need to "globalize" global education through literature, theories, and diverse perspectives that reflect the complexity of the planet in the early twenty-first century. Global education in the United States needs to be informed by interdisciplinary and multidisciplinary scholarship from many cultures and by the issues and concerns of people who are often invisible in the social studies curriculum in the United States.[16]

However, the task involves more than finding the right content to help students understand the felt needs and realities of the majority of the world's peoples. More importantly, students must examine the assumptions that underlie mainstream academic knowledge and attain a better understanding of the historical and contemporary role of the United States in the world.

Notes

1. Robert G. Hanvey, *An Attainable Global Perspective* (New York: Center for War/Peace Studies, 1975).
2. Chadwick F. Alger, *Your City and the World/The World and Your City* (Columbus, OH: Mershon Center, 1974); Chadwick F. Alger and James E. Harf, "Global Education: Why? For Whom? About What?" in Robert. E. Freeman, ed., *Promising Practices in Global Education: A Handbook with Case Studies* (New York: National Council on Foreign Language and International Studies, 1986): 1-13.
3. Lee Anderson, *Schooling for Citizenship in a Global Age* (Bloomington, IN: Social Studies Development Center, 1979); James Becker, *Schooling for a Global Age* (New York: McGraw Hill, 1979).
4. The NCSS position statement on global education was published in *Social Education* 46, no.1 (January 1982): 36-38.
5. Ibid, 37.
6. www.socialstudies.org/positions/global/whatisglobaled
7. See Kenneth Cushner, "Assessing the Impact of a Culture-General Assimilator," *International Journal of Intercultural Relations*, 13 (1989); 125-146; Kenneth Cushner, *Human Diversity in Action* (New York: McGraw-Hill, 1999); K. Cushner and Richard Brislin, *Intercultural Interactions: A Practical Guide* (Thousand Oaks, CA: Sage, 1996); K. Cushner, Averil McClelland, and Philip Safford, *Human Diversity in Education: An Integrative Approach* (New York: McGraw-Hill, 1992); Graham Pike, "Global Education and National Identity: In Pursuit of Meaning," *Theory Into Practice* 39, no. 2 (1992): 64-73. Graham Pike and David Selby, *Reconnecting from National to Global Curriculum* (Toronto: International Institute for Global Education, University of Toronto, 1995). Chapter 4 focuses on global education within the world history curriculum.
8. Steven L. Lamy, "Global Education: A Conflict of Images" in Kenneth Tye, ed., *Global Education from Thought to Action* (Alexandria, VA: Association of Supervision and Curriculum Development, 1990): 49-63.
9. Schukar, 1993.
10. Merry M. Merryfield, (Ed.), *Making Connections Between Multicultural and Global Education: Teacher Educators and Teacher Education Programs* (Washington D.C.: The American Association of Colleges for Teacher Education, 1996) and Merry Merryfield, *Joint Guidelines for Multicultural and Global/International Education* (Washington DC: The American Association of Colleges for Teacher Education, 1997).
11. The critics here reviewed: Eric Buehrer, *The New Age Masquerade* (Berentword, TN: Wolgemeith & Hyatt, 1990); Jonathan Burack, "The Student, the World, and the Global Education Ideology," in James Leming, Lucien Ellington, and Kathleen Porter, eds., *Where Did Social Studies Go Wrong?* (Washington; Fordham Foundation, 2003) retrieved at www.edexcellence.net/foundation/publication/publication.cfm?id=317#907 March 24, 2004. Gregg Cunningham, *Blowing the Whistle on Global Education* (Denver, CO: Region VII Office, United States Department of Education, 1986); Chester E. Finn, "Teachers, Terrorists, and Tolerance," *Commentary* 112, no. 5 (2001): 54-57; K. Kersten, "The Radicalization of Minnesota's Public School Curriculum" (Minneapolis, MN: Minnesota Association of Scholars, 1988); and Phyllis Schlafly, "What Is Wrong with Global Education?" *St. Louis Globe Democrat* (March 6, 1986): 23. For a description of several attacks on global education in different states, see Ron Schukar, "Controversy in Global Education: Lessons for Teacher Educators," *Theory Into Practice* 32, no. 1 (1993), 52-57.
12. All the references in this section on globalization are listed under Resources on Globalization at the end of the chapter.
13. G. Chen and W. J. Starosta, *Communication and Global Society* (New York: Peter Lang, 2000); Bettina Fabos and Michelle D. Young, "Telecommunication in the Classroom: Rhetoric versus Reality," *Review of Educational Research* 69, no. 3 (1999): 217-259; W. Harcourt, *women@internet: Creating New Cultures in Cyberspace* (London: Zed Books, Ltd, 1999); S. Kiesler, *Culture of the Internet* (Mahwah, NJ: Lawrence Erlbaum, 1997); Mark Warschauer, *Electronic Literacies: Language, Culture and Power in Online Education* (Mahwah, NJ: Lawrence Erlbaum, 1999).
14. Nelly P. Stromquist and Karen Monkman, eds., *Globalization and Education* (New York: Rowman & Littlefield, 2000); Patrick O'Meara, Howard Mehlinger, and Roxana Ma Newman, eds., *Changing Perspectives on International Education* (Bloomington, IN: Indiana University Press, 2001); Walter C. Parker, A. Ninomiya, and John Cogan, "Educating World Citizens: Multinational Curriculum Development," *American Educational Research Journal* 36, no. 2 (1999): 117-145; Graham Pike, "Global Education and National Identity: In Pursuit of Meaning," *Theory Into Practice* 39, no. 2 (2000): 64-73. Graham Pike and David Selby, *Reconnecting from National to Global Curriculum* (Toronto: International Institute for Global Education, University of Toronto, 1995).
15. Alger and Harf; Anderson; Becker; Roland Case, "Key Elements of a Global Perspective," *Social Education* 57, (1993): 318-325. Hanvey; Willard M. Kniep, "Defining a Global Education by its Content," *Social Education*, 50 (1986): 437-466.
16. See Merry M. Merryfield, "Moving the Center of Global Education," in William B. Stanley, ed., *Critical Issues in Social Studies Research for the 21st Century* (Greenwich, CT: Information Age Publishing, 2001): 179-207.

Resources on Global Education

WEBSITES

The American Forum for Global Education, www.globaled.org. Newsletter, publications.

The Centre for Global Education, www.yorksj.ac.uk/centres/cge/. Publications, projects.

The Choices Program, www.brown.edu/Research/Choices/. Curriculum development, publications, materials that respond to current events

Global TeachNet, www.rpcv.org/pages/globalteachnet.cfm. Newsletter, listserv, study tours, awards.

The International Education and Resource Network (iEARN), www.iearn.org and Intercultural E-Mail Classroom Connections, www.iecc.org. These organizations connect teachers and students with projects and people in other countries.

Ohio State University, www.coe.ohio-state.edu/mmerryfield/. Listserv, online global education courses for teachers, and www.teachglobaled.net for extensive online resources on Africa, East Asia, Latin America, The Middle East, Slavic and Eastern Europe and global issues.

Resource Center of the Americas, www.americas.org. Children's books and other resources on Latin cultures, issues, daily life.

Rethinking Schools, www.rethinkingschools.org. Journal for teachers, publications on teaching for equity and justice, globalization.

The Stanford Program on International and Cross-Cultural Education (SPICE), stanford.edu/about.

Teaching for Change, www.teachingforchange.org. Videos, children's books, and materials for teachers on diverse cultures and countries, issues of inequity, prejudice and conflict.

Teaching Tolerance, www.splcenter.org/teachingtolerance/tt-index.html. Magazine, teaching ideas, videos, book reviews.

PUBLICATIONS

Diaz, Carlos, Byron G. Massialas, and John A. Xanthopoulos. *Global Perspectives for Educators.* Boston: Allyn & Bacon, 1999.

Gaudelli, William. *World Class: Teaching and Learning in Global Times.* Mahwah, NJ: Lawrence Erlbaum, 2003.

Merryfield. Merry M. "Pedagogy for Global Perspectives in Education: Studies of Teachers' Thinking and Practice." *Theory and Research in Social Education* 26, no. 3 (1998): 342-379.

Parker, Walter C., A. Ninomiya, and John Cogan, "Educating World Citizens: Multinational Curriculum Development." *American Educational Research Journal* 36, no. 2 (1999): 117-145.

Pike, Graham and Selby, David. *Reconnecting from National to Global Curriculum.* Toronto: International Institute for Global Education, University of Toronto, 1995.

Resources on Globalization

WEBSITES

The Globalization Website, www.emory.edu/SOC/globalization/.

BBC Special Report on Globalisation, news.bbc.co.uk/1/hi/special_report/1999/02/99/e-cyclopedia/711906.stm.

Globalisation Guide of the Australian Asia Pacific Economic Study Centre, www.globalisationguide.org.

The Globalist, www.theglobalist.com. Interactive site on global issues.

Globalization101.org: A Student's Guide to Globalization at the Center for Strategic & International Studies, globalization101.org

Web Sites for Teachers on Globalization at the University of Wisconsin-Milwaukee, www.uwm.edu/Dept/CIE/Resources/globalization.

Earth Charter, www.earthcharter.org.

World Bank on Globalization, www.worldbank.org/economicpolicy/globalization. Also see Globalization: Threat or Opportunity? from the International Monetary Fund, www.imf.org/external/np/exr/ib/2000/041200.htm.

Globalization from AlterNet.org, a media watchdog organization, www.alternet.org/issues/index.html?IssueAreaID=21.

Globalization from the Social Science Research Council, www.ssrc.org/sept11/essays/globalization.htm.

Globalization Research Center (Globalization Research Network), www.globalhawaii.org/home.html.

PUBLICATIONS

Barber, Benjamin R. *Jihad vs. McWorld: How Globalism and Tribalism Are Reshaping the World.* New York: Random House, 1995.

Burbules, N.C., and C. A. Torres. *Globalization and Education.* New York: Routledge, 2000.

Cvetkovich, A., D. Kellner. *Articulating the Global and the Local.* Boulder, CO: Westview Press, 1997.

Friedman, Thomas L. *The Lexus and the Olive Tree: Understanding Globalization.* New York: Farrar, Straus and Giroux, 1999.

—————. *The World is Flat.* New York: Farrar, Straus and Giroux, 2005.

Huntington, Samuel P. *The Clash of Civilizations and Remaking of the World Order.* New York: Touchstone Books, 1998.

Kaplan, Robert. *The Coming Anarchy.* New York: Random House, 2000.

Lechner, Frank J., and John Boli, eds. *The Globalization Reader.* Malden, MA: Blackwell, 2000.

Martin H., and H. Schumann. *The Global Trap: Globalization and the Assault on Democracy and Prosperity.* London: Zed Books, 1997.

McCarthy, Cameron. *The Uses of Culture: Education and the Limits of Ethnic Affiliation.* New York: Routledge, 1998.

Meyer, B. and P. Geschiere, eds. *Globalization and Identity.* Oxford: Blackwell, 1999.

Sassen, Saskia. *Losing Control? Sovereignty in an Age of Globalization.* New York: Columbia University Press, 1996.

Stiglitz, Joseph E. *Globalization and its Discontents: Essays on the New Mobility of People and Money.* New York: The Free Press, 1998.

Spring, Joel, *Education and the Rise of the Global Economy.* Mahwah, NJ: Lawrence Erlbaum, 1998.

CHAPTER 2

Experience and World-Mindedness

But some ventures refuse to be over. I never sleep one night without dreaming of Arabia.

Colonel West, quoted above, is remembering his experience as a British army officer serving in the Arab Legion in Jordan. The venture—the experience in Arabia—is not over for the now successful pig farmer, one of the characters in Ronald Blythe's *Akenfield*, the story of a small English village and its people in the 1960s.

Experiences with people different from ourselves can have a powerful impact on our "worldmindedness." Whether people are immersed in another culture overseas or in the United States, they can learn and change, and people with such experiences can make important contributions to teaching and learning from a global perspective. As a Liberian proverb says, the alligator does not cross the river without getting wet. Cross-cultural experiences can launch people on the road toward worldmindedness, as they give other places and people the same serious attention and concern as those at home and recognize that both those people and the people of home belong equally to the world.

Perhaps the bigger challenge is figuring out how to integrate people who have cross-cultural experiences into the curriculum and classroom. Blythe doesn't say whether the English village school ever invited Colonel West to talk with the children about Arabia, but the schoolmaster recognized a need. He says, "We are concerned with roots when we should be spreading."[1] Like that schoolmaster, we 21st century teachers want to be sure our students understand their roots and also grow wings and go out into the world.

This chapter examines the impact of cross-cultural experiences, both those taking place overseas and within the United States. We look at five dimensions of that impact: substantive knowledge, perceptual understanding, personal growth, interpersonal connections, and cultural mediation. We then translate those into attributes of global competence. We discuss the concept of double consciousness, another especially important possible result of cross-cultural experience. Teaching ideas 7-12 illustrate how experiences can be utilized and created in the classroom, including how students could complete a portfolio that would demonstrate global competence in the five dimensions. (See pp. 31-39 below.)

Impact of International and Cross-Cultural Experience

A seventh grade social studies teacher returned from a six-month deployment in Crete as part of Operation Enduring Freedom/Noble Eagle before the Iraq War. An enlisted seaman in the Navy after September 11, he also visited places in Asia, such as Bangkok and Okinawa. He enjoys answering questions his students ask about those places. He also shares what he has learned about other perspectives on U.S. actions, and he relates his experiences to his teaching about Alexander the Great and the Roman Empire. For spring break 2004, he headed to Mexico on the migrants' bus to practice his Spanish.

The five dimensions of the impact of international experience were developed after research into the impact of that experience on people like David. Four dimensions of the impact—substantive knowledge, perceptual understanding, personal growth, and interpersonal connections—overlap and merge into each other. The fifth dimension—cultural mediation—seems to grow out from the others and into the community. The following sections will define each of these dimensions, offer a few examples of supporting research, and include a teaching idea.

Of course, people can also have cross-cultural experiences within the United States. Some people, in fact, have no choice. For example, new immigrants and most so-called minorities are inevitably bicultural; many negotiate expertly in what is considered mainstream culture, as well as in their own ethnic or religious culture. Others may be immersed in situations in which they have the opportunity to gain new perspectives, grow personally, and develop new relationships. Although the dimensions we consider in this chapter come out of research on the impact of international experience, we believe they can apply to cross-cultural experience more generally.

We recognize, too, that it is possible for people to have an experience and miss the meaning. Although Mark Twain is supposed to have said "travel is fatal to prejudice, bigotry, and narrow mindedness," sometimes experiences confirm stereotypes. Perhaps more problematic, some travelers or sojourners or those with cross-cultural experiences inside the United States believe they are experts after their experience. They offer answers rather than ask questions, thinking they can now explain what Iraqis or Italians or Indians (American or Asian) are like. Reflection on experiences and continued openness are critical for the development of worldmindedness.

Substantive Knowledge

Substantive knowledge is the content learning, both practical and intellectual, that is essential if one is in a new place. It ranges from knowing how to spend *naira* in Nigeria or ride the Metro in Paris to speaking appropriate Australian English or conversational Russian. It includes using the metric system in Great Britain and learning what exams mean in Malaysian schools. It is not restricted to U.S. Americans going elsewhere, of course. It is learning that snow is water (not fallout from a bomb), as Yolanda, an immigrant schoolgirl from the Dominican Republic, does in *How the Garcia Girls Lost Their Accents* by Julia Alvarez.[2]

One gains knowledge from reading books—a variety of books, from tour guides to novels. One's knowledge also grows from living in a place. (See, for example, Penina Goldstein's College Entrance Essay on this page.) It is often learned by making mistakes, particularly when the language is different. For example, a U.S. student abroad in the Netherlands found that ordinary activities like grocery shopping proved the most confusing—once she bought vinegar thinking it was grape juice. A Peace Corps volunteer in Thailand remembered trying to tell someone she was afraid and saying "I am a banana" instead, because of the tonal nature of the Thai language. One learns, too, by watching others, asking questions, and trying new things—like eating cloudberries in Sweden!

Substantive knowledge includes the history and geography and culture of a country lived in or visited. It is the immediacy of eye-witness accounts, being able to show one's own pictures of the Dachau concentration camp in Germany or the Great Zimbabwe ruins in Zimbabwe and say with the authority of having been there that pictures don't do these

---

College Entrance Essay
by Penina Goldstein, senior at Paul Laurence Dunbar High School in Lexington, Kentucky in spring 2004

Thinking back on the time I spent in Malaysia, I taste the way roti canai peels apart in my mouth, the intense glow of sambal on my tongue, and the coating sweetness of nasi lemak in my throat. I see the women's vibrantly colored fabrics, maroon and orange. I feel the daily rain soaking through my pinafore. I hear the melodic Muslim call to worship from the minaret of a nearby Masjid.

Australian memories smell like coffee and eucalyptus and feel like the wooden oars of a crew boat and the heaviness of my woolen school uniform. They sound like a kookaburra laughing over the tranquil Yarra River.

Lexington is green: parks, horse farms, and fields. It smells like cut grass and feels familiar and comfortable. I recognize people in the grocery store and anticipate the newest messages on the church marquee I pass daily. Lexington is home, a place of belonging, of departures and returns.

I have lived in Lexington, Kentucky for 15 of my 17 years. My second-grade year in Malaysia and ninth-grade year in Australia account for the other two. In each of these places I have been outsider and insider. My Chinese-Malaysian peers compared their dark smooth bodies to mine, poking at my pale skin and hairy arms and laughing at my Caucasian features. In Australia, American words sounded plain and rough against Aussie accents and slang. My school friends coached me in Australian colloquialisms so we would laugh at my contorted accent. At home in the Bible Belt, Judaism sets me apart from my peers. I follow the strict dietary laws of kashurt, celebrate Jewish holidays, observe Shabbat, and speak to my father in Yiddish. However, friends outside of Jewish circles often "worry about my soul."

I relish immersing myself in new situations, forming friendships, and playing an active role in communities. I was a flower girl in a Tamil-Catholic wedding in Malaysia, rowed crew for my Australian school, and sing with the Bluegrass Youth Chorus. These and other experiences have taught me both independence and interdependence.

Although the diverse cultures and foreign traditions of these three places have changed me, I continue to stand up for my beliefs. In Malaysia we practiced Judaism quietly for fear of being the target of anti-Semitism. Yet, even that memory inspires—to strive to live in a morally conscious way without being judgmental.

No matter where I find myself I look forward to forming new bonds. I challenge myself to keep my mind open to new experiences and to learn from people with ideas different from mine. I want to continue cataloguing colors, smells, sounds, textures, and flavors. And as I grow through these senses, I set the goal for myself to gain sensibility.

Teaching Idea 7
Interactive Postcards and Photographs

Goal: Students will "read" pictures and ask questions to learn about a specific country.

Procedures: The sixth grade geography teacher gives each student one of a stack of postcards brought back from her own or a friend or relative's international travel experience. She asks each student to "read" and share the picture and to ask a question about the picture. She answers questions if she can, adding interesting information. This interactive strategy replaces the passive showing and narrating of slides or a even a fancier Powerpoint presentation. A variation would be to have students find pictures on websites or in magazines of countries they are studying and to read and question the pictures.

Further Ideas and Resources: An extension of this activity could ask students to look at postcards or pictures from the country and photographs taken by a visitor to compare the "eyes." What does a nation want to highlight? What does the visitor see? Are they the same? Why? Why not?

places justice. Teachers who have traveled report that they teach with more accuracy, authority, creativity, enthusiasm, and understanding about places they visited, and, after a homestay program, high school students report considerable knowledge of the people and culture of their host country and an understanding of that country's role in world affairs.[3] New Zealand, for example, is no longer just a country at the bottom of the world, but a place graced with natural wonders the teacher or student has seen.

Perceptual Understanding

Perceptual understanding includes open-mindedness, perspective consciousness, complexity of thinking, resistance to stereotyping and chauvinism, the inclination to empathize, and the ability to be reflective. A person with perceptual understanding considers how people in Colombia might view Sir Francis Drake, a hero in England, after visiting the museum in Cartagena and seeing the results of his piracy. Such a person will say: "I just can't explain Liberia and Liberians in a few sentences." Teachers with perceptual understanding can get beyond AIDS in Africa or SARS in China and try to see the larger context of people's lives. They will know more than the five pillars of Islam or the caste system in India. As well as beautiful traditional Fijian tapa cloth, they will appreciate a McDonald's menu from Fiji and note the vegetarian adapta-

tions for the Indian population there.

Perceptual understanding is complicated by the fact that sometimes internationally experienced people become very attached to and invested in another culture. For instance, it may seem easy to condemn Colonel West, in *Akenfield*, as an imperialist in Arabia. He says: "I was lost to the Western world and utterly absorbed in and devoted to what I was doing. I felt I was part and parcel of an effort. I didn't try to assimilate Jordan or anything like that but my spirit was with this country and I felt that I was living to a purpose and creating something... Toward the end of the life in Jordan... We [were] becoming part and parcel of the destruction of the thing which we have spent our lives creating."[4] West saw what was happening even if he didn't entirely understand the problem of "we" trying to create something in someone else's place. Sometimes we "understand" others, but in the end still want to have or indeed do have the power to exclude or include on our own terms. Being even graciously inclusive is different from being a believer in equitable pluralism in spite of difficult differences. As Catherine Hall explains in *Civilising Subjects, Metropole and Colony in the English Imagination 1830-1867*, whether the English missionaries and others who considered themselves "friends of the negro" in Jamaica were talking about "the family of man" or later "manly citizenship," they were defining black people as children, according to their stereotypes, and not considering the "complexity or agency of other human beings."[5]

Perceptual understanding certainly doesn't happen automatically. Attitude change is difficult to measure and may be affected by many things, including the facts that people go abroad with different preparation and personalities, stay varying lengths of time, and have varying amounts of contact with host country people. However, in one study of high school exchange student returnees, 85% indicated that the exchange experience caused an attitudinal change which led them to begin to individualize people; another study of a college service and study abroad program found increased interest in reflective thought and tolerance for ambiguity, an increase that persisted a year later.[6]

Really experiencing another culture and really listening to someone from another culture are crucial steps toward perceptual understanding. As Hall points out, "Being on the island (Jamaica) changed how men thought." When one of the English "friends of the negro" went to Jamaica, he saw that Jamaica was indeed a different kind of society from the metropolis and had its own culture.[7]

Goal: Students will listen to a dialogue between an American teacher in Afghanistan and an Afghan boy; afterward, they will explain how their assumptions about and perceptions of the two people change.

Procedures: Ask students to read "Boy in a Mulberry Tree" in trios, one person as narrator, one as the Peace Corps volunteer, and one as the Afghan boy in the tree. Or the teacher can be the narrator and ask two students to do the dialogue for the whole class. Use the following questions to debrief: Why is this a positive, equal interaction between two people of different cultures? What would be your first impression of an Afghan shepherd boy before reading this story? What would be your first impression of the American before reading the story? How do those perceptions change? What might life be like for Afghan boys and girls today? How would you find out?

Another Idea: Look for "A Pilgrim's Diary" of a young female Saudi journalist who goes on the *hajj* to Mecca for more cross-cultural listening and learning. The five part series was in *The Christian Science Monitor* from January 30 through February 5, 2004 and can be found at csmonitor.com.

Boy in a Mulberry Tree

By Bill Witt, a Peace Corps volunteer in Afghanistan from 1973 to 1975.[8]

A mid-September sky stretched still and cloudless over the Kakrak Valley. Earth and men were nearly done with their yearly tasks: here or there, one more cutting of hay, or a few sehrs of potatoes were about all that remained for gathering. No one seemed in a hurry to finish the work, the tawny, stubbled fields stretched out in the warm sun, the threshing floors were silent.

Water harvested from the Koh-e-Bara rushed with power down to the valleys. The water was being harvested by the sun from snows that had been the heaviest in recent memory, snows so deep that a few fissures on the north face of Shah Foladi still showed white. Down-valley, I'd stopped to talk to a farmer who was sickling clover. Drowsy bees attended the clover to drain the purple blossoms' fragrant nectaries ahead of the felling strokes. It had been a very good year, praise God, the farmer said. He'd sold the vegetables early, the wheat stalks had been heavy with grain. Potatoes, onions, carrots, beans lay in surplus in his bins. All these years, he said he'd never had anything but a sickle for cutting his wheat and hay. "But this year, God willing, I will have enough money to buy a scythe!"

I'd walked for a half-hour since talking with that lone farmer and, here in its middle reaches, the valley now seemed emptied of people—no boys shying stones at imagined wolves, no girls with little siblings like ungainly squirrels clinging to their hips, no voices, no laughter in the air...

But I thought I heard someone singing. To my left a scattered rag-bag of sheep soundlessly gleaned a stubble-field, and beyond them, some 60 or 70 yards away, stood a grove of mulberry trees. From somewhere in their rasping, slowly shedding foliage, a voice was flowing. The voice came like a chant, piping a while, then pausing, then piping again. I followed it, and as I drew closer to the grove, I could hear the quatrain-fall of the lines and the melting of their rhymes.

Locating the singing tree, I ducked beneath its canopy, and there, about eight feet up, was a boy of about 12. He sat on one branch and rested his forearms on a higher, parallel one. His dangling feet stroked the air, keeping the meter. He'd been chanting his words toward the mountains and the sky, but now he looked down at me and grinned.

"Salaam aleikum! Welcome to my country! Is it not beautiful?"

"And Peace upon you, young friend." (Ah, what a welcome change from the Kabuli kids' 'Hello Mistart, howareyou-givemoney? Pen? One thing?') "Yes, your country is very beautiful!"

"Yes, so beautiful, the most beautiful

place. Have you seen other places?"

"Yes, Kabul, Jalalabad, Paghman, Istalif, Salang, Panjshir, Samangan, Faizabad..."

"Many places. And isn't this the most beautiful?"

"It is very beautiful, thanks be to God."

"How do you come to my country? Where are you from?"

"I'm from Amriko. I'm a teacher here, for the Peace Corps."

"Peace Corps? Yes, they are very good people. Do you know Mr. Mike? From Bamiyan?"

"Of course."

"He is a good person and a good teacher."

"Is he your teacher?"

"Oh, no. I've never gone to school. What do you teach?"

"I teach English, at the School for Male Nurses, in Kabul. I also love poetry. What poem were you saying?"

"Ah, it is Sa'adi, the 'Gulistan.'"

"Gulistan—Land of Roses. A famous poem. I've read some parts of it."

"I don't read, I just say it, like this. Isn't it beautiful?" And the flow of words resumed... Then came a pause. "You know poetry? Let me hear a poem from Amriko!"

(Oops. What do I have to say now? Let's see, something that's short, that rhymes...Kho. Ok. Got one.) "Kho, this is a poem about a man who is driving home in his tonga on a winter night, and he stops for a little while to think about something."

"Why does he stop outside if it's cold?"

"Maybe he likes the quiet, and also he wants to let his horse rest for a little while. 'Whose woods these are, I think I know....'" I struggle through the dozen lines, but stressing the rhythm and rhymes as much as I can. Whew. Made it.

"A beautiful poem! But short, I think. Do you know Rumi?"

"Ah, yes Jalaluddin Rumi: another famous poet. Sufi?"

"Sufi, yes. From Balkh. Afghan. Yes, listen." And Rumi's lines weave through the branches, into the sky, verse on verse. "Let me hear another English poem!"

"Kho. Kho. Here's a poem about a man who wants to live alone in a little house where he can raise vegetables and keep honeybees: 'I will arise and go now, and go to Innisfree....'"

"A nice poem, but so short, also. Why does he want to be away from his family?"

"He's maybe like a Sufi, and he wants to be able to think about God."

"Is he an old man?"

"No, he's a young man."

"This is strange. Why doesn't he want a wife, children?"

"I don't know."

"Do you have any long poems in Amriko? Poems about love?"

"Oh yes, there are many beautiful poems about love."

"Let me hear a long one this time."

(Now what?! Oh, wait yes, it's coming back—the Balcony Scene—yes, I think I can remember that!) "Here's part of a long poem by our most famous

poet. His name is Shakespeare. It's a story about a young man who loves a young woman, but his father and her father and all their families are enemies. The young man's name is Romeo, and the young woman is Juliet. In this part Romeo goes at night to the qallah of Juliet's father, to the rose garden beneath her balcony. He says, 'But soft! What light through yonder window breaks? It is the east, and Juliet is the sun...' (Amazing: I've made it through the soliloquy and got it mostly right. Good thing this kid doesn't speak English; if I'd missed something, he'd've nailed me!)

"What happens to this boy and girl?"

"They love each other, and they marry, secretly. But they fall into a trap when they try to escape from their village. Then they kill themselves."

"This is a good story! It sounds like Rabia Balkhi. Do you know about Rabia Balkhi?"

"A little bit."

"Rabia Balkhi is also Afghan. She was a great poet, and she died like that, for love. Do you want to hear Rabia Balkhi?"

"How about just one more, and then I think I should go." (I'm about out of poems!)

"Kho. Listen , here is Hafez: 'Mazra-e-sabz-e falak didom-o-mah-e-no...

Fields of green in the sky I saw

Cut down by a sickle moon.

I recalled the clouds of seeds I'd sown,

Concerned for my harvest with oncoming dawn...'"

Personal Growth

The third dimension of impact is personal growth. Many internationally experienced people, and not only younger people, talk about how they gained self-confidence and independence, especially if they went alone or were involved in a homestay program. "I did it, and now I feel I can do anything," they say. Although personal growth seems less directly related to what happens in a classroom—in contrast to a returned exchange student being able to describe the social welfare system in Sweden or a teacher sharing her changed perceptions of Kenyans after a study tour—growth remains important because education is about growth and change.

Based on their research, Kauffmann, Martin, and Weaver propose a model for understanding international experience or study abroad. They state that growth in cognition (similar to gaining substantive knowledge and perceptual understanding) goes hand in hand with growth in other aspects of personality as the student interacts with the new environment. Their developmental "education as change" model suggests five other variables besides cognition that mediate the interaction: autonomy, belonging, values, vocation, and worldview. Autonomy in their model is related to the changes in self-confidence and feelings of independence noted by many returnees from international experience. They also quote Bruggemann who asserts that "personal development is...about...interaction in which the person is evoked, assaulted, and impinged upon in formative and transformative ways."[9]

Adler[10] offers another more linear model. He begins at contact with the other culture and moves to disintegration (depression and withdrawal may result from impact of cultural differences), then to reintegration (differences are rejected by a person who is angry, frustrated, rebelling, but assertive), then to autonomy (when differences and similarities are legitimized and one becomes confident and empathic), and finally to independence (when differences and similarities are valued, significant, and understood and the person exercises choice and responsibility).

Our cross-cultural experiences, even when they are difficult and include culture shock, have the potential for personal development. Kohls,[11] for example, in his best-selling *Survival Kit for Overseas Living*, writes about the stages of cross-cultural adjustment as initial euphoria, irritability and hostility, gradual adjustment, and adaptation or biculturalism. Teachers can encourage their internationally and cross-culturally experienced students to talk about and write about their adjustment and development.

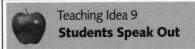

Teaching Idea 9
Students Speak Out

Goal: Students will learn about how recent immigrants and exchange students adapt to American culture.

Procedures: Organize a panel of internationally and cross-culturally experienced students, such as new immigrants and returned and current exchange students, to talk at a club meeting, brown bag lunch in the library, or a social studies class. Ask the students to focus on what they found difficult to adjust to in a new culture, here or elsewhere, what strategies helped them cope and learn, and how other people assisted them.

Further Ideas and Resources: In a psychology class, the teacher might introduce the concept of culture shock and describe several models of growth, using Kohls' book as one resource. Or a teacher might talk about models of growth with immigrants and exchange students as an after-school activity to help them understand their adjustment.

Interpersonal Connections

Interpersonal connections are the fourth area of impact. Long term intercultural relationships are one result of international experiences.[12] So a young woman who completed student teaching in South Africa returned for a month following her first year of teaching to implement an AIDS curriculum in schools in Capetown. Several teachers who spent their student teaching semester in England welcomed their hosts to their own homes in subsequent years.

Cross-cultural interaction can happen in the United States, too, one example being that between international and American students. Teacher education students matched for a semester with students in an English as a Second Language program gained in the areas of substantive knowledge and perceptual understanding, and also learned how to develop a cross-cultural interpersonal relationship.[13]

Sometimes interpersonal connections come first and are the catalyst for impact in the dimensions of substantive knowledge and perceptual understanding. In the Democracy Education Exchange Project (DEEP), a high school photography/social studies class in Boulder, Colorado, was paired with a high school civics class in Yerevan, Armenia to work on social documentary photography. In spring 2003 groups of four to six students in each of the classes began the project by introducing themselves to each other; they then discussed their own family backgrounds, wrote their own views of their school and schooling, and identified one local social issue per group. They also exchanged photos, using digital cameras and Photoshop. Following the exchanges, the students began to ask each other clarifying questions so that the small groups could begin to think about potential issue resolution. Through sharing visual and written information, the students gained insight into their own and another culture. Students began to understand that social problems are not necessarily unique to one place or culture. The iEARN (International Education and Resource Network) and other networks listed under Resources are other opportunities for students to gain interpersonal connections that can lead to knowledge and understanding.

Teaching Idea 10
Peace Corps Partnership Program

Goal: Students will learn about a community in a Peace Corps country, organize a service project, and develop a relationship with Peace Corps volunteers and the community.

Procedures: A high school teacher decides to have her Global Issues class join the Peace Corps Partnership Program as a service project. On the website www.peacecorps.gov/worldwise, the teacher reads about Corcoran High School in Syracuse, New York which has supported since 1983—through the sale of student-drawn notecards—projects ranging from building a maternity ward in Burkina Faso to building latrines in Ivory Coast to building a community kindergarten in Ghana. For each project students exchange letters, photos, and cultural artifacts with a Peace Corps volunteer and the community they are helping.

Further Ideas and Resources: Peace Corps has a CyberVolunteer Program that sends teachers monthly email notices of featured letters—in 2004-2005 from Bulgaria, Nepal and Togo. That program includes accompanying lessons, such as a geography plan that begins with the question: How does where you live influence how you live? National Peace Corps Association has initiated a new PeaceMatch program that brings returned volunteers into classrooms as speakers and plans with fellow teachers for the annual Peace Corps Day on March 1. Check their website at www.rpcv.org.

Cultural Mediation

Finally, the fact that people have been strangers in another country or have had cross-cultural experiences in the Unit-

ed States often encourages them to be cultural mediators or bridges across cultures. In his examination of the effects of living in another culture, Brislin lists "improved ability to act as a cultural mediator."[14] He gives as examples people who act as guides for sojourners in their own country and people who mediate between cultures by creating opportunities for monocultural people to communicate with people in other countries.

As Brislin notes, sometimes the cultural mediation is done with people from the culture in which the internationally or cross-culturally experienced person was immersed. So an exchange student returnee from Japan helps a Japanese woman newly arrived in the United States with her shopping. But often the bridge-building is more generalized. Returned Peace Corps volunteer teachers know that students who have traveled enjoy talking with them. They report that they encourage students to apply for exchange programs and help make the transition of foreign and immigrant students in their classes easier.[15]

Teachers with international experience will find ways in which students with such experiences can share them in classroom, school, and community. Students can organize a front hall exhibit focusing on "my country"; host a brown bag library lunch series on "Schooling Around the World"; participate in morning announcements with questions on the Nation of the Week; write one of a series of articles entitled "Bringing a Global Perspective to Our Community" for the school or community newspaper; or initiate a pen pal or email exchange with the home or host school. Cross-culturally experienced teachers will also be able to deal with and explain cultural differences, for instance, why some cultures don't value being "on time" in the same way Americans do or why face-saving may be important.[16]

A person without international or cross-cultural experiences may have to learn to be a cultural mediator in our country, with that role becoming the impetus for further learning. Pipher, author of *The Middle of Everywhere, The World's Refugees Come to Our Town*,[17] calls such people cultural brokers. They act as introducers and do everything from explaining why we wear seat belts, to what to do if the tornado siren sounds, to who to go to with immigration problems. She believes the most important cultural brokers are schoolteachers. Indeed, both teachers and students can be thrust into the roles of cultural mediators and then learn about a particular country, become empathetic about another person's situation, and develop a friendship.

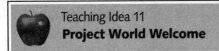

Teaching Idea 11
Project World Welcome

Goal: Students will develop a project to welcome newcomers from other countries to their school.

Procedures: A class or an international club, using the expertise of those in the school and community who have international and cross-cultural experiences, researches what would be helpful for new arrivals at the school. They might organize a buddy program, or set up monthly social gatherings, or raise money for flags from countries represented in the school to be hung in the school's front hall.

Further Ideas and Resources: Project World Welcome could also be extended into the community with students getting involved with resettlement of a refugee family, for example.

A Portfolio of Tasks of Global Competence

To be presented at the end of the school year in a World History or Global Issues Class or as a senior portfolio. The culminating task could be to apply for a passport. One rural Kentucky high school principal raised money so he could present passports to each senior as he or she walked across the stage at commencement.

Substantive Knowledge: Choose a world issue. Describe its historical roots, its current significance, and its global reach, including its relevance to you and your U.S. community. Then outline several possible human choices about the future of the issues and their ramifications and, finally, your own choice. Prepare your product as an article for your local newspaper's opinion page.

Perceptual Understanding: You are a delegate from a small country to the United Nations. Do enough research on your chosen country so that you can prepare a three-page speech to the General Assembly from that country's perspective. The topic for the speech is your view on the United Nations role in peacemaking, peacekeeping, and peace enforcing. In the speech, compare your country's perspective on this issue with that of the United States government perspective.

Capacity for Personal Growth: With another person, prepare an itinerary and budget for a two-week visit to a part of the world with which you are not very familiar. You may decide the purpose of the visit, for example, looking at trade possibilities for a local company, meeting a friend who is on leave from his or her military post, or visiting an international non-governmental agency involved in refugee work. Include a map with locations marked and an itinerary for sightseeing and other activities, as well as a budget and schedule for transportation and room and board.

Ability to Develop International Interpersonal Relationships: Submit the transcript of a substantive (a minimum of three exchanges) conversation between you and a person from another country who is currently living in the United States, or submit copies of an exchange of electronic mail between you and someone in another country. If you can do so, use another world language than English. Attach to the transcript your reflections on the exchange, particularly what you learned "from" as opposed to "about" the other person. You may also include pictures.

Ability to be a Cultural Mediator: With several other people, organize an educational program at your school or in the community about a group such as newly arrived refugees or migrant workers or international students at the local university or exchange students at your school. Work with and involve the group if you can. Submit a plan for the program and evaluations of the program from the audience.

In Ghana, I was in the white person category, so schoolchildren would say "Good morning, *oburoni*" and toddlers would point at me and shout "Oburoni." For United States Americans, double consciousness involves recognizing, as well, the power differential between us and others and the assumptions that come with power. For example, Kentucky teachers engaging in dialogue with Ghanaian teachers during a teleconference asked: "What are your local issues?" They did not realize that, when the Ghanaian teachers talked about the World Bank and the International Monetary Fund, they were talking about institutions that were local to them in terms of the impact of the policies.

Angene Wilson

The Importance of Double Consciousness

A concept that has particular potential to deepen our understanding of the impact of international and cross-cultural experience is "double consciousness," described by W.E.B. DuBois in 1903 as follows:

It is a peculiar sensation, this double-consciousness, this sense of always looking at one's self through the eyes of others, of measuring one's self by the tape of a world that looks on in amused contempt and pity. One ever feels his twoness—an American, a Negro; two souls, two thoughts, two unreconciled strivings; two warring ideals in one dark body, whose dogged strength alone keeps it from being torn asunder.[18]

International and cross-cultural experiences can give an individual a feeling of what it is like to be considered different, even inferior, to be placed on the periphery of society, to be looked at an outsider who does not and will never belong. For people of color, such experiences happen as they grow up in the United States. Some white educators have international experiences that help them understand the concept of double-consciousness. Those of us who are white often have our first or strongest periphery or outsider experiences overseas because we are accustomed to being the "normal" ones in our society.[19]

We Americans also tend to talk about interdependence in the world rather casually. However, the concept is not a benign one that can be easily explained in the long popular chocolate candy bar activity. We need to ask: Who is setting the price for cocoa? Who is processing it? Who has the money to eat the chocolate bar? Joaquim Chissano, President of Mozambique, offered another description of interdependence at a 1998 conference on debt relief: "Interdependence between the north and south is like the interdependence between the cow and its owner. The owner needs the cow because of its milk. The cow needs the owner because he provides it with hay. But when the cow ceases to produce milk, the owner may well decide to slaughter it. The cow cannot do the same to the owner."[20]

Yao Quashigah of Ghana writes that we need "an appreciation of global issues which would lead to the realization that the world has a common course and then we can talk about a common future. We have been emphasizing this is America, this is Africa, instead of emphasizing this is the earth... The U.S. is rich and powerful and exploits resources so it has tons of garbage to be dumped elsewhere. Should that garbage be exported to West Africa?"[21] He is asking for a double consciousness that might lead to a common future.

Conclusion

Because we lived there as Peace Corps volunteers, we care deeply about two neighboring countries in West Africa. Like Colonel West who dreams of Arabia, we still dream about Liberia and Sierra Leone, ventures that have profoundly affected our lives. In our mind's eye, we can see the capitals Monrovia and Freetown (at least what they looked like when we lived there) and the places upcountry where we taught. We can still speak a bit of Liberian English and Krio and Mende. We can still feel the washboard roads and taste the sweet pineapple. And many years later we still remember what we learned from Liberians and Sierra Leoneans, teachers and students and neighbors who taught us so much. We are still in touch with friends there and some now here in the United States.

Our worldmindedness is born of our experiences living in Liberia, Sierra Leone, Fiji, Ghana, Nigeria, Malawi, Botswana, Indonesia, the Philippines, and China. These lived experiences bring these countries into the center of our world rather than leave them at the periphery. Recent events of civil war, child soldiers, and blood diamonds in several of these countries have a different meaning for us because of the knowledge and caring that come from living in a country. Our experiences in other cultures have taken root and grown into life-long interests and study and connections that we use in our teaching, as do countless other teachers who have had such experiences. Cross-cultural experiences do make a difference.

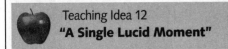

Goal: Students will understand the concept of double consciousness.

Procedures: Ask students in a World Cultures or Global Issues or a Sociology class to read the story "A Single Lucid Moment." Be sure they understand what the title means: a moment in which the writer sees his or her own world in a different way. Some questions to raise in discussion are: How are life and values in Maimafu village in Papua New Guinea different from life and values in Chicago, USA? Why is homelessness possible in one place but not in the other? How are differences related to differences between rural and urban places, maybe small and big places?

Further Ideas and Resources: Challenge students to role play this story to illustrate the dual perspectives or the communalism and the individualism of the two societies. For additional lesson plans to use with this story, see Reading and Responding to "A Single Lucid Moment," in Voices from the Field (pages 162-172) at peacecorps.gov/wws/guides/voices/. For additional stories, visit peacecorps.gov/www/stories and www.peacecorpswriters.org. A new online publication, "Uncommon Journeys," with stories of Peace Corps volunteers across the world, along with lesson plans, can be downloaded from peacecorps.gov/wws in a pdf file.

A Single Lucid Moment
By Robert W. Soderstrom,
Returned Peace Corps Volunteer,
Papua New Guinea

As the plane buzzed back over the mountains, it was now just us and the villagers of Maimafu. My wife, Kerry, and I were assigned to this village of 800 people in the Eastern Highlands Province of Papua New Guinea. It looked as if we were in for a true Indiana Jones adventure!

The mountains were dramatic and thick with rain forest. No roads had ever scarred them. We had loaded a four-seater plane with cargo (we would fly out every three months to resupply) and flew for 30 bumpy minutes southwest to the mountain ridges. From the plane, the village looked very much like a shoe-box panorama from a grade-school science project.

My wife and I were the first Peace Corps Volunteers ever in Maimafu. We had been greeted by a large group of beautiful people, all wearing gorgeous, curious smiles. Giggling, naked children hid behind trees during the trek down the mountain to our new home, and a lively entourage followed using their heads to carry out boxed supplies through the muddy trails. It was quickly becoming clear that we had just been adopted by a very large and unique family.

The basic culture of subsistence living had not been replaced; there were no cars, electricity or telephones—just grass huts, large gardens, and a whole lot of rain forest. The women spent the day in the gardens planting, weeding, and harvesting. The men grew coffee, from which they generated their sole income of about $200 a year. The village had lived in harmony with its natural surroundings for millenniums.

The villagers had built us a beautiful bamboo thatched hut on short stilts. Planted behind the house was a three-acre garden carefully tended and ready to harvest. Its bounty included corn, greens, tomatoes, beans, peanuts, onions, potatoes, and pineapples. To top it all off, the path to our new home was sprinkled with flower petals the day we arrived.

It quickly became clear that Maimafu was a preserved example of communal living. Men rallied to the building of a new home, the elderly worked and lived with their families, and mothers breastfed their neighbors' children. In fact, the one parentless, Down's syndrome man in our village was fed, housed, and clothed by everyone; he would spend a few days with one family before wandering in to work or play with the next.

It was when we had settled in that it happened. We were sitting in a circle on the ground with a large group of villagers to "tok stori," Papua New Guinea's favorite pastime of "telling stories." I had passed around photos I had snapped back home in Chicago. A villager was staring intently at one of the photos.

He had spotted two homeless men on a Michigan Avenue sidewalk with crude signs propped between their legs.

"Tupela man wokem wanem?" he asked. (What are these two men doing?)

I attempted to explain the concept of homelessness to the group, and the desire of these two men to get some food. Crowding around the photograph for a good stare, the villagers could not comprehend how the men became homeless, or why the passersby in the photo were so indifferent. They bombarded me with questions and I did my best to make sense of the two ragged beggars in the midst of such glittering skyscrapers. I read from their questions and solemn mood that they had made an important observation—these two men must lack not only food and shelter but also a general sense of affection and purpose in their community.

Early the next morning, we were startled to hear a sharp rap at the door. Opening it, I was greeted by Moia, Kabare, Kavalo, and Lemek. Kerry and I went out into the bright, beautiful day and sat with them in a circle. Each man gave us a pineapple. Moia spoke: "After you left last night, all of us men on the village council had a very big meeting. For a long, long time we discussed the two men in your picture. We have reached a conclusion and have a proposal for you."

"What could this possibly be?" we wondered.

"Please contact those two men as well as your government. Ask the government if they will fly those two men to Maimafu, just like they did for you. We have marked two spots of land where we will build houses for those two men, just like we built for you. Our men will build the houses and the women will plant the gardens to feed them."

They were offering to do what? I was stunned and overwhelmed. Their offer was bold and genuine. It was innocent and naive. It was beautiful. And, like the twist of a kaleidoscope, my worldview had completely changed.

What does one say to such an offer? We stammered for a response and stumbled over explanations of difficult logistics, scarce money, and government bureaucracies. But the councilmen would not accept no for an answer. In their simple lives, it was impossible to comprehend that humanity was host to such an injustice. They wanted action.

The villagers were serious. They were offering everything they had. We reluctantly matched their enthusiasm with a few letters to America and long conversations with the village council. We toured the sites where the homes were to be built. We listened to the women discuss the type of gardens they would plant, which would even include coffee trees to generate a small income. And we answered numerous questions over time from villagers amazed with this foreign thing called homelessness. The plan

could not work, we hearts sank, and I could that this dream would n

"Sori tru, sori tru we r dospela samting," they told us (We are sorry this cannot happen). They clicked their tongues and shook their heads in disappointment.

Initially inspired by the episode, I began mulling questions over and over in my mind. Fetching water in the ink-black night and looking up the hill at our small hut, light from the lantern inside splitting the bamboo-thatched walls, I would think of the spiritual wealth of Maimafu and the material wealth of America: Can a community reach a balance of material wealth and spiritual wealth? Why do these two societies exhibit so much of one and not much of the other? Do those two ends interfere with each other? How much spiritual wealth can we have? How much material wealth do we need? How has the world evolved so that some people own mansions and others lack shoes? How many people have love in their souls but diseased water in their drinking cups?

The villagers worked with us on newer projects. And, I discovered, like many Peace Corps volunteers before me, that the world's purest form of brotherhood can often be found in the smallest of villages.

1. ~~~nald~~ Blythe, *Akenfield: Portrait of an English Village* (New York: Dell, 1969), 181.

2. Julia Alvarez, *How the Garcia Girls Lost Their Accents* (New York: Plume, 1991), 166-167.

3. Angene H. Wilson, "Teachers as Short-term Sojourners: Opening Windows on the World," *The Social Studies* 75, no. 4 (1984): 184-92.

4. Blythe, 192.

5. Catherine Hall, *Civilising Subjects: Metropole and Colony in the English Imagination 1830-1867* (Chicago and London: University of Chicago Press, 2002).

6. David Bachner and U. Zeutschel, *Students of Four Decades: A Research Study of the Influences of an International Exchange Experience on the Lives of German and U.S. High School Students* (Washington, DC: Youth for Understanding, 1990); Norman L. Kauffmann, Judith N. Martin, and Henry D. Weaver, with Judy Weaver, *Students Abroad: Strangers at Home, Education for A Global Society* (Yarmouth, ME: Intercultural Press, 1992).

7. Hall, 420.

8. Published in *WorldView Magazine* 14, no. 4 (Fall 2001). *WorldView Magazine* is published by the National Peace Corps Association, Washington, DC.

9. Kauffmann, Martin, and Weaver, 124, 127.

10. Peter Adler, "The Transitional Experience: an Alternative View of Culture Shock" in *Humanistic Psychology* 15, no. 4 (1975): 13-23.

11. L. Robert Kohls, *Survival Kit for Overseas Living* (Yarmouth, ME: Intercultural Press, 1996).

12. J. Koester, *A Profile of U.S. Students Abroad* (New York: Council on International Educational Exchange, 1985); Barbara Burn, The Impact of the Fulbright Experience on Grantees from the United States," *ADFL Bulletin* 14, no. 1 (1982): 39-43.

13. M. P. Sharma and L. B. Jung, "How Cross-cultural Participation Affects the International Attitudes of U.S. Students," *International Journal of Intercultural Relations* 10 (1986): 377-387; Angene H. Wilson, "Conversation Partners: Gaining a Global Perspective Through Cross-Cultural Experiences," *Theory into Practice* 32, no. 1 (1993): 21-26

14. Richard W. Brislin, "Why Live Abroad?: Outcomes, Human Relations, and Contributions to Task Effectiveness as Key Variables in Educational Exchanges," *East-West Culture Learning Institute Report* (Honolulu, HI: East-West Center, 1981).

15. A. Wilson, "Returned Exchange Students: Becoming Mediating Persons," *International Journal of Intercultural Relations* 9 (1985): 285-305; Wilson, "Returned Peace Corps Volunteers Who Teach Social Studies," *The Social Studies* 77, no. 3 (1986):100-107.

16. Kenneth Cushner, Aaveril McClelland, and Phillip Safford, *Human Diversity in Education, An Integrative Approach* (New York: McGraw Hill, 1992), includes many critical incidents about cultural differences that are relevant for teachers.

17. Mary Pipher, *The Middle of Everywhere: The World's Refugees Come to Our Town* (New York: Harcourt, 2002).

18. W. E. B. DuBois, *The Souls of Black Folk* (New York: Signet Classic, 1969), 45.

19. Merry Merryfield, "Moving the Center of Global Education: From Imperial World Views that Divide the World to Double Consciousness, Contrapuntal Pedagogy, Hybridity, and Cross-cultural Competence," in William B. Stanley, ed., *Critical Issues in Social Studies for the 21st Century* (Greenwich, CT: Information Age Publishing, 2001), 179-208.

20. As quoted in A. Yao Quashigah and Angene H. Wilson, "A Cross-National Conversation about Teaching from a Global Perspective: Issues of Culture and Power," *Theory into Practice* 40, no. 1 (Winter 2001): 55.

21. Ibid, 61.

Resources

Websites

Council on Standards for International Educational Travel (CSIET), www.csiet.org. This private, not-for-profit organization establishes standards for, monitors, and disseminates information about reputable international youth education and exchange programs. Their advisory list contains information about programs that meet their standards.

EPALS: Classroom Exchange, www.epals.com. ePALS members connect with peers around the world through writing email, participating in a discussion board, and engaging in projects. The site also features instant language translation technology embedded within an email browser and seven language versions (Arabic, English, French, German, Japanese, Spanish, and Portuguese) and others in development.

The Fulbright Teacher Exchange Program, www.fulbrightexchanges.org. This program helps teachers and administrators participate in exchange. There are also links to other opportunities.

Fulbright-Hays Seminars Abroad Programs, www.ed.gov/offices/OPE/HEP/iegps/sap.html. The U.S. Department of Education funds primary and secondary school teachers in the social sciences and humanities to participate in short-term (four to six weeks) summer study/travel seminars abroad. There are about seven to ten seminars annually with 14 to 16 participants in each. The deadline for the summer seminars is in November of the previous year.

iEARN International Education and Resource Network, www.iearn.org. This network offers a myriad of projects for students to participate. Recent newsletters report on projects such a creative and visual arts gallery started by teachers in Sierra Leone, a discussion on cloning led by a teacher in Egypt, a Music in Your Life project begun in Brazil, and a Youth of the World Narcotism project started in Azerbaijan.

World Links, www.world-links.org/english/. A global learning network linking thousands of students and teachers around the world via the Internet for collaborative projects in 26 developing countries. Also accessible through worldbank.org.

Books

Cushner, Kenneth. *Beyond Tourism: A Practical Guide to Meaningful Educational Travel.* Lanham, MD: Scarecrow Education, 2004.

CHAPTER 3

Teaching for Understanding of World Cultures

Until the lion tells his side of the story, the tale of the hunt will always glorify the hunter.   AFRICAN PROVERB

American students cannot understand the world without knowledge of other people on the planet. And yet there have often been profound differences between what is taught about the world's cultures in American classrooms and the lived experiences, beliefs, and worldviews of people in those cultures. International visitors and students are often shocked by how their cultures are portrayed in American textbooks and the misperceptions "educated" Americans have about their beliefs or way of life. Teachers who take our study tours often return to reassess their instructional materials as outdated or misleading or their curricular content as not very useful in helping students understand people in that culture. Of course some people do not like having their illusions challenged by the realities of other cultures. "But those people don't act like Africans," said an American teacher in Nairobi for a study tour. "They're wearing suits and reading newspapers. I want to see real Africans who live in huts, and hunt lions. I can't teach about businessmen in cities!"

Out of all that could be taught about people on the planet, what content has meaning and utility in the real world? What knowledge will give young Americans insights into the ways other people live, think, and act? In this chapter we discuss elements of substantive culture learning that can prepare young people for a world characterized by human diversity and interconnectedness.

Culture has been defined in many ways.[1] For the purpose of this chapter, culture includes the shared assumptions, values, and beliefs of a group of people that shape their norms of behavior, worldviews and use of technology. Culture is dynamic and constantly changing. Historically, cultural change has gone hand in hand with military conquest and colonialism, religious conversion, immigration and migration, trade and economic development, new technologies, and environmental problems. In the 20th century culture change accelerated as globalization threatened the survival of many indigenous cultures and created new regional and global cultures.[2]

In this chapter we draw from research in intercultural education and global education to recommend strategies for teaching about the world's cultures from global perspectives. First we identify the characteristics of substantive culture learning, and the knowledge and skills that prepare young people for citizenship in a multicultural democracy in a globally interconnected world. Second we demonstrate how to assess students' levels of intercultural competence and provide developmentally appropriate methods and materials to meet their needs. The last part of the chapter outlines five strategies for teaching world cultures that integrate cultural knowledge with skills in intercultural competence.

Substantive Culture Learning

Substantive culture learning includes knowledge of both internal and surface culture plus skills in intercultural competence, the knowledge, and ability needed to interact and work effectively across cultures. Several scholars have used the analogy of an iceberg to explain the significance of surface versus internal culture.[3]

The small visible tip of the iceberg represents surface culture, those things we notice when we visit a village in southern France or a city in Mexico. We can see how people behave in public, watch their body language, listen to their music, eat their food and observe their dress and decoration, their architecture, their use of space, and their arrangements of homes, farms, markets, or towns. Students often enjoy these topics much as a tourist does—laughing at some customs, surprised at how 'strange' others seem, enjoying the novelty of differences and recognizing some commonalities.

The attributes of surface culture have long been popular topics in regional geography or world cultures courses. But surface culture by itself is not only inadequate for understanding other cultures, it may actually constrain students' ability to develop global understanding.

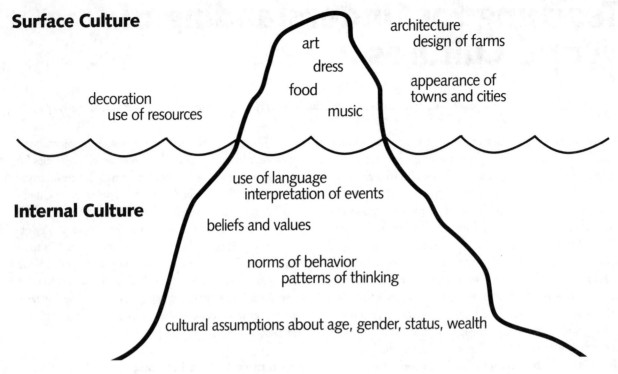

Surface Culture

art
dress
food
music

architecture
design of farms

appearance of
towns and cities

decoration
use of resources

Internal Culture

use of language
interpretation of events

beliefs and values

norms of behavior
patterns of thinking

cultural assumptions about age, gender, status, wealth

Although surface culture has its place in the social studies classroom, students also need to study internal culture if they are to understand their world today. When used exclusively, the surface approach to culture denies students the opportunity to acquire cross-cultural understanding, practice perspective-taking and develop skills in communicating and working with people from other cultures.

Look below the surface of the iceberg in the figure on this page. Internal culture acts as a lens through which people perceive and interpret information, people, events, and experiences. Internal culture includes the values, beliefs, and tacit assumptions that cause people to behave, speak, think, and interact the way they do. In effect, internal culture is what shapes our thinking and actions and makes people Korean, Mende, or Irish. To begin to understand the Japanese or Russians, Arabs or Hmong, we have to get beyond their dress, food, or architecture and study their beliefs, values, patterns of thinking, and norms of behavior. Teaching Ideas 13 and 14 suggest activities that will help students understand differences and similarities between cultures.

Given the diversity within many cultures and dynamic changes going on across the planet, we also want students to recognize that cultures are complex and their norms are constantly evolving. We want them to understand that there are diverse cultures within most countries that came about because of patterns of colonialism and linguistic differences (French Canadians), racism (African Americans in the U.S.), colonialism and immigration (Asians in the United Kingdom), and imperial borders (the borders of African nations were drawn without regard for where nations were already living).

Cultures are not defined by national borders. The breakup of Yugoslavia could be used as a case study of the tensions between national borders and cultures. Because of the partition of Germany following World War II, German reunification has had to deal with the two cultures of East and West. There are many other reasons why we want students to look critically at the cultures within and across national borders.

The foundation of substantive culture learning is knowledge of internal culture. As students learn about people's values and beliefs, their norms of behavior, and their interaction and communication styles, they begin to understand their perspectives and worldviews. Often a first step is helping students recognize and appreciate the power of internal culture by having them identify their own assumptions about some fundamental aspects of human interaction and then compare them with those of people in another culture.

Teaching Idea 13
Behavioral Norms

Goal: Student will be able to identify how cultural patterns of thinking affect behavioral norms.

Overview: Students compare what is perceived to be proper behavior in individualistic and collectivist cultures.

Procedures: After an introduction to the concept of internal culture and the "iceberg" graphic, students are asked to circle which of the choices below they themselves have been taught is the right thing to do in each of the situations:

#1 You have been nominated for an award for work that you did on your debate team. Should you (a) agree and hope you win the award or (b) feel embarrassed and turn down the nomination because you don't want other team members to feel bad?

#2 Your uncle's business has a job opening. Should he (a) give the job to the most qualified applicant or (b) to you, his niece, whom he knows needs a job?

#3 A new person at school whom you met running track wants to be friends with you. He recently moved from another city and wears different clothes than you do and speaks with an accent. (a) Should you stick with your own friends or (b) get to know him better?

Share with students that 1a, 2a, 3b are answers frequently given in individualist cultures; the others would be preferred by people in collectivist cultures where children are taught that harmony of the group is more important than other considerations. They would not want to stand out from the group. They would favor people in their own group over others.

Ask students what they think might happen when a person from an individualist culture goes to school in a collectivist culture?

Stages in Culture Learning

Students come to social studies classrooms at different stages in culture learning. Within cross-cultural psychology, sociology, and intercultural communication there has been extensive research on how young people develop understanding of cultures different from their own. Milton Bennett's *Developmental Model of Intercultural Sensitivity* is particularly relevant for the social studies as it provides insights into how teachers can help young people overcome ethnocentrism and develop intercultural competence.[4] Figure 2 (p. 44) is an overview of Bennett's stages of intercultural development and some suggestions for teaching strategies at each stage.

In discussing each of the six stages, Bennett describes the psychology of peoples' thought processes and identifies educational strategies that meet the needs of people in that stage. For example, if students are at the early stage ("there are no cultural differences I need to know about"), activities such as holding an international festival or visiting an exhibit of Chinese art would help them develop recognition of some differences without overwhelming them with profound cultural contrasts. However, if they are at the stage of minimization where cultural differences are recognized but trivialized (the "one world" view of "we are really more alike than different, so I don't have to worry about all those differences"), activities are needed to help students recognize the importance of cultural contexts.

From his research on how students move from one stage to the next, he recommends using experiential learning such as simulations and shared experiences with people from other cultures for the last three stages. Cross-cultural experiential learning reinforces students' recognition of profound cultural differences as it helps them acquire cross-cultural interaction skills to mediate differences.[5]

My first year of teaching included five "world cultures" classes at Riverdale Junior High School in Jonesboro, Georgia. To motivate my students and get beyond the deadly boring "exports and imports" of my textbook, I taught surface culture. Looking back now, I see it was much like a tourist perspective of other cultures. I decorated my room with travel posters and created bulletin boards that focused on surface differences. I motivated my students as though they were experiencing a travelogue: "Let's go visit India and see the Taj Mahal and the Red Fort. We will eat samosas, drink tea, listen to Ravi Shankar (who was playing with the Beatles back then), try on *saris*, and see a video of Hindu temples." The comments of a guest speaker from Nigeria woke me up to the inadequacies of this approach. He told me how disappointed he was that my students not only knew nothing significant about Nigerian people but did not want to listen to what he thought or cared about. "They just want to learn a game or eat some food—what does that teach them that is important?" were the words I shall never forget. I had been training them to think that surface culture was all they needed to know. And I had done nothing to help them learn from or interact with people from other cultures.

Merry Merryfield

Stage	Examples of Developmentally Appropriate Strategies
1. Lack of awareness of cultural differences	Demonstrate cultural differences that are obvious but not threatening. • A guest speaker shares her video of Gaborone where she lived and taught as a Peace Corps volunteer in Botswana.
2. Denigration of cultural differences	Focus on commonalities and contributions. • Demonstration of how the Yoruba show respect to their parents and older people in the community; • Instruction on how Arabs have contributed to scientific achievement.
3. Minimalization of differences	Illustrate how ignorance of differences can have profound effects. • Body language acceptable in one culture can be insulting or forbidden in another (for example, passing food with the left hand or direct eye contact with a superior)
4. Acceptance of behavioral and value differences	Teach cultural complexity. • Case studies of how people within a culture can differ based on their social class, gender, age, etc. • Academic study of culture's effects on behavior
5. Adaptation of skills for interacting and communicating	Focus on real-life interaction and skill development across cultures. • Cooperative learning through shared tasks and goals • Experiences where people have more/less power
6. Integration of intercultural competence	Experiences with different cultures, social classes, etc. • Sustained intercultural experiences with different groups • Academic study of cultural hybridity and change

It is important that children learn that there are times when "just being themselves" with people of another culture is inappropriate or even insulting.[7] Unlike cultural studies that are solely academic, substantive culture learning requires students to use their cultural knowledge and intercultural skills in everyday life to recognize, manage or resolve real cultural misunderstandings and conflicts. Teaching Ideas 14-19 offer class activities that are appropriate for increasing intercultural competence (pp. 45-50 below).

How can knowledge of intercultural stages help teachers? The stages provide ways to assess students' development of intercultural competence and identify appropriate methods and materials. Here are some illustrations of how teachers can recognize where their students are in culture learning and develop appropriate activities.

1: Stage of Lack of Awareness of Cultural Differences

Students in this stage may be genuinely unaware of cultural differences due to the cultural homogeneity of their environment (either from accidental isolation or deliberate separation).

• Are your students isolated physically or psychologically from interacting with people different from themselves as equals?
• Are they unaware that people in the U.S. and the world have different norms of behavior, different values, and different lifestyles?

When teachers recognize this stage, they can provide students with readings, videos, websites, and other visuals that introduce them to some easily understood cultural differences in a developmentally appropriate way.

Teaching Idea 14
Cultural Differences

Goal: Students will recognize cultural differences.

Overview: Students examine materials that allow them to compare Japanese and American perceptions of each other.

Procedures: Students explore the website "Experience a Day in a Student's Life in Higashiharima" (www.yoshiyuki.com/explore/morning1.htm) and take notes on how going to school in Japan is both different and similar to their own experiences. Then, to move beyond recognition of differences, the teacher shows the video "Common Experiences, Different Visions," a documentary that shows how Japanese and American students have stereotypes of each other and what two groups of students in Japan and the U.S. actually have done to overcome their misinformation.[8]

Teaching Idea 15
Arab Americans

Goal: Students confront stereotypes of Arab Americans and replace them with information on contributions.

Procedures: In a unit on immigration, students examine the lives of famous Arab Americans and the contributions they have made to the United States. The teacher directly addresses their stereotypes of Arabs in America through websites and resource people in the community. See 100 Questions about Arab Americans and a special section on stereotypes at www.freep.com/jobspage/arabs.htm and descriptions of famous Arab Americans at www.aaiusa.org/famous_arab_americans.htm

2: Stage of Denigration of Cultural Differences

Students in this stage often criticize people different from themselves. They may make derogatory remarks, refer to stereotypes as knowledge, or exhibit overt hostility. Students may openly demonstrate their feelings of superiority with others whom they view as inferior. However, some students in this stage will have a reversal of attitudes and denigrate their own culture or express feelings that the other culture is superior.

- Do your students demean people different from themselves?
- Do they believe stereotypes of Asians, Africans, Arabs or others?
- Do they act as though they are superior to people of other cultures or other world regions?
- Are they hostile towards people based on their race, ethnicity, language, religion, or national origin?
- Do they assume people in other countries would be better if they were "more like us"?

When teachers recognize this stage, they find it helpful to plan activities where students learn about positive attributes of other cultures and recognize their own culture's similarities to the values, experiences or norms of behavior in other cultures.

3: Stage of Minimizing Differences

Students in the minimization stage play down cultural differences. They may focus on physical similarities (all people have the same physical needs) or transcendence (we are all God's children). This stage of universalism usually develops when people become comfortable in recognizing differences across and within cultures but they do not yet appreciate the significance of those differences or they are not yet comfortable in dealing with such differences. "So what?" a student says as he learns that extended families are extremely important to Iraqis and affect their political and economic infrastructure. "I have a grandmother, too."

- Do your students want to ignore cultural differences?
- Do they lack appreciation of the depth of cultural differences?
- Can the students explain how cultural differences can lead to important misunderstandings and conflicts?

When teachers recognize that their students exhibit minimizing behaviors, they can develop activities that show how cultural differences can create critical problems and conflicts that affect everyone's lives. Critical incident scenarios, case studies, and cultural assimilators can provide students with real-life instances of misunderstandings that arise when cultural, religious, or linguistic differences are not taken into account. Teaching Idea 16 provides an example of misunderstandings based on cultural differences (see p. 46).

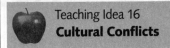

Goal: Students will identify misunderstandings and conflicts based on cultural differences.

Overview: Students examine a case study of a cultural conflict.

Procedures: Select a small group of students to be Cultural Mediators and have them read the entire handout including the "Cultural Norms" section. Have them sit apart from the rest of the class.

Ask a student to read "Mr. Bevis speaks" and then another to read "Mariam speaks."

Have the class identify the problems and hypothesize what differences in cultural and religious norms may be contributing to the problems.

Then ask the Cultural Mediators to present the substance of the "Understanding Cultural Norms" section and begin the discussion of ways that the conflict can be resolved. Final questions might be: If you were to talk to Mariam and her teachers, what would you say? How do we know when cultural misunderstandings are taking place in our school or community?

Mr. Bevis speaks

We have this new Asian student, Mariam, who is not getting off to a very good start. She won't speak in class and ignores me when I try to help her. I heard she has been giving Ms. Walker trouble in gym, and she walked off in a huff in the lunchroom today. She needs to improve her behavior or she will be in serious trouble. We have other Asian students, and they don't have to cover their hair. I don't think she is going to fit in.

Mariam speaks

I just completed my second week here at Cross Keys Middle School. After begging my father to come along with him while he is a visiting professor, I find myself wishing I had stayed at home in Bandung where people are friendly, and I can enjoy my Javanese dance and music. I've studied English since primary grades, but American schools are truly awful places. My PE teacher is very upset with me because I won't wear those indecent clothes and said she will have to fail me in gym. Why can't I play sports in long pants? Mr. Bevis in maths doesn't like me. He told me today I had better pay attention. I don't know what he means. I was trying my best.

People here have no manners. The cafeteria lady actually handed me food with her left hand. I guess they think it is okay to insult me since I am a foreigner. Some boys told me in the hall that they knew I was a terrorist because I cover my hair. I don't know what to do. I can't tell my father. He will think I am bringing shame on the family. I wish I were home.

Understanding Cultural Norms

Mariam is from Indonesia. Her Muslim religious norms and her Javanese cultural norms conflict with many norms in her new school. Many Muslim women believe that they must dress modestly (covering hair, shoulders, and legs). She has never worn shorts and is embarrassed seeing the American girls in them. She has been taught the left hand is dirty, never to be used to touch food or another person or to hand someone something. In her school at home, students honor their teachers and show respect by listening and lowering their eyes when spoken to. They don't question their teachers. Yet when she looks down to show her American teachers respect, they act as though she is not listening.

There are many books with resources on critical incidents and cross-cultural misunderstandings, and students can even develop their own as they research and learn about other cultures. Case studies and simulations are also often very effective in demonstrating why people need to understand cultural differences. See the recommended resources at the end of the chapter.

When people recognize the importance of cultural differences, they enter the three ethnorelative stages of culture learning:

4: Stage of Acceptance of Cultural Differences

Students in the acceptance stage recognize and respect behavioral and value differences. They perceive most cultural differences as neither good nor bad, just different. They acknowledge that across cultures people have different ways of thinking about the group versus the individual, privacy, male/female interactions, showing respect or resolving conflicts, as well as the more obvious differences in dress, food, housing, music, body language, etc.

- Do your students accept cultural differences as real and important?
- Do they know that people from different cultures will interpret events or issues based on their own cultural norms and perspectives?
- When they interact with people from other cultures, do they try to understand the others' points of view?

At this stage most of the students' knowledge is academic, and they need interaction with people different from themselves to develop intercultural skills in applying what they have learned to real-life situations. In this stage teachers often plan activities to develop basic skills in intercultural communication and interaction. In the last decade electronic technologies have created many new opportunities for students to interact with people from diverse cultures.

While there is extensive literature on the power of face-to-face cross-cultural experience in developing the knowledge, skills, and dispositions of worldmindedness, there is much less consensus on the effects of electronic cross-cultural exchanges.[9] Online projects have promised to increase cultural sensitivity and awareness as they develop the skills and experiences needed in a global society. Some scholars have identified positive outcomes, such as perspective taking, critical thinking, increased task engagement, sensitivity to cultural diversity, and social cognition, in some of these projects.[10] However, others who have reviewed such projects and programs have

Teaching Idea 17
Learn About Democracy Online

Goal: Students learn about democracy with students in another country.

Procedures: Students in a school in the US can be linked to students in Poland, Lithuania and Russia to enhance knowledge of democracy. See www.iEARN.org for this and many projects that connect American social studies classes to people across the globe.

Learning Democracy through International Collaboration

One of the main reasons to continue the project, which started last year, is the necessity to improve the teaching of democracy education, and establish a continuous exchange of information and suggestions on different civic issues. The project focuses on children's rights and duties, tolerance and freedom, civic responsibilities and engagement. This way secondary school students in the United States, Poland, Lithuania, and Russia will be able to enhance democracy knowledge, which hopefully will lead to their active participation in the community. For five weeks the participating classes will be posting their responses to the project questions presented prior to the project start and respond to the messages posted by their international partners. Students and teachers will also have an opportunity to dialogue individually with one another in the "student dialogue" and "teacher dialogue" section of the message board. LA CRF, the main facilitator of the project, will host the project material.

Copied from www.iearn.org/projects/democracy.html on February 21, 2004.

found the results to be inconclusive, overly optimistic and even contradictory.[11] Some researchers have noted that online discourse needs to be supplemented with visual images (video-conferencing, videotapes, photos, or other images) to have an impact on changing students' misperceptions.[12]

5: Stage of Adaptation

Students in the adaptation stage have developed some skills in interacting and communicating across cultures. Their affective skills—such as empathy or an understanding of pluralism through multiple cultural frames of reference—are enhanced and expanded in frequent cross-cultural interaction. Students in the adaptation stage exhibit these kinds of skills and knowledge:

- Are your students able to put themselves into the position of another person in a different cultural context and begin to see events and issues through that person's eyes?

- Can they get beyond their own cultural norms and envision events or issues through another set of cultural norms?

- Do students have the knowledge and skills to switch back and forth to examine the realities of an event or issue from two or three cultures' norms?

Empathy is the ability to leave one's own cultural baggage behind and mentally walk a few steps in another person's shoes. Empathizing involves knowing enough about another person's values and thought patterns to be able to imagine what that person is thinking or feeling as she or he experiences an event, makes a decision or considers an issue.

Empathy is a high level intercultural skill because what it requires goes beyond perspective taking. In global education, we refer to perspective consciousness as the ability to recognize that each of us has a culturally-based view of the world that is not universally shared. In fact, some people have worldviews that are profoundly different from our own. To feel empathy, students must learn about other peoples' situations, their beliefs and values, and their norms of behavior, and then try to think about what the other person would feel in a particular situation. The key attribute of empathy with someone of another culture is the ability to put one's own cultural lenses aside and for a few minutes to try to see the world through the other person's cultural lenses.

For example, look back at the scenario of Mariam, the Indonesian student who is having problems in her new school. In the lesson idea above, the task was to identify cultural differences that led to Mariam's problems in the school. If students were in the adaptation stage, they could be asked to role-play Mariam's conversation with a sister or friend back home. Such an exercise would require students to take a few steps in thinking like Mariam and provide an opportunity for students to empathize with her.

The second element in this stage is an understanding that people need to be within a culture in order to understand its cultural frames of reference. As noted in Chapter Two, W.E.B. DuBois wrote about this element in the early 1900s in his explanation of double consciousness. African Americans were able to understand white frames of reference because they grew up within a white society that they had to understand in order to survive. Most minorities within a nation develop

Teaching Idea 18
The Experiences of Refugees and Immigrants

Goal: Students understand the diverse experiences of immigrants and refugees.

Procedures: In the study of refugees, immigration, ethnic conflict and the global movement of people, students will increase their understanding of historical events and current issues if they have opportunities to develop empathy with individuals who have left their homes to find peace and a better life in another place. Ideally students read stories, examine online case studies and meet face to face with refugees past and present in order to understand multiple cultural frames of reference and the significance of differences in both why people leave their homes and what they go through during resettlement.

Resources: Stories of immigrants and refugees can be found in books, CDs and online through organizations such as Amnesty International, university ethnic and area studies programs, school collections, and publishers, such as PBS and Scholastic. These sites have stories about and by immigrants and refugees:

- www1.umn.edu/humanrts/
- teacher.scholastic.com/immigrat/tguide.htm
- www.archq.org/meetref.shtml
- www.otan.us/webfarm/emailproject/grace.htm
- www.birmingham.gov.uk/GenerateContent?CONTENT_ITEM_ID=9513&CONTENT_ITEM_TYPE=0&MENU_ID=5249
- www.refugeeaction.org/stories/refugee_stories.htm
- www.education-world.com/awards/past/2001/r0901-10.shtml
- www.pbs.org/newamericans/6.0/html/immstories.html
- www.perry-lake.k12.oh.us/phs/American%20Experience%20Class/American%20Dream%20Project/collection_of_immigration_storie.htm

multiple frames of reference as children or young adults. White Americans often develop multiple frames of reference by living in neighborhoods where they are a minority or by living in another country.[13]

The cultural pluralism that comes from developing multiple cultural frames of reference has two effects: people internalize two or more different cultural worldviews and they are able to switch back and forth as the situation requires. This process is similar to linguistic facility in speaking different languages or code switching between two forms of English.

It is important to note that understanding pluralism through multiple cultural frames of reference only develops from actual experience within one's own and other cultures. If there are at least two cultures within the school or community, teachers can provide ways for students to learn and interact within those cultures. Ideally all students would graduate from high school with multiple frames of reference which they had learned through long-term intercultural study and on-going cross-cultural experiences.

6: Stage of Integration Across Cultures

Students in the integration stage are able to evaluate new cultural contexts, learn how to interact within them, and deal with constructive marginality, a state in which a person is "always in the process of becoming a part of and apart from a given cultural context."[14] Unlike the adaptation stage, people in the integration state are constantly in the process of integrating within other cultures. The integrated person recognizes the cultural changes that come with living and working in multiple cultures and knows the difference between being of a culture and being on the periphery or margins of a culture. Students in the integration stage have well-developed cross-cultural skills and knowledge and considerable experience in culture learning.

- Have your students integrated themselves within more than one culture (i.e., learned norms and language so they can act, think and feel as do people in that culture)?
- Can the students evaluate the cultural contexts of new situations?
- Can the students appreciate the perspectives, knowledge, and skills that come from being on the margins of a culture?

In integration, people develop skills in contextual evaluation, the ability to analyze and evaluate situations from more than one cultural context. A teacher enters a meeting between a Vietnamese family and her school principal. If she is at the integrative stage she is able to inform her responses and interactions during the meeting from both Vietnamese perspectives and knowledge and the school's norms. Tacitly she recognizes the minefields of cultural conflicts and has the skills to work through them with the others during the meeting. She also knows implicitly that the dynamic for resolution of the problems changes when two Latina teachers join the meeting because they bring their own cultural assumptions about proper behavior and their considerable [...] with immigrant students.

In contextual evaluation people are consci[...] everyday interactions, events, and decisions are [...] upon a specific context. The ability to evaluate cultural contexts is a critical skill for young people growing up in a multicultural society as it teaches them to stop and consider the cultural contexts of situations before proceeding to act from their own cultural norms or make assumptions about other people's motives. It should be noted that contextual evaluation rests upon the assumption that people want to appreciate the significance of cultural differences and want to work effectively with others who are different from themselves. It builds upon previous stages and it takes practice.

Another characteristic of the integration stage is constructive marginality, a concept interpreted in new ways by Janet Bennett.[15] Often Americans perceive people who are on the cusp of two different cultures as misfits and assume cultural marginality is negative. Teachers may see Hiroshi, a student who moved from Japan to Ohio four years ago, as not fitting into his American school, and they become even more concerned when they hear that he is not considered really Japanese when he goes to visit his grandparents in Osaka. They might feel sorry for Miata, an African American girl who grew up on Army bases around the world and now feels different from the students in her new high school in rural Georgia.

Although past generations might have assumed that people would be better off if they stayed "home" and lived monocultural lives, the reality of a globally connected world is that more and more people must be able to work across several cultures within their own community and nation. In some places cultural diversity is already a way of life, and people with bicultural identities can use their bicultural knowledge and bilingual skills to their advantage. Teachers who grew up in Mexico and now help Spanish speakers find success in American schools use their constructive marginality to improve their lives and those of others. Students who are experiencing constructive marginality can help others with intercultural sensitivity and cross-cultural understanding.

Goal: Students understand constructive marginality by collecting data from people who have been placed on the margins by circumstances of movement or social change.

Example: Identify people in the community who have lived in more than one culture and bring them in for a panel discussion of the nature of culture learning, bicultural identity and marginality.

Example: In the study of urbanization, have students work in small groups to interview and email people who have had different experiences with rural and urban settings. Some would be people who have moved from farms or small towns to a big city. Some would be people who grew up in big cities and moved to small towns. And some would be people who have lived in the same place all their lives. The students collect data to answer the question: what is gained or lost when people move to a new environment?

Five Strategies

To develop substantive cultural knowledge and skills, students must confront their stereotypes, acquire indepth knowledge of some cultures, examine other peoples' perspectives and experiences, identify the effects of cultural change and recognize ways in which European imperialism continues to shape American worldviews.[16] Explanations of these strategies are followed by lesson ideas.

1. Addressing Stereotypes, Exotica, and Myths of "The Mysterious Other"

When students enter social studies classrooms they bring with them powerful images of other cultures from the media and other influences in their environment. Their stereotypes, exotic images, and myths about other cultures are barriers to learning about cultures because they distort reality and go hand in hand with prejudice and ethnocentrism.[17] Addressing stereotypes is one of the first steps toward a global perspective.

It is easy to identify stereotypes and other misinformation students have acquired. All we have to do is ask students to tell us what comes to mind when they think of Chinese, Mexicans, Germans, new immigrants, or other cultures under study. Cultural stereotypes are traits assigned to a group of people that are negative, incorrect, or overgeneralized.

Often stereotypes are used as shortcuts so that people do not have to deal with cultural complexity and can justify their own culture's status and behavior.

Researchers have found that students individualize the characteristics of people in their in-group and perceive their behavior as "normal," but they view out-groups in terms of generalized traits and other stereotypical characteristics.[18] For example, white Americans will usually recognize the traits and behaviors of other whites as belonging to individuals but often perceive African Americans or Arabs in terms of generalized characteristics. This tendency to stereotype people different from oneself has several outcomes, which can include justifying prejudice. "I don't have to listen to Abdi because he's Muslim and all Muslims are …." Often the effect of stereotypes is to obfuscate learning, as one student said about a lesson on Christian Arabs: "I know Arabs are Muslim. Don't confuse me with that Christian stuff!" Social studies teachers spend much of their instructional time providing students with information and activities to help them overcome stereotypes.

Because of their seductive qualities, exotic images of other cultures are perhaps even more enduring than stereotypes. Although they have changed over time, these images continue to romanticize and misrepresent other cultures to the point of creating myths of cultures that people may prefer to realities. Exotic images are so embedded in American culture that they are used to sell movies, clothes, sheets, high priced vacations, home decorations, furniture, even ceiling fans and mixed drinks—think about it.

There is "the mysterious Orient" with the riches of the Forbidden City, inscrutable Chinese wearing kimonos, the glamour of *Madame Butterfly* and the beauty and passivity of "oriental" women, the mystique of Geisha girls, exotic temples, fearless Samurai warriors, and the danger of ninjas. Africa's exoticism revolves around images of brave white hunters and near naked, painted Africans dancing or holding spears (Masai *moran* have become the image most frequently used) or running barefoot. Wild animals, safaris, jungles, diamond mines, and danger provide the backdrop for thrilling adventures. The "noble savage" myth is accessorized with pith helmets, khakis, and mosquito nets.

Perhaps the ultimate exotic images are located in the Middle East. What is more exotic than handsome but dangerous sheiks, Arabian horses racing across the desert, the beauties of the harem, the dance of the seven veils, turquoise-tiled fountains, scantily clad belly dancers, adventures in the bazaar and intrigue with nomads or caravans? How can teachers replace the *Arabian Nights/Indiana Jones* images of the Middle East with the realities of life today in Cairo, Baghdad, or the West Bank?

There are many ways to address stereotypes and exotic images. Some teachers begin with a pretest or attitude inventory to identify student beliefs, knowledge, and perceptions about the culture under study. For example an attitude inventory for a unit on East Asia in a 9th grade World Cultures course might include open-ended items such as:

1. When I think of Asia, I think of...
2. Most Chinese families are...
3. Japanese customs include...
4. The climate in Korea is...

Or factual information might be assessed in a true/false pretest:

1. Chinese people have very large families.
2. South Koreans are communists.
3. Some of the largest cities in China are Beijing, Hong Kong, and Taipei.
4. The climate in East Asia is tropical.

Items are selected that highlight content important to the unit such as an understanding of Taiwan's and Hong Kong's special relationships with China. Once teachers learn that students cannot distinguish Chinese from Japanese or think only of panda bears, Geisha girls and Samurai warriors when they think of Asia, they can plan activities that directly counter their students' misinformation with knowledge of every-

day life in the cultures under study. Resources often include excerpts from literature or histories written by the people of the culture and primary source documents such as letters, speeches or diaries.

Teachers can also compare the stereotypical images of other cultures with photographs that show the reality of contemporary life in those cultures. Using the image and photograph on this page, teachers could ask students what impression of Japanese women they have. Is it exotic or is it similar to the realities of Japanese girls and women today?

Researchers have found that words are not nearly as effective as visuals are in helping students overcome stereotypes and exotica.[19] However, many films and videos in use are dated or focus on exotic content—temples, ceremonies, traditional clothes, special celebrations—while omitting the realities of everyday life for average people. Websites and webcams can be powerful resources in helping students actually see life in other places as it really is and they are, for the most part, free and do not become outdated. Teaching Idea 20 shows how they can be used in an activity in Japan.

Teaching Idea 20
Stereotypes and Exotica

Goal: Students juxtapose stereotypes with actual images using the internet.

Procedures: Write down what you think would be the stereotypes and exotic images your students have of the Japanese. Make a list of at least ten items that they associate with Japanese people today. Then go to www.hbc.co.jp/news/hbc-newsi-e.html and click on each of the webcams. You will see people walking down the street, disc jockeys, and other scenes. If your students looked at these webcams in Sapporo, would they see anything to support their stereotypes? Students could compare images from several webcams across Japan (just about every Japanese city has a website with several webcams on day and night). School websites and sites developed by Japanese students are other excellent resources that can dispel stereotypes and exotica.

Ask your students: Do books and media use words that are stereotypical, patronizing or inaccurate? STOP when you see these words in books about Africa and substitute more accurate ones.

STOP words	SUBSTITUTE	NOTES
Jungle	Rainforest	Only 5% of Africa is rainforest
Backward, Primitive	Indigenous or traditional	These words are demeaning and used to indicate inferiority.
Bush	Savannah	About 40% of Africa is grassland
Native	Tanzanian, Hausa, African	This word is demeaning and used to indicate inferiority.
Witch doctor	Herbalist, indigenous doctor	We call traditional medicines "home remedies"
Native costume	Clothes, national dress	Incorrect use of the word "costume"
Pagan religion	Traditional or indigenous religion	This term is inaccurate and used to indicate inferiority.
Juju or superstition	Faith, belief system	Beliefs are faith. This term is inaccurate and used to indicate inferiority.
Hut	Home or house	Used to denote inferiority
Many wives	Polygamy	Although Islam allows four wives, less than 10% of Africans have more than one wife.
Bantu people	Bantu languages	Bantu is a language group, not the name of a people.
Pygmy	Mbuti	This is a derogatory name made up by Europeans.
Bushman	Basarwa	This is a derogatory name made up by Europeans.

Researchers have found that prejudice and stereotyping can be reduced though two steps. First students engage in activities with new knowledge that disconfirms specific stereotypes and replaces them with new information. Figure 3 and Teaching Idea 21 suggest ways of substituting accurate expressions for stereotypical language about Africa, while the box on page 53 offers cautions about the use and misuse of the word "tribe" in discussions of African peoples. Second, the new information is reinforced through meaningful real-life experiences.[20] For example, a teacher who recognizes her students perceive people in China as poor, uneducated, and starving has them work with maps and statistics on Chinese demographics and shows a video on a day in the life of a middle class family in Beijing. Once they have more knowledge, she has them interact in small groups with six Chinese (some professionals, some working class) who live in the local community to reinforce the academic work with first-hand experiences.

Teaching Idea 21
STOP Words

Goal: Students identify stereotypes and pejorative language and replace them with new knowledge.

Procedures: After identifying students' stereotypes, pejorative language and misperceptions about Africa in general, the teacher has them use the STOP words listed in Figure 3 to critique books and videos from the school library. This lesson could be a first step in addressing stereotypes and derogatory language. See also www.africaaction.org/bp/ethnic.htm

Teaching against stereotypes and exotic images goes beyond addressing misinformation. Students need to understand how stereotypes and exotic images have been used as political, cultural, even military weapons. Since history began, some

CONTINUED ON PAGE 55

Thinking about the Use of the Word "Tribe"

Few current K-12 texts use the word "tribe" in their discussion of African peoples, and most scholars today agree that the word promotes misleading stereotypes, has no consistent meaning, carries historical and cultural assumptions, and blocks accurate views of current African realities. The use of the word "tribe"— a term coined by European anthropologists to describe the organization of groups sharing common language, culture and territory—obscures our understanding of the complexities of the African continent. The word has been used to describe the Zulu who became a powerful state only two centuries ago, and the !Kung hunter-gatherers, for Masai herders and Kikuyu farmers and members of those groups who live in cities.

Tribe is particularly inappropriate in describing the Rwandan civil war. Not only do Hutus and Tutsis share the same language and culture, but their relationships have been mediated by modern institutions such as states with armies, identity cards, state-run newspapers and radio (and a secret hate-radio station for Hutus), cash-crop markets, and complicated by regional and urban-rural tension among Hutus.

Historically, Donald R. Wright writes in *The World and a Very Small Place in Africa, a History of Globalization in Niumi, The Gambia* (2004), "ethnicity as we think of it—a clear identity with, and strong loyalties to, an ethnic group — almost certainly did not exist in precolonial West Africa."[†] He describes Niumi's early population as a conglomeration of peoples who had various and fluid individual and group identities, spoke several languages, and existed comfortably together. However, Europeans assumed Africans identified with a tribe or ethnic group as they did, and so the British colonial administrators demanded that people be identified as Mandinka or Jola or Serahuli.

"Talking about Tribe," published by the Africa Policy Information Center,[††] explains that "Calling nearly all African social groups tribes and African identities tribal in the era of scientific racism turned the idea of tribe from a social science category into a racial stereotype." While Africans themselves often still use the term "tribe," the word does not have the same connotation for them as for many Americans for whom tribe conjures up timelessness and primitive savagery and hides the modern character of African ethnicity.

"Talking about Tribe" concludes: "To say African groups are not tribes and African identities are not tribal, in the common-sense meanings of those words, is not to deny that African ethnic divisions exist. It is to open questions: what is their true nature? How do they work? How can they be presented from taking destructive forms? It is, moreover, to link the search for those answers in Africa to the search for answers to the similar questions that press on humanity everywhere in the world today."

So what are the alternatives to tribe? Sometimes "ethnic group" or "people" or "group" or just the name may be appropriate, as in the Ewe in Ghana or Togo. However, that Ewe person may prefer to be called by his nationality first.

What is important is that students learn that the history and meanings of words do matter.

There is much academic literature on "tribe," but particularly accessible to teachers is the article "The Trouble with 'tribe'" in *Teaching Tolerance*, Spring 2001, based on the Africa Policy Information Center background paper "Talking about 'Tribe,'" quoted above. *Mistaking Africa: Curiosities and Inventions of the American Mind* by Curtis Keim (Boulder, CO: Westview Press, 1999) includes an excellent chapter entitled "Africans Live in Tribes, Don't They?" and would also be helpful to teachers who want their students to understand how they learn about Africa from television, the print media, and other sources.

†   Donald R. Wright, *The World and a Very Small Place in Africa: a History of Globalization in Niumi, The Gambia* (Armonk, NY: M.E. Sharpe, 2004).

††   Chris Lowe et al, "Talking about 'Tribe': Moving from Stereotypes to Analysis" (Washington, DC: Africa Policy Information Center, 1997).

Concept of Self *A continuum from individualist to collectivist*	The more a culture is individualistic, the more people are expected to look after themselves. Individualist cultures value independence and self-reliance. They work hard for recognition. Children are taught to take care of themselves. In collectivist cultures identity is the function of one's group. Students or employees do not want to stand out. The group demands harmony and loyalty, and, in return, looks after its members their whole lives.
Tolerance for Inequities[23] *A continuum from low to high*	The higher the tolerance, the more people tolerate inequities as part of life. Cultures with low tolerance for inequities see power inequities as unjust and want to overcome them.
Uncertainty avoidance *A continuum from low to high*	The more a culture has high uncertainty avoidance, the more people want structure, rules, and strict codes of behavior. People in cultures characterized by high uncertainty avoidance are active, aggressive, security-seeking and intolerant. Cultures with weak uncertainty avoidance are contemplative and do not want a lot of rules. They are accepting of personal risk, and relatively tolerant.
Gender *Masculine/ feminine*	The more a culture is masculine, the more people enforce strict gender roles. They stress material success and respect whatever is big, strong and fast. Very feminine cultures encourage overlapping roles for both sexes and stress interpersonal relationships and concern for the weak.
Time *Monochronic to Polychronic*	The more monochronic a culture is, the more time is a valued resource. People take deadlines and schedules very seriously. Getting to class on time is more important that stopping to greet a friend. People do one thing at a time and finish one task before beginning another. People stay in line to wait their turn. Polychronic cultures bend time to meet needs. Schedules and deadlines are flexible. People will get there when they can but human relationships are more important than time. People can work on many tasks and interact with several people at the same time. People don't stand in line.
Responsibility *Universalist to Particularist*	The more universalist a culture is, the more people know what's right is always right. There are no exceptions. Fair treatment means everyone is treated the same. Favoritism and nepotism are frowned on. People succeed because of what they do. In particularist cultures, there are no absolutes. What is right depends on the situation. Fair means treating everyone uniquely, and people know everything is not fair. Favoritism is the norm because the system is not fair. Whom you know is more important than your performance.
Locus of Control *A continuum from internal to external*	The more the locus of control is internal, the more people believe they make their own luck. Unhappiness is one's own fault. Where there is a will, there is a way. In other cultures the locus of control is external. People believe in luck and think that fate controls their lives. They accept that things happen and destiny cannot be changed.
Importance of Face *A continuum from little to very important*	In cultures where face is very important, people want to preserve harmony and are likely to say whatever makes the other person feel good. Strengthening interpersonal relations is more important than the telling the truth. In cultures where face is less important, telling the truth is more valued than worrying about someone's feelings. People say no or confront people when they need to do so.
Degree of Directness *A continuum from indirect to direct*	The more a culture is direct, the more people say what they think. And when they say yes, they mean it. In indirect cultures people must read between the lines. People suggest or hint at what they think or take some action that lets someone know that there is a problem. People may say "yes" when they mean "maybe" or "no" as it is more polite to agree.

people have used stereotypes to categorize and demean those whom they view as inferior or the enemy. (See Teaching Idea 22.) In the video, *Faces of the Enemy*, Sam Kean shows an amazing collection of posters and cartoons from World War II and other conflicts that demonstrate how different countries have used the same images to demonize their enemies—the enemy is a devil, a barbarian, a beast, reptile, insect, an animal.[21]

Students need practice in identifying how stereotypes and other cultural misinformation have been used throughout history to justify aggression and colonialism and condone slavery and genocide. Teachers can help students practice their research and critical thinking skills by looking at how stereotypes are used today by hate groups, terrorists, and others who want to rally their group against The Other.[22]

Teaching Idea 22
Demonizing the Enemy

Goal: Students analyze how enemies are portrayed across cultures and time periods.

Procedures: Have students examine cartoons about enemies from different countries or countries under study. How do cartoonists portray enemies? What are commonalities and differences across different countries and different time periods?

Resources:

- www.cartoonstock.com/newscartoons/directory/e/enemy.asp
- www.utexas.edu/coc/journalism/SOURCE/j363/lecturenotes/lecture5/sld015.htm
- abcnews.go.com/sections/world/DailyNews/demonizing_enemy030129.html

---

2. Understanding Internal Culture

Knowledge of internal culture provides a framework for understanding and interacting with people of diverse cultures. Although people may make different choices and hold different opinions from others in their culture, there are cultural patterns of thinking that shape people's assumptions and norms of behavior.

Figure 4 presents some of the thought patterns that shape cultural behaviors and worldviews.[23]

There are many other cultural thought patterns that prescribe behavior.

Case studies, simulations, cultural assimilators and cross-cultural experiences can be used to teach students how cultural thought patterns affect communication, interaction and understanding. Craig Storti's *Figuring Foreigners Out* has a series of activities in which students identify their own cultural norms on a continuum from the extremes of individualist to collectivist (and other patterns of thought such as those in Figure 4) and then compare them to norms in a dozen other cultures. His dialogues (similar in structure to the following lesson idea) demonstrate how differences in thought patterns create significant cultural misunderstandings.

Several publications of Intercultural Press (www.interculturalpress.com) offer dialogues, case studies, and culture-specific information that can help students become familiar with cultural thought patterns. We highly recommend Seelye's *Experiential Activities for Intercultural Living*, Archer's *Living with Strangers in the U.S.A.* and Storti's *Cross-Cultural Dialogues* for resources on cross-cultural interaction. It is important that K-12 students recognize how cultural differences affect the ways in which people make judgments, ask questions, make sense of body language, develop expectations, and interact with others. Teaching Idea 23 suggests an activity to help students understand cultural differences (p. 56).

3. Teaching Perspective Consciousness and Multiple Perspectives

In developing skills in perspective consciousness, students learn to look at past or present events and issues through the cultural lenses of other people and explore the diversity of perspectives that exist within societies.

In the first stage students develop the ability to recognize how their own perspectives (sometimes referred to collectively as a person's world view) are cultural constructions that change over time and are not universally shared by others. In the second stage, students examine the perspectives of people in several cultures and work on understanding their patterns of thought. What cultural beliefs, values, and norms shape the perspectives of people in that culture? What knowledge and experiences influence their ways of seeing and interpreting an event or issue? Why do people within a culture see things quite differently at times? In the third stage, students begin to develop the ability to put themselves into the position of another person and see an event or issue through that person's eyes in order to more fully understand the other culture and the event or issue under study. (See Teaching Idea 24, p. 57.)

Figure 5 (p. 57) shows how stages of perspective consciousness might be used in teaching about Germany in a unit on World War II.

Goal: Students are able to identify misunderstandings that come from cultural differences.

Procedures: Give students the two dialogues to read or let them act them out in class. Ask students to hypothesize what the cultural misunderstandings might be. Then share the "Notes" with them and have students discuss ways that cultural differences can cause problems and suggest strategies on how these misunderstandings can be overcome.

#1 Help Me

Kim comes up to Ms Garcia's desk.

Ms. Garcia: Kim, how are you? Let me see your paper.

Kim: Here you are. What do you think of the second section?

Ms. Garcia: Kim, your writing has improved. Can you tell me why you used this quote?

Maria and Jose approach Ms. Garcia.

Maria: Hey Ms. Garcia, can you help me find that reference you mentioned?

Ms. Garcia: Sure Maria. I think it is on my desk. Let me look.

Jose: I've finished now, Ms Garcia. Can you see if it is okay?

Ms. Garcia: Hi Jose. I'd love to look at your paper.

Kim: But Ms. Garcia, you were going to help me. I want to talk about my paper.

Ms. Garcia: We are talking about your paper.

- What is the problem here?
- What cultural differences exist?
- How are belief systems in conflict?

Notes: #1 is an example of the misunderstandings that can result when someone from a monochronic culture interacts with someone from a polychronic culture. Ms. Garcia feels comfortable working on many tasks and interacting with several people at the same time. She would feel badly if someone came up to her desk and she did not greet them. She feels she is responding well to all. Kim, however, comes from a monochronic culture and expects her teacher to finish working with her before she talks to the others. She thinks Ms Garcia is ignoring her and resents the other students not waiting their turns.

#2 The Interview

Mr. Allen: Well, now we have five applicants for the job. Whom shall we interview first?

Mr. Ali: My nephew has applied.

Mr. Allen: Well, that is nice. Whom should we see first? Should we take them in alphabetical order?

Mr. Ali: My nephew is here.

Mr. Allen: We will get to him in time.

- What is the problem here?
- What cultural differences exist?
- How are their belief systems in conflict?

Notes: #2 is an example of how two different cultural patterns can merge together. First Mr. Allen comes from a universalist culture and believes all the applicants should be treated the same. The most qualified person should be hired. Mr. Ali demonstrates particularist norms of wanting to hire his nephew. After all, he needs a job and Mr. Ali knows he can do the work. Second, Mr. Ali also demonstrates norms of an indirect culture in that he does not say directly "hire my nephew." He hints at it in a rather indirect way, and since Mr. Allen comes from a direct culture, he misses the point entirely and has no idea that Mr. Ali expects his nephew to be hired.

Teaching students to understand how their own perspectives are not universally shared is relatively easy as many students today live in culturally diverse communities and know from experience that friends from different backgrounds often see situations differently or their families have different norms or beliefs. However, most students do need some practice in recognizing how their own cultural beliefs, values, norms, knowledge and experiences shape the ways in which they process information.

Figure 5: Stages of Perspective Consciousness

STAGE	Possible activities for a U.S. History unit on World War II
STAGE 1 Students are able to recognize that their own points of view are cultural constructions that change over time and are not universally shared by others. Students understand that it is normal for people of different cultures to have diverse, even conflicting, perspectives.	What rights should religious, racial or ethnic minorities have within a nation? Students compare their own points of view on the rights of minorities with statements made by Germans, French, Poles, Americans, and others in the World War II period. When does a country have the right to invade another country? Students compare their own points of view on when countries should send armies into another with statements made by Americans, Germans, and French in the World War II period and today.
STAGE 2 Students are able to explain how people's cultural beliefs, values, norms of behavior, and experiences shape their world views. Given appropriate data, students can identify how people's world views influence their interpretation of an event or issue. Students recognize that cultures are complex and there is diversity of thought within every culture.	Students read primary sources on why Germans felt they had the right to invade and control other countries. And they read primary sources on how diverse Europeans and Americans perceived and reacted to German expansionism during the 1930s and into the war. They identify underlying value assumptions, knowledge, and experiences that shaped people's perspectives. Students examine cultural norms and values of German culture in the 1920s and 1930s and identify events and issues that triggered the country's political leadership and eventual aggression. They answer the questions: how did Germans view the Treaty of Versailles? Why was Hitler able to target Jews and other minorities as scapegoats? How did some Germans resist Nazi beliefs and actions?
STAGE 3 Students learn how cultural knowledge can be used to "try on" the perspectives of a person in another culture. Students hypothesize what it would be like to experience an event or discuss an issue as that person.	Given profiles of diverse Jewish and Christian young people in pre-war and World War II Germany, students try to put themselves in the place of one young person as they hear about Jews being removed from their neighborhood. What do you know? What do you feel? What do you do?

Teaching Idea 24
Perspective Consciousness

Goal: Students demonstrate perspective consciousness.

Procedures: Take an event from the news that has a strong cultural component and is related to the topic under study. Ask students to interpret that event. Then give them reactions from people of other cultures (or religions, ethnicities, etc.). For example, during a global cultures unit on Europe, a middle school teacher brought in an article about the French decision to ban Muslim girls' wearing of head scarves in school. The students agreed that the girls should be able to wear a scarf if they wanted to and truly did not understand why anyone would want to ban them.

Then the teacher had one half of the class read the points of view of people in favor of the ban and the other half read points of view of those people in France who were against it. When the class came back together and debated the issue from those data, they were all able to explain how people's perspectives are related to their cultural assumptions and experiences. And they had learned the valuable lesson that all French people do not think alike.

Figure 6: One Point of View vs. Multiple Perspectives

Topic	One point of view	From multiple perspectives
Democracy	Based on perspectives of people who have always had political rights; based solely on European and American perspectives.	Balance with perspectives of those Americans who were disenfranchised by their gender or skin color and the experiences of people whose democracies are different from the US, such as Great Britain, France, Botswana, India, Japan, Indonesia.
Colonialism	Based on perspectives of people who colonized others.	Balance with perspectives of people in Africa, Asia, the Americas, etc., who experienced colonial rule in different time periods and with different colonizers.
Slavery	Based on the perspectives of ancient Greeks and Romans who allowed slavery, or white Americans and Europeans from 1500-1865.	Balance with perspectives of slaves in different situations in different countries, freed slaves, people who sold slaves, those who escaped from slavery, people who are enslaved today.
The American westward movement	Based on the perspective of manifest destiny.	Balance with perspectives of diverse Native Americans, Mexicans, African Americans and whites who had different perspectives on expansionism.
Communism	Based on American foreign policy perspectives	Balance with perspectives of people who lived under communism in diverse places, communist party members, people who fled communism.
Islam	Based on white Christian perspectives	Balance with perspectives of diverse Muslim men and women in several parts of the world, Muslim scholars, minorities of other religions who have lived or live in countries that are mostly Muslim.
Christianity	Based on white Christian perspectives	Balance with perspectives of diverse Christian men and women in several parts of the world, and of minorities of other religions who have lived or currently live in countries that are mostly Christian.
World trade	Based on official U.S. government policies	Balance with perspectives of workers in different places around the world, people who have both lost and gained jobs through trade agreements and decisions of multinational corporations, people who run companies both large and small, labor unions, people who work in energy, manufacturing, service, agricultural and tech sectors; environmentalists and people who disagree with environmentalist agendas.

To teach perspective consciousness, social studies teachers incorporate multiple perspectives into lessons about topics that cannot be understood if students only have access to one point of view. (See Figure 6.) Perhaps the most popular application of multiple perspectives has developed around the study of Christopher Columbus and other European explorers. Students read primary sources not only by Columbus and other Europeans but also by Native Americans and other peoples affected by European exploration. They examine how people's cultural norms provide very different interpretations of the European/American encounters past and present. *Rethinking Columbus* is a prime example of instructional materials that are popular with teachers who want students to understand the ways in which Indians and other groups experienced and thought about the actions of Columbus and how events 500 years ago affect people's lives today.

Think about the difference in what students would understand about their world if they only are taught perspectives of one point of view versus multiple perspectives on important topics in the social studies.

Multiple perspectives add complexity and depth to social studies topics whether they be events (the Vietnam conflict), issues (free trade), or concepts (revolution). Students need to compare diverse European and Middle Eastern perspectives on the Crusades, African and European perspectives on colonialism, and North Korean, South Korean, Russian, Chinese, and American perspectives on a divided Korea. If students are to understand the Middle East today, they need to understand diverse perspectives from the region, including those that are in conflict with American foreign policy.

4. Teaching the Dynamics of Cultural Change

One of the perennial problems in American social studies is the tendency to teach about other cultures as pure, static, isolated, and unchanging. There are three dimensions to this problem. First is the issue of access to current information and the latest scholarship. We often have teachers in our courses who last studied other world regions 25 or more years ago. Every place on the planet has changed in the last three decades and some changes have been astounding. Think of how computers and the internet, AIDS, immigration, pollution, biotech, and terrorism have affected people's lives across the world. The Cold War is over and along with the reunification of Vietnam and Germany we have many new countries and the new European unification to learn about. What we knew about South Africa under apartheid is only history now since we need to be able to teach about how South Africa has changed under majority rule.

There was a time (at least for those of us who have been teaching awhile) when social studies teachers may have taught about Taiwan, South Korea, or Turkey as Third World, non-industrialized countries. Now we can use these countries to teach about relationships between economic prosperity and social and political change. Although teachers may learn from conferences and journals or keep up with changes in a particular country or region of interest, it is very difficult for any social studies teacher or professor to stay up to date on all world regions. This problem is often compounded by diminishing school budgets and aging films, videos, library books, and texts.

The second dimension of the problem is the practice of "pigeon-holing" cultures within a particular time period or within the context of a particular topic as though that is the only time they existed and they are not connected to other cultures or world events. If American students only study Koreans during the Korean War in the 1950s, how can they possibly appreciate economic, political, and cultural changes that have changed Koreans' lives over the last 50 years? If Americans only study Russians in the context of communism or Brazilians in the context of environmental issues, how can they understand these people today?

No doubt many students have no idea that there are Native Americans alive today since they rarely study them beyond the contexts of white settlement in the past. Ask your students to describe what they think of when you say "Indian." Then think about what students learn about how the world works today when whole cultures, countries or regions are ignored in the curriculum except when Europeans settled there or when Americans went to war or traded with them.

The third dimension is the preference for teaching cultural "purity" over cultural synthesis, hybridity or global connections. This preference can be seen when teachers choose to teach minority "traditional" cultures (once called primitive cultures) within a country rather than the cultures of the majority of people. The myth of the noble savage comes to mind as a part of some people's efforts to romanticize so-called untouched "primitive" cultures. For example, a teacher spends the two days allotted to southern Africa on what she refers to as "the Bushmen," the San, who are a very small minority and live in many ways quite differently from the majority of people in Botswana, South Africa, and other countries in southern Africa. In research with such teachers, we have found that they desire to teach about people who are pure, "untainted" Africans, as opposed to those Africans who have been influenced by Europeans, Arabs, Asians or even other Africans. Unfortunately, by focusing on the most unusual people within a region, the teacher has denied her students access to the majority of African cultures and everyday life within these countries. It would be similar to a teacher looking for Americans who have not been influenced by other cultures over the last 200 years and deciding to teach about the Amish as the real Americans. If the goal is global understanding, cultures should be selected for study based on their representativeness. Since the American curriculum does not have room for the study of every culture, the question is, which cultures will help students understand regions and the state of the planet?

One of the most important dimensions of teaching culture is helping students understand how all cultures are constantly changing and evolving as people connect with new ideas, products and ways of thinking. Often we teach about how cultures have changed because of conquest. We know how the peoples who came under the power of the Roman Empire, the Ottoman Empire, or the Soviet Union changed because of that rule. What we often don't teach about is how those societies that in one way or another ruled or dominated others also changed. Traders, explorers, soldiers, religious missions, and settlers were always influenced by the people they came into contact with. Since early humans walked the earth, cultural borrowing, cultural diffusion, and cultural hybridity have characterized the human experience.

There are many opportunities within the social studies to teach about cultural change, hybridity, and connections across cultures. Every culture and time period has some relevant illustrations of how people made accommodations for new ideas (for example, the ways in which many Africans blended aspects of their indigenous religions with Christianity so that both sets of beliefs were accommodated), borrowed ways of doing things (Europeans learned about the use of quinine to treat malaria from people in South America), or adapted new resources or products to their own needs (think of the effect of the American potato on Irish and other European peoples). See "Gandhi is Fasting" in Teaching Idea 25 on this page, which shows how an Indian leader who got his start in South Africa influenced the African American movement for civil rights in the United States.

In *Culture and Imperialism*, Edward Said articulates a pedagogy for teaching about hybridity and cultural complexity that fits well within the social studies. He suggest that students can "look back at the cultural archive" and "reread it not univocally but contrapuntally, with a simultaneous awareness both of the metropolitan history that is narrated and of those other histories against which (and together with which) the dominating discourse acts."[24] By examining the blending and fusion of cultures, contrapuntal pedagogy goes beyond multiple perspectives. Instead the focus is on the interaction and integration of cultures, the dynamic process in which the peoples who came into contact were changed as they experienced each other's lifestyles, technologies, goods, and ideas about the natural world, community, spirituality, and governance.

By organizing contrapuntal history or cultural studies by events or ideas valued by people in many cultures (not only Americans), students can identify the power that comes with who frames the questions. They can recognize the limitations of knowledge that focuses on a single perspective or only on cultural differences. In *Uses of Culture*, Cameron McCarthy

Teaching Idea 25
Global Protest and Prejudice

Goal: Students recognize the significance of the interconnectedness of protest and prejudice across the world.

Overview: Students make connections between the ideas and experiences of Indians and African Americans.

Procedures: Ask students why an African American in 1943 would write a poem about an Indian halfway around the world. Have students read *Gandhi Is Fasting*, written by Langston Hughes in 1943. What did African Americans and Indians have in common in the early 1940s?

This activity can kickoff student research on the interconnectedness of ideas of protest and reform for people of color across the Americas, Africa, and Asia. Martin Luther King Jr. studied Gandhi's strategies and adapted many within the American context. Gandhi first practiced non-violent protest when he was a young attorney in South Africa.

Gandhi is Fasting
By Langston Hughes

Mighty Britain, tremble!
Let your empire's standard sway
Let it break entirely –
My Gandhi fasts today.

You may think it foolish –
That there's no truth in what I say –
That all of Asia's watching
As Gandhi fasts today.

All of Asia's watching.
And I am watching, too,
For I am also jim crowed –
As India is jim crowed by you.

You know quite well, Great Britain,
That it is not right
To starve and beat and oppress
Those who are not white.

Of course, we do it too.
Here in the U.S.A.
May Gandhi's prayers help us, as well,
As he fasts today.

Teaching Idea 26
Balancing Perspectives of The Other

Goal: To make connections across time and place, students can analyze white people's perspectives of Africans and African Americans and then compare those ideas to Africans' and African Americans' perspectives on whites.

Procedures: Depending upon the curricular topic, the focus could be on Europeans' depictions of African women, African women writers' descriptions of whites; or white American literature on African American women compared with African American women's writing, such as Michelle Wallace's "Negative Images: Towards a Black Feminist Cultural Criticism."[25]

criticizes multiculturalists, who in their efforts to view the world through the lens of racial or ethnic identity "stack African Americans, Latinos, and Native Americans against Polish Americans, Italian Americans, Jewish Americans, etc."[26] Instead of continuing these divisions, he encourages educators to "study the historical and contemporary heterogeneity of human interactions and lives."[27] Thus the curriculum does not focus on or try to reconstruct "pure" or "authentic" cultures. It focuses on understanding the mutual shaping and blending and connections that characterize world cultures today.

5. Recognizing the Inheritance of Imperial Worldviews

We need to learn again how five centuries of studying, classifying and ordering humanity within an imperial context gave rise to peculiar and powerful ideas of race, culture, and nation that were, in effect, conceptual instruments that the West used both to divide up and educate the world.[28]

John Willinsky

In *Learning to Divide the World*, John Willinsky examines how histories and literature written under imperialism "live on, for many of us, as an unconscious aspect of our education."[29] An imperial worldview can be recognized by its framework of opposition, the ways in which the world's peoples are divided and described, or by its "scientifically underwritten racism."[30] Whether the terms are The Orient/The Occident, First World/Third World, free/communist or industrialized/developing nations, imperial worldviews demand an "us"–usually the white middle class descendants of Western Europeans who are said to have developed de-

mocracy and today make the world safe—and "them," the Others who are divided from real Americans by their culture, skin color, language, politics, or other differences. The legacy of imperialism may be visible in the curriculum through the teaching of European diffusionism (as discussed above), racialized identities, and a reliance upon American and European scholars and writers.[31]

How can students learn about the legacy of imperialism? Teachers can begin with students examining the European struggle from the fifteenth to eighteenth centuries to make sense of the unprecedented sights that they came unto contact with in their explorations of Africa, Asia, and what they named "the new world." (See Teaching Idea 27.)At first mythical creatures from Pliny's *Historia Naturalis* filled the navigators' maps and biblical prophecies were used to explain new lands and phenomena. Eventually the contrast between accepted knowledge of the world and their own experiences led the early European explorers and colonizers to recognize that "much of their learning had been shaken, if not undone, and they needed to rebuild that world anew."[32]

Teaching Idea 27
Inventing America through Maps

Goal: Students compare European maps over several centuries.

Procedures: Rabasa's chapter "Allegories of Atlas" in *Inventing A-M-E-R-I-C-A: Spanish Historiography and the Formation of Ethnocentrism* offers insights into the construction of Mercator's 1636 Atlas, his world maps, and their impact on education.[33] Students can analyze maps, histories, literature, and visuals to trace early changes in European thinking about other places and cultures and juxtapose constructions by the people they were interacting with in Africa, Asia and the Americas.

Resources: See Antiquarian Maps at www.library.yale.edu/MapColl/africa.html

Instructional materials that pull together literature, primary sources, and critiques for such a lesson are available from Rethinking Schools, The Network for Educators on the Americas (NECA), and many of the African, Asian and Middle Eastern Title VI area studies centers in the U.S. See the resources at the end of the chapter for collections that are especially pertinent to the social studies.

As exploration led to empire, the interpretation of these

Goal: Students analyze books and media to see if imperial frameworks continue to affect their ideas.

Procedures: Does the imperial framework still shape ideas, books and media today? Students can test these ideas by examining the mainstream academic knowledge of their school or community. They could also compare scholarly publications or texts from previous generations with those of today. In deciding what should serve as data for analysis of mainstream academic knowledge, teachers could choose to focus on academic scholarship (textbooks, journals) in libraries and museums or include popular knowledge through trade, business or government documents, cultural or leisure attractions (theme parks, plays, exhibitions, fairs, circuses), and media (newspapers, TV, films, music, cartoons). Below is a checklist students could use in their inquiry.

Does an Imperial Framework Live On?

1. Is there a portrayal of "The Other" (people of color in the U.S. or peoples in Africa, Asia, Latin America, the Middle East) based only upon European or American perceptions and scholarship?

2. Are there unstated assumptions that Americans or Europeans are superior to people of other cultures? Or is it implied that those "people over there" would be better off if they were more like Americans?

3. Is learning structured to focus on differences between Americans and other cultures?

4. Are people in the other cultures portrayed as ignorant, amusing, violent, exotic or bizarre?

5. Do people in other countries appear as backdrops for American or European experiences, decisions, wars, and other actions? Are people in other cultures less frequently named or treated with much less attention, voice, or complexity of character?

6. Are there justifications for European imperialism in Africa, the Americas, Asia, the Middle East? Is it implied that whites had the right to take land away from people of color, segregate them, tax then, move them or take their resources?

7. Is it implied that racism or imperialism ended long ago and no longer exists today?

8. Do people who suffered from, resisted or overcame imperialism, colonialism, or other acts of discrimination receive little attention?

9. Are culture or nationality linked to racial differences or ethnic purity?

10. Is colonial or imperialist literature used (Conrad's *Heart of Darkness*, for example)? Is colonial or imperialist language used (such as oriental, bushman, pygmy)? And are there assumptions of superiority (rationalizations for imperialism as in manifest destiny)? Are the language, literature, and perspectives of colonized peoples present?

new worlds developed into a vast scholarship that provided new explanations and a reordering of both past and present knowledge. "Like architects after an earthquake, many lettered Europeans saw a chance to rebuild a world."[34]

Over five centuries, knowledge was generated in the name of imperialism's intellectual interests by scientists, naturalists, ethnographers, historians, geographers, journalists, painters, and poets. This "research and development arm of imperialism" informed education and made "the whole world coherent for the West by bringing all we knew of it within the imperial order of things."[35] Literature from "the colonies," visual images from sketches, paintings and photos, and the incredible physical acquisitions brought back to Europe provide fertile ground for students to examine how Europeans interacted with and made sense of their new environments. What did they choose to paint, to write about, to collect?

Willinsky's meticulous details and references are rich resources in themselves for the social studies classroom. In "The Imperial Show and Tell," he provides many examples of how not only animals and artifacts were exhibited for European edification, but also people of color. For example, in 1810 a Xhosa girl of sixteen was brought to London where she was exhibited nude as the "Hottentot Venus."

Her body became the subject of cartoons and vaudeville plays and, as she became famous, the show moved to Paris. When she died at 25, her body was dissected by Georges Cuvier, the founder of comparative anatomy, who took this opportunity to compare her organs to those of orangutans and then prepare and present them to the Académie Royale de Médecine to demonstrate the "African perversity, deforma-

tion, and pathology" said to be caused by Africans' primitive sexual appetites and lack of morals.[36]

Students can examine connections between the racism of imperialism and the knowledge of European social scientists. Students can also examine how their zoos, museums and fairs developed from the European dedication to describing, organizing, labeling and interpreting everything they perceived of interest as they "discovered" the new world.

Students can explore how colonial rule and trade gave rise to many structures and processes for storing and expanding knowledge about the world: experimental agriculture and the import of exotic plants and animals for botanical and zoological gardens, lectures before learned societies on theories of race, encyclopedias, ethnographies of "primitive peoples" and museums in which to view their artifacts, and travel literature, plays and fiction that takes the reader into different cultures through European eyes. Many of the ways we still learn about the world are based on the practices and assumptions of colonialism.

In analyzing the effects of museums, exhibitions, zoos, and other collections from the Empire, Willinsky provides many ideas on teaching about how these "instruments of public instruction" have passed off European constructions of the cultures, geographies, and histories of Africa, Asia, and the Americas as scientific truth. In chapters such as "History and the Rise of the West," "Geographies of Difference," and "Science and the Origin of Race," he details the imperial framework of knowledge production and its legacy in today's schools. After all, it was the best anthropological, geographical, and historical knowledge that Europe could offer that defined the differences between civilized and uncivilized, East and West.

The inheritance of European imperial worldviews lives on in American classrooms today when students are taught only to see other countries through western frames of reference or study other cultures through the eyes of conquerors, tourists, or adventurers. Teaching Idea 28 suggests ways for students to examine these imperial frameworks.

Integrating the Strategies into the Curriculum

These strategies fit well into many social studies units. Figure 7 (p. 64) presents an example from a middle school unit on Chinese cultures.

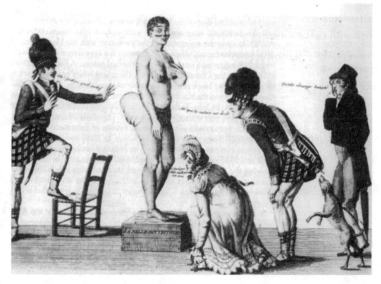

The UNIT	The STRATEGIES
The teacher begins the unit by asking the students to contribute to a collage on what they know about Chinese people. In their work he recognizes that there are many stereotypes (lots of photos of martial arts and women in kimonos) and some misinformation (students confuse Japanese, Vietnamese, and Indians with Chinese).	*Identifying students' stereotypes and exotic images*
He organizes student research on patterns of internal culture that are central to Kenneth Cushner's Culture-General Framework.[37] Cushner provides a structure for studying other cultures that addresses substantive cultural attributes instead of superficial characteristics such as clothes, food, or holidays. Groups of 3 students each collect data on eight elements identified by Cushner: (1) values and assumptions of what is good, (2) how people think about ingroup/outgroup distinctions, (3) learning styles and assumptions about education, (4) communication styles, (5) how people attribute or judge the causes of behavior, (6) time and space, (7) face, status and power, and (8) gender and family roles and norms.	*Understanding internal culture*
They collect data from the library, approved websites, and Chinese people living in the community so that they can learn how beliefs affect behavior.	*Teaching perspective consciousness and multiple perspectives through literature, online resources and people in the community*
They read short stories written by people in Indonesia, Malaysia, Canada, and the U.S. who identify as Chinese as well as people in China and Taiwan.	
They interact online with students their own age in Hong Kong and discuss differences between their lives today and the lives of their grandparents. They see videos and websites that portray everyday life, schools, and communities in China, Hong Kong, Taiwan, the U.S. and Malaysia.	*Teaching about cultural change, hybridity, and global connections*
At the conclusion of the project, the students construct a new collage that comes from their research and interaction. They compare it with the first one and recognize that they had some negative stereotypes (Chinese are poor and uneducated), exotic images (they wear long gowns and big hats and live in temples), and other misinformation (Chinese people do not all look the same or even speak the same language).	*Addressing stereotypes, and exotica* *Recognizing the inheritance of imperial worldviews*
The students also learn that Chinese people have changed in many ways over the last 20-30 years. As they come to understand some of the diversity of contemporary Chinese people in East Asia and other parts of the world, they also recognize how their own cultural patterns are transmitted and changed over generations, yet rarely examined.	*Teaching about cultural change, hybridity and global connections*

These strategies reinforce each other as they address cultural complexity, change, and connectedness. Teaching culture is complicated as it involves not only knowledge of factual information but also skills in intercultural competence and perspective consciousness. Culture is an integral part of every social studies course: what, after all, is history without culture? How can students understand politics or economics without cultural contexts? After all, social studies is centered on people and the human condition.

Notes

1. Intercultural Press (www.interculturalpress.com) has numerous publications on culture and culture learning that are useful to teachers. We highly recommend chapters 1 and 2 of Richard Brislin, *Understanding Culture's Influence on Behavior* (Fort Worth, TX: Harcourt, Brace, 1993).

2. For descriptions of the effects of globalization on world cultures, see Mike Featherstone, ed., *Global Culture* (Newbury Park: CA, 1992); Frank J. Lechner and John Boli, eds., *The Globalization Reader* (Malden, MA: Blackwell, 2000).

3. For other "iceberg" models, see Gary R. Weaver, *Contrasting and Comparing Cultures* (Boston, MA: Pearson, 2000),72-77; Kenneth Cushner, *Human Diversity in Action* (Boston, MA: McGraw- Hill, 1999), 3-7. The terms "internal culture " and "external culture" were probably first used by Edward T. Hall in his book *Beyond Culture* (Garden City, NY: Doubleday, 1976). Hall conceptualized "internal culture" as the mind and argued that the only way to understand another society's internal culture is to actively participate in its culture. It is the collision of cultures that can lead to understanding.

4. Milton J. Bennett, "Towards Ethnorelativism: A Developmental Model of Intercultural Sensitivity," in R. Michael Paige, ed., *Education for the Intercultural Experience* (Yarmouth, ME: Intercultural Press, 1993): 21-71.

5. Ibid.

6. Ibid.

7. Ibid.

8. *Common Experiences, Different Visions* (Urbana, IL: Asian Educational Media Service, Center for East Asian and Pacific Studies, University of Illinois at Urbana-Champaign, 1994). This 55-minute video documentary presents the differing perceptions of common experiences of two teams of high school students—an American team of students from high schools in the state of Indiana and a Japanese team of students from Kaminokawa High School in Tochigi Prefecture. In the program, the two groups of students participate together in common experiences in both Indiana and Tochigi Prefecture, taping their activities and recording their impressions. The everyday activities the students choose to explore include going shopping, participating in sports, and going on vacation. Each group produced its own program with comparisons about how the two groups viewed these activities. The two versions were edited with professional help and brought together for this program. A study guide with questions to stimulate classroom discussion accompanies the video. Available for $10 plus $5 shipping and handling from Asian Educational Media Service, UIUC, MC-025, Urbana, IL 6180. E-mail: aems@uiuc.edu.

9. Richard Brislin, *Understanding Culture's Influence on Behavior* (Fort Worth, TX: Harcourt Brace, 1993); Richard Brislin and T. Yoshida, eds., *Improving Intercultural Interactions* (Thousand Oaks, CA: Sage Publications, 1994); Martha H. Germaine, *Worldly Teachers: Cultural Learning and Pedagogy* (Westport, CT: Bergin & Garvey, 1998); Theodore Gochenour, ed., *Be-*

yond Experience: The Experiential Approach to Cross-cultural Education (Yarmouth, ME: Intercultural Press, 1993); Angene H. Wilson, "A Case Study of Two Teachers with Cross-Cultural Experience: They Know More," *Educational Research Quarterly* 8, no. 1 (1983): 78-85; Angene H. Wilson," Returned Peace Corps Volunteers Who Teach Social Studies," *The Social Studies* 77, no. 3 (1986): 100-107; Wilson, "Conversation Partners: Helping Students Gain a Global Perspective Through Cross-Cultural Experiences," *Theory into Practice* 32 (1993): 21-26; Wilson, *The Meaning of International Experience for Schools* (Westport, CT: Praeger, 1993). Angene H. Wilson. "Oburoni Outside the Whale: Reflections on an Experience in Ghana," *Theory and Research in Social Education* 26, no. 3 (1998): 410-429.

10. Curtis, J. Bonk, R. Appelman, and K. E. Hay, "Electronic Conferencing Tools for Student Apprenticeship and Perspective Taking," *Educational Technology*, 36 no. 5, (1996): 8-18; Curtis J. Bonk and Vanessa Dennen, "Frameworks in Web Instruction: Fostering Research, Design, Benchmarks, Training, and Pedagogy" in M. G. Moore and B. Anderson (Ed.), *Handbook of Distance Education* (Mahwah, NJ: Lawrence Erlbaum, 2003); Curtis J. Bonk, and K. S. King, (Eds.), *Electronic Collaborators: Learner-Centered Technologies for Literacy, Apprenticeship, and Discourse* (Mahwah, NJ: Lawrence Erlbaum, 1998); M. Daniels, A. Berglund, and M. Petre, "Reflections on International Projects in Undergraduate CS Education," *Computer Science Education*, 9, no. 3, (1999): 256-267; Cynthia S. Sunal and Lois Christensen, "Culture and Citizenship: Teachers from Two Continents Share Perspectives Via a Website," *The International Social Studies Forum* 2, no.2, (1999): 121-140.

11. Bettina Fabos and Michelle D. Young, "Telecommunication in the Classroom: Rhetoric Versus Reality," *Review of Educational Research* 69, no. 3(1999): 249. 217-259; Mark Warschauer, *Electronic Literacies: Language, Culture and Power in Online Education* (Mahwah, NJ: Lawrence Erlbaum Associates, 1999)12. R. Garner and M. G. Gillingham, *Internet Communication in Six Classrooms: Conversations Across Time, Space and Culture* (Mahwah, NJ: Lawrence Erlbaum, 1996).

13. For research on this topic see Merry M. Merryfield, "Why Aren't American Teachers Being Prepared to Teach for Diversity, Equity, and Interconnectedness? A Study of Lived Experience in the Making of Multicultural and Global Educators," *Teaching and Teacher Education* 16(4), 2000, pp. 429-443.

14. Peter Alder, 1977, as quoted in Milton Bennett, 1993, p. 59.

15. Janet Bennett, "Cultural Marginality: Identity Issues in Intercultural Training," in R. Michael Paige, (Ed.), *Education for the Intercultural Experience* (Yarmouth, ME: Intercultural Press, Inc., 1993), pp. 109-136.

16. We recognize it is impossible to study hundreds of cultures in depth. However, in the 13 years of K-12 education we feel that students should study at least a dozen cultures from across the planet in considerable depth.

17. In Weaver (2000, cited above) there are several chapters, including ones on Arabs, Russians, Germans, Japanese, that describe the effects of mass media on Americans' images of other cultures and global issues.

18. For a review of research on stereotyping see Chapter 1 in Walter Stephan, *Reducing Prejudice and Stereotyping in Schools* (New York: Teachers College Press, 1999).

19. Researchers Garner and Gillingham monitored online discourse between American children in Illinois and Yup'ik children in Alaska. Despite email that said that Yup'ik do not wear furs and live in igloos, the Illinois children maintained those stereotypes until they viewed a video. R. Garner & M. G. Gillingham, *Internet Communication in Six Classrooms: Conversations Across Time, Space and Culture* (Mahwah, NJ: Lawrence Erlbaum, 1996).

20. Ibid., pp. 7-17.

21. *Faces of the Enemy*. 58 minutes. $74.95. Distributed by Catticus Corporation, 2600 10th Street. Berkeley, CA 94710 or call (510) 548-0854 or email skgarden@aol.com

22. The Southern Poverty Law Center (www.SPLCenter.org) monitors hate

groups and their activities through Hatewatch online. Free publications for teachers include periodicals such as Intelligence Report and Teaching Tolerance as well as videos.

23. Craig Storti, *Figuring Foreigners Out: A Practical Guide*. Yarmouth. ME; Intercultural Press, 1999.

24. Edward Said, *Culture and Imperialism* (New York: Alfred A. Knopf, 1993):.51. Also see Edward Said, *Orientalism* (New York: Random House, 1978).

25. Michelle Wallace, "Negative Images: Towards a Black Feminist Cultural Criticism," in S. During (Ed.), *The Cultural Studies Reader* (New York: Routledge, 1993): 118-131. Patricia Hill Collins, *Black Feminist Thought* (New York: Routledge, 1990).

26. Cameron McCarthy, *Uses of Culture: Education and the Limits of Ethnic Affiliation* (New York: Routledge, 1998) p. 156.

27. Ibid, p. 160.

28. John Willinsky, *Learning To Divide the World* (Minneapolis, MN: 1998), 3.

29. Ibid., p.4.

30. Ibid.

31. J. M. Blaut, *The Colonizer's Model of the World: Geographical Determinism and Eurocentric History* (New York: The Guilford Press, 1993). Patrick Brantlinger, "Victorians and Africans: The Geneology of the Myth of the Dark Continent," in Henry L. Gates (Ed.), *Race, Writing and Difference* (Chicago: University of Chicago Press, 1986) pp. 185-222. Paulo Freire, *Pedagogy of Hope* (New York: Continuum, 1995). Paul Gilroy, *The Black Atlantic: Modernity and Double Consciousness.* (Cambridge, MA: Harvard University Press, 1993). M. Omi & H. Winant, "On the Theoretical Status of the Concept of Race," in Cameron McCarthy and Walter Crichlow (Eds.), *Race, Identity and Representation in Education* (New York: Routledge, 1993) (pp. 3-10). B. Parry, "Problems in Current Theories of Colonial Discourse," *Oxford Literary Review* 9(1&2),1987, 27-58. Mary Louise Pratt, *Imperial Eyes: Travel Writing and Transculturation* (London: Routledge, 1992).

32. Willinsky, 1998, p. 23.

33. J. Rabasa, *Inventing A-M-E-R-I-C-A: Spanish Historiography and the Formation of Ethnocentrism* (Norman, OK: University of Oklahoma Press, 1993). H. J. Mercator, *Atlas or a Geographicke Description of the World* (Facsimile edition in two volumes. Amsterdam: Theatrum Orbis Terrarum., 1636).

34. Willinsky, 1998, p. 24.

35. Ibid., pp. 10-11.

36. Gilman, 1985, as quoted in Willinsky, 1998, pp. 59-60. For an in-depth examination of using science to define moral differences as well as others in colonial Europe see S. L. Gilman, "Black Bodies, White Bodies: Towards an Iconography of Female Sexuality in Late Nineteenth-Century Art, Medicine, and Literature," *Critical Inquiry* 12 no.1, (1985) 204-242. See also Barbara Chase-Riboud, *Hottentot Venus* (New York, Doubleday, 2003).

37. Kenneth Cushner, *Human Diversity in Action* (New York: McGraw-Hill, 1999). See also Kenneth Cushner & Richard W. Brislin, *Intercultural Interactions: A Practical Guide* (Thousand Oaks, CA: Sage, 1996) and Kenneth Cushner, Averil McClelland & Philip Safford, P. *Human Diversity in Education*, third edition (New York: McGraw-Hill, 2000).

Resources on Intercultural Education

ONLINE

Building Bridges: A Peace Corps Classroom Guide to Cross-Cultural Understanding, www.peacecorps.gov/wws/bridges

Electronic School Book - Southern Africa, www.school.za/tes

Experiment in International Living, www.experiment.org

Intercultural E-Mail Classroom Connections, www.iecc.org

International Education and Research Network, www.iearn.org

Institute of International Education, www.iiepassport.org

Intercultural Communication Institute, www.intercultural.org

Multicultural Pavilion, www.edchange.org/multicultural

The Odyssey: World Trek for Service and Education, www.worldtrek.org/odyssey

BOOKS

Archer, Carol M. *Living with Strangers in the U.S.A.* Englewood Cliffs, NJ: Regents/Prentice Hall, 1991.

Bennett, Milton. J. "Towards Ethnorelativism: A Developmental Model of Intercultural Sensitivity," in R. M. Paige, ed. *Education for the Intercultural Experience.* Yarmouth, ME: Intercultural Press, 1993: 21-71.

Brislin, Richard W. *Understanding Culture's Influence on Behavior.* Fort Worth, TX: Harcourt Brace , 1993.

Brislin, Richard W., and T. Yoshida, eds. *Improving Intercultural Interactions.* Thousand Oaks, CA: Sage Publications, 1994.

Cushner, Kenneth, and Richard W. Brislin. *Intercultural Interactions: A Practical Guide* (Thousand Oaks, CA: Sage, 1996).

Cushner, Kenneth, A. McClelland, and P. Safford. *Human Diversity on Education: An Integrative Approach*, third ed. New York: McGraw-Hill, 2000.

Dasen, Pierre R. "Cross-Cultural Psychology and Teacher Training," in James Lynch., C. Modgil, and S. Modgil, eds. *Cultural Diversity and the Schools: Prejudice, Polemic or Progress?* London: Falmer Press, 1992: 191-204.

Gochenour, Theodore, ed. *Beyond Experience: The Experiential Approach to Cross-Cultural Education* (Yarmouth, ME: Intercultural Press, 1993).

Hall, Edward. *Beyond Culture* (Garden City, NY: Anchor, 1976).

Paige, R. Michael, ed. *Education for the Intercultural Experience* (Yarmouth, ME: Intercultural Press, Inc. 1993).

Seelye, H. Ned, ed. *Experiential Activities for Intercultural Living* (Yarmouth, ME: Intercultural Press, 1996).

Storti, Craig. *Cross-Cultural Dialogues* (Yarmouth, ME: Intercultural Press, 1994).

Resources for Teaching Multiple Perspectives and Hybridity

ONLINE

Culture of the Other, www.vistavisuals.nl/worldmix_uk/ideas/main7.html#1

Post-colonialism, www.postcolonialweb.org/poldiscourse/discourseov.html

BOOKS

Ashcroft, B., Gareth Griffiths, and Helen Tiffin, eds. *The Post-Colonial Studies Reader* (New York: Routledge, 1995).

Blaut, James. M. *The Colonizer's Model of the World: Geographical Determinism and Eurocentric History* (New York: The Guilford Press, 1993).

Brantlinger, Patrick. "Victorians and Africans: The Geneology of the Myth of the Dark Continent," in Henry Louis Gates, ed, *Race, Writing and Difference*. Chicago: University of Chicago Press, 1986: 185-222.

Clark, Leon. ed. *Through African Eyes*, vol. 2. New York: CITE, 1997.

Diawara, Manthia. *In Search of Africa*. Cambridge, MA: Harvard University Press, 1998.

Gilman, S. L. "Black Bodies, White Bodies: Towards an Iconography of Female Sexuality in Late Nineteeeth-Century Art, Medicine, and Literature," *Critical Inquiry* 12, no.1 (1985): 204-242.

Gioseffi, Danielle, ed. *On Prejudice: A Global Perspective*. New York: Doubleday, 1993.

Hammond, D., and Jablow, A. *The Africa That Never Was: Four Centuries of British Writing about Africa*. Prospect Heights, IL: Waveland Press, 1992.

Harding, Sandra. *Is Science Multicultural? Postcolonialisms, Feminisms, and Epistemologies*. Bloomington, IN: Indiana University Press, 1998.

Henry, Annette. *Taking Back Control: African Canadian Women Teachers' Lives and Practice*. Albany, NY: SUNY Press, 1998.

McCarthy, Cameron. "The Problems with Origins: Race and the Contrapuntal Nature of the Educational Experience," in C. E. Sleeter and P. L. McClaren, eds. *Multicultural Education, Critical Pedagogy and the Politics of Difference*. Albany, NY: State University of New York Press, 1986: 245-268.

—————. *The Uses of Culture: Education and the Limits of Ethnic Affiliation*. New York: Routledge, 1998.

—————. and Crichlow, Warren, eds. *Race, Identity and Representation in Education*. New York: Routledge, 1993.

Ngugi wa Thiong'o. *Decolonizing the Mind*. London: Heinemann, 1986.

—————. *Moving the Centre: The Struggle for Cultural Freedom*. London: James Curry, 1986.

Pratt, Mary Lou. *Imperial Eyes: Travel Writing and Transculturation*. London: Routledge, 1992.

Pratt, Mary Lou. "Me llamo Riboberta Menchu: Autoethnography and the re-coding of citizenship." In A. Carey-Webb and S. Benz, eds. *Teaching and Testimony: Rigoberta Menchu and the North American Classroom*, Albany, NY: State University of New York Press, 1996: 57-72.

Rabasa, J. *Inventing A-M-E-R-I-C-A: Spanish Historiography and the Formation of Ethnocentrism*. Norman, OK: University of Oklahoma Press, 1993.

Said, Edward. W. *Orientalism*. New York: Random House, 1978.

—————. *Culture and Imperialism*. New York: Alfred A. Knopf, 1993.

Willinsky, John. *Learning to Divide the World: Education at Empire's End*. Minneapolis, MN: University of Minnesota Press, 1998.

CHAPTER 4

Global World History

The world is a glass you drink from.

In *The Space Between Our Footsteps, Poems and Paintings from the Middle East*, selected by Naomi Shihab Nye, Simon and Schuster Books for Young Readers, 1998.

To include the whole world in what we teach is challenging, and the challenges are perhaps most apparent in our teaching of world history, the focus of this chapter.

We begin with a brief history of the teaching of world history, followed by sections entitled: Organizing the Course, Remembering People, Relating Past and Present, and Dealing with Eurocentrism. Besides Teaching Ideas 29-32 (see pages 74-78 and 82 below), we have included the Advanced Placement World History themes and habits of mind because they seem relevant to teaching any world history course.

A Brief History of Teaching World History

In the United States we have had a long tradition of teaching western civilization instead of a global world history. *Readings in World History*, edited in 1962 by Leften S. Stavrianos, was an early collaboration of six college and high school teachers who believed that world history courses should be "truly global in scope and not limited merely to Western civilization."[1] The book was divided into sections on ancient, classical (including India and China), and medieval civilizations (including Islam), followed by "Civilized Man Lives in Global Unity," focusing on modern history. Readings also included regional units on the United States, Soviet Union, Latin America, Middle East, India, China, and sub-Saharan Africa and a concluding section on "Our World Today" with four primary sources on the United Nations.

Although attempts to add so-called non-western studies began in the 1960s and 1970s, it was in the early 1980s that a number of events propelled curriculum change. The World History Association was founded in 1982, and William H. McNeil stated in a 1983 newsletter: "The circumstances of our age demand a global account of how things got to be the way they are. Only so can the world in which we live make sense." In 1983 Ernest Boyer's *Carnegie Report, High School*, advocated three and a half years of social studies. The report stated that "the history curriculum must extend beyond

American history and Western Civilization to include non-Western studies. Specifically, we recommend that all students discover the connectedness of the human experience and the richness of other cultures through an in-depth study of a non-Western nation." A College Board booklet at that time, *What Students Need to Know and Be Able to Do*, urged the study of world civilizations as a part of a pre-collegiate curriculum.[2]

In the 1990s world history became recognized as a field. The *National Standards for History* were published in 1994, setting out nine eras of world history in terms of periodization, focusing on historical thinking, and offering specific examples of student achievement for each standard. *Bring History Alive, A Sourcebook for Teaching World History* was published in 1996 and supports the world history standards, including examples, plus essays on conceptualizing world history and essays to introduce each era. Also in 1997, the National Council for History Education published *Building a World History Curriculum*. This publication lists 12 "central strands and significant questions to be carried throughout courses and across the grades"—K-12. It also includes four possible course patterns for middle and high school, one of which splits history of western civilization and world history/geography into two years and another that suggests two years of combined world and western history before and since 1789; both sequences are for ninth and tenth grades. By 2000 World History had joined the ranks of Advanced Placement courses, and in spring 2002 the first 20,000 high school students took the exam. The *Teacher's Guide* and course description are sources for this chapter, as well as the previously mentioned books. A *World History Best Practices* book was published in 2002 by the College Board and the Advanced Placement Program and is also referenced here.[3]

High school teachers have been crucial partners with college teachers in the development of the national standards and AP courses and of the World History Association. In the 1990s teachers also became much more involved in providing alternatives and supplements to textbooks. In 1991 *Rethinking Columbus*,[4] published by Rethinking Schools in cooperation with the Network on Educators on the Americas, challenged the way we have taught about the arrival of Columbus in the Americas and provided strategies and materials for "talking back" to Columbus and for considering both the effects of what many would call the "invasion" instead of the "discovery," as well as contemporary struggles of Native Americans. A revised version was published in 1998. Also in the 1990s, the Teachers' Curriculum Institute (History Alive!) began to publish lessons based on their seven teaching strategies—interactive slide lecture, experiential exercise, social studies skill builder, response groups, writing for understanding, problem solving group work, and interactive student notebook. At present, they have an Ancient World History Program, a World History from 500 to 1700 Program, and a Modern World History Program.[5]

Title VI area studies centers and global education groups have contributed to our knowledge and pedagogy as well. Area studies centers at universities have provided outreach services to schools for many years. The world area studies centers at Indiana University, for example, organize interactive video programs for 60 to 80 teachers each year. Programs such as SPICE (Stanford Program on International and Cross-Cultural Education) produce excellent materials on world cultures and world history, for example, their "Silk Road Encounters Education Kit." The American Forum for Global Education has produced curricula on specific countries such as India and Turkey, as well as regular issues papers. The Global TeachNet program of the National Peace Corps Association hosts a weekly listserv and publishes a bimonthly newsletter with articles, resources, and lesson ideas. The Association for Asian Studies has a helpful website and excellent magazine for teachers, *Education about Asia*.[6]

Organizing the Course

Organizing a truly global world history course is a monumental challenge. The questions are many. What are the eras of world history, as opposed to those of western civilization? Should we just use dates rather than come up with descriptions for those eras? What if my state or school system begins high school world history at 1500? Does it make sense to interrupt chronology for current events? How do I integrate world regions? Or should I teach regions, civilizations, or cultures separately? Are there reasons to focus on encounters instead? Or patterns as part of the "big picture"? Are case studies the way to deal with the particular in the "big picture"? How, if one is teaching comparative themes, does one choose the themes to use comparatively? What is the role of individuals in world history? How do I ensure that students see today's global issues as growing out of the past?

The mother of all the questions above is simply: How do I organize my course?

There are at least four possibilities. One is a combination of traditional western civilizations and what once were called non-western cultures or civilizations or the rest of the world. A second model focuses on universal patterns. A third possibility is a combination of universal patterns and particular cultures. A fourth approach is to teach world history as part of a global cultures course based on geographic regions.

Western Heritage/Different Cultures

The first combination, what Ross Dunn[7] calls the Western Heritage and Different Cultures model, seems to prevail in textbooks, standards documents, and classroom practice. This model evolved out of the traditional world history course that was mostly western until at least the 1960s, when sometimes a semester or even a year of so-called non-western history was added or integrated.

The advantages of this approach are that the combination seems familiar and is supported by many excellent materials based on good scholarship from specialists in the history of particular parts of the world. The World History units from the National Center for History in the Schools include, for instance: "The Golden Age of Greece," "The Byzantine Empire in the Age of Justinian," and "Kongo: A Kingdom Divided." The SPICE program, mentioned earlier, has excellent units, too, ranging from "Castle Towns: An Introduction to Tokugawa Japan" to "Collapse of a Multinational State: The Case of Yugoslavia." Teachers also use lessons from the Teachers Curriculum Institute's world history programs. The Modern World History Activity Sampler contains the following activities: "Debating the Ideal Form of Government: A Meeting of the Minds," "The Unraveling of the Soviet Economy," "Exploring Continuity and Change in China through Art," "The History of Modern Mexico Through Murals," "Constructing a Timeline of African History," and "Impressions of the Middle East."

However, there are major disadvantages to the Western Heritage/Different Cultures approach. Dunn describes the combination as follows: "The first half of the text or standards guide presents major civilizations *ad seriatum*, each covered in a discrete unit encompassing several hundred to several thousand years. Diversity and internationalism thus honored, the scene shifts to Europe, whose internal history, together with the activities of Europeans abroad, dominates the second half of the document."[8] His next sentence relates to the problem of Eurocentrism as he points out that "the idea of the West as *entity*, whose 'rise' may be ascribed almost entirely to internal mechanisms and foundational traits, remains largely unchallenged."[9] Thus, he argues, this combination is often inevitably Eurocentric. It is usually not comparative and doesn't help students deal with the "big picture" or make sense of the global world in which they live. Even when this model is not Eurocentric, it may be biased toward large, hierarchical civilizations. So seventh graders may spend a great deal of time on ancient Egypt and Greece and Rome and never connect ancient civilizations across world regions or understand global issues that began to evolve in that period.

Universal Patterns

The universal patterns framework looks at history quite differently. Dunn describes what he calls the Patterns of Change Model as advancing "the idea that social and spatial fields of historical inquiry should be open and fluid, not predetermined by fixed cultural or geographical categories." Designing the curriculum then consists of "framing substantive, engaging historical questions that students might be invited to ask, unconstrained by predetermined order lines of civilizations, nations, or continents."[10]

The Advanced Placement course, based on the Patterns of Change Model, highlights six overarching themes and three habits of mind, specific to World History.[11] It lays out very carefully what students are expected to know (and not to know). The major time periods are 8000 BCE to 600 CE, then 600 to 1450, 1450 to 1750, 1750 to 1914, and 1914 to the present. As examples of what is studied in the time period 1450 to 1750, students compare European monarchy with a land-based Asian Empire and compare coercive labor systems like slavery and other such systems in the Americas. The focus is on the themes and habits of mind, not on individual facts. For instance, students are expected to know the importance of European exploration but not individual explorers and the Ottoman conquest of Constantinople but not the Safavid Empire.

Themes

In the Course Description of Advanced Placement Program World History[12]

- Patterns and impacts of interaction among major societies: trade, war, diplomacy, and international organizations.
- The relationship of change and continuity across world history periods.
- The impact of technology and demography on people and environment (population growth and decline, disease, manufacturing, migrations, agriculture, weaponry).
- Systems of social structure and gender structure (comparing major features within and among societies and assessing change).
- Cultural and intellectual developments and interactions among and within societies.
- Changes in the functions and structure of states and in attitudes toward states and political identities (political culture), including the emergence of the nation-state (types of political organization).

Habits of Mind for World History

In the Course Description of Advanced Placement Program World History[13]

- Seeing global patterns over time and space while also acquiring the ability to connect local developments to global ones and to move through levels of generalizations from the global to the particular.
- Developing the ability to compare within and among societies, including comparing societies' reactions to global processes.
- Developing the ability to assess claims of universal standards yet remain aware of human commonalities and differences; putting culturally diverse ideas and values in historical context, not suspending judgment but developing understanding.

One way for teachers to understand this big picture way of looking at history is to read J. R. and William H. McNeill's *The Human Web, A Bird's Eye View of World History.* A teacher we know assigned the book to her AP students for summer reading. The McNeills interpret human history as webs in "an evolution from simple sameness to diversity toward complex sameness."[14] Throughout the book, their comparisons also jar the reader out of any western civilization bias. The Atlantic Europeans are the "Mongols of the sea." Martin Luther is described as the German Wang Yangmin (1472-1529), "an influential thinker who held that truth, knowledge, and virtue could be achieved by ordinary people without lengthy instruction in Confucian lore."[15] Given the time we usually spend teaching about the two World Wars and the Cold War, it is interesting to see the McNeills speculate that environmental issues such as climate change and the reduction in biodiversity may turn out to "the most important development in the period after 1890, more so than ideological struggles or world wars."[16]

The advantages of the universal patterns model are almost a mirror of the disadvantages of the first model. Looking at universal patterns involves macro-history and the "big picture." It should be less Eurocentric. It can encourage thinking about globalization as an historical as well as current phenomenon. One disadvantage for the teacher is that most textbooks and materials still cater to the first model. However, because Patterns of Change is the model for AP world history, the themes and habits of mind may begin to affect "regular" world history texts and teaching.

Authors in the World History Association are working to develop helpful materials, including those mentioned earlier in the history of the field section of this chapter. Another disadvantage is that students may not understand how central culture can be to peoples' lives and that differences among cultures may not be appreciated because they are not studied in enough depth for students to thoroughly understand multiple worldviews. This is not to say that culture, any more than geography, determines history. However, collectivist and individualist cultures do differ; for example, the concept of *ubuntu* (a person is a person through other people) is important in South African culture and contrasts with the American focus on the individual.

Universal Patterns and Particular Cultures
A third way of organizing a world history course is to combine universal patterns and particular cultures. Jean Elliott Johnson suggests we recognize the debates between materialist and culturalist historians and universalist and particularist historians but not get caught in them. Instead we might try to "imagine the importance of both material and cultural dimensions of the human past" and help students "move chronologically through time and space so they see history

Summarized Sample Syllabus of Patterns of Change
Gloria Barnes, Franklin Learning Center High School, Philadelphia[17]

Unit 1 —World Trade and Economy
Case studies of Venice, Cairo, Jenne, Kilwa, and Hangchow. One topic is the Bubonic Plague. The project compares merchants from various parts of the world

Unit 2—Migrations and Colonization
Topics include Columban voyages and also Zheng He, the Columban Exchange, and European Hegemony and Global Trade Network. One assignment is reading an article about the treatment of slavery in various textbooks and participation in a class forum on the issues raised.

Unit 3—Revolutions and Their Export
The study of Intellectual and Scientific Revolutions, the American/Haitian Political Revolutions, British and Japanese Economic Revolutions, and a student-chosen case study on the Mexican, Russian, or Chinese Revolutions.

Unit 4—Technology and the Twentieth Century
Nationalism, imperialism, the global economic network, the World Wars, the Cold War and post Cold War are topics covered. One assignment is small group research and presentation on a topic such as colonial and semi-colonial regions, or on significant personalities and their roles as winners and losers.

as a seamless web involving both the universal and particular, both cultural and materialist factors."[18]

The advantages of this model are that it uses recurring patterns and cases to show students both the universal and particular. It deals not only with materialist and economic themes such as technology and trade, but also with cultural achievements. Its disadvantages are probably organizational difficulties and lack of teacher background in cultures beyond Europe. Of course, the universal patterns model has to use particular cultures, at least as illustrations, so this hybrid may not be so different from the second model.

Johnson describes her world history course, which begins at 3500 BCE and comes forward to 1600 as a drama in nine acts. The Acts begin with Origins of the Human Community:

Learning to Cooperate (3500 BCE) and come forward to Act Nine: The Expanding Synthesis (15th to 17th centuries CE). Each act has subheadings. Those for Act Seven are as follows.

ACT SEVEN: THE FLOWERING OF HUMAN CULTURES
(400 to 1200 CE)
  A. "Setting the Stage: Make Art, Not War."
  B. The Golden Age in India: Gupta and South Indian Kingdoms
  C. The Flowering of the Byzantine Empire
  D. The Islamic Achievement
  E. Cultural and Technological Achievements of the T'ang and Song
  F. Reflections and Innovation from the Japanese Archipelago
  G. Achievements of the Maya in Mesoamerica
  H. Community Solidarity in Africa
  I. Church and Manor: A Flowering of Christendom in Europe[19]

World Cultures

A fourth approach that some schools and textbooks have followed is to focus on different world cultures in a regional integration of history, geography, anthropology, and political science. So students study regions (Africa, Europe, Latin America, the Middle East, and so on) learning in sequential chapters about the region's environment, the history, the society, the government, and religion and arts.

This approach has the advantages of being more interdisciplinary and of the linking of historical past immediately to the present—both often attractive to students. However, the history is definitely truncated; in fact, world historians would probably not consider this organizational pattern really world history. Because the regions are taught autonomously and difference is emphasized, there is little comparison across time and space.

Still, in what course do students learn about the lives of people today? Where do they learn about the influence of the environment? Is enough emphasis placed on the arts? Is enough emphasis placed on world religions? Where do students deal seriously with the stereotypes and assumptions they bring to the study of a particular part of the world? Because of the latter two questions, after September 11, some teachers decided to begin their world history courses with a unit on world religions. Others stopped in their world history courses to focus especially on Islam and on the Middle East.

Which Approach?

A teacher may well decide to use a combination of the approaches. Some teachers will choose to focus on individual civilizations until about 1450 and then pull the world together. Some schools use a World Cultures approach in middle school, a Western Heritage/Different Cultures or Universal Patterns and Particular Cultures approach in the general world history in high school, and Universal Patterns in AP World History.

Teaching the French Revolution in Different Approaches

Western Heritage/Different Cultures: The French Revolution is part of a sequence in a unit entitled Age of Revolutions that begins with the English and American Revolutions, followed by the Industrial Revolution and Revolutions in Europe (1830 and 1848 in France) and Revolutions in Latin America.

Universal Patterns: Under Political and Economic Revolutions, students address the questions: How can the Industrial Revolution be compared to the Neolithic Revolution? What are the commonalities between the political revolutions in the Americas and in France from 1775 to 1830?

Universal Patterns/Particular Cultures: Political revolutions (China, Cuba, France, Iran, Mexico, Russia, U.S., Haiti) are studied together across time with attention to similarities and differences.

World Cultures: The unit on Europe includes the history of the French Revolution and the Napoleonic Age.

Whichever organizational pattern a teacher uses, there seems to be consensus that teaching chronologically makes sense, though in a way that emphasizes thematic linkages that tie history together rather than a timeline of specific dates and events. As Robert Bain points out, comparing can be done across time or space (culture or region) or both. He makes good suggestions for collecting information and analyzing each case, then making an initial comparison, then summarizing results, then reconsidering each case and making a final comparison.[20]

Also, ideally, all students (not just AP students) should develop the habits of mind for world history: seeing global patterns over time and space and connecting the local to the global; comparing within and among societies; and developing the ability to assess claims of universal standards while remaining aware of human commonalities and differences and taking into account historical context in order to gain understanding.

Models and other syllabi are helpful. However, teachers will still need to develop their own frameworks or plans, taking into consideration state and national standards. Roupp's suggestions for developing a world history course seem particularly useful: form a study group, take a workshop, select several good texts, consider your students' skills and expertise, draft a course outline from your conceptualization and goals, trade and peer review units, develop a unit a summer, and organize your own teacher improvement program.[21] Of course, we know that world history may be only one of the courses a social studies teacher teaches. It may not even be the teacher's first love—at first.

Remembering the People

One of us once observed a world history class in which students had been given the task of deciding who were the most influential people in history. They rose to the occasion with various evidence and arguments that launched a heated and serious discussion. Students enjoy activities such as a Women of the World reception, as they introduce themselves to each other as Queen Zubaydah of Baghdad or Queen Amina of the Hausa or a Trung sister of Vietnam, or other women they have never heard of before.[22] People, the famous and the ordinary, are just plain interesting to most of us. Perhaps our western emphasis on individualism is one reason.

Although the Advanced Placement course description states that students are expected to know the importance of European exploration, but not individual explorers, we remain intrigued by such people. In the year 2003, we focused on explorers of history, Lewis and Clark (and Sacajawea and York), and we also watched as our explorers of space lost their lives in the *Columbia* space shuttle disaster.

"The power of one" fascinates many of us. We know individual national leaders make a difference. Nelson Mandela made a difference for good in South Africa, for example, while Hitler made a difference for evil in Europe. We know particularly inventive people make a difference since we reap the benefits (and the problems) of the car, the television, the computer.

Teaching Idea 29
Using the PBS TV program "The Crucible of the Millennium"[23] and Resource Guide To Begin and End a World History Course[24]

"The Crucible of the Millennium," originally shown on New Year's Eve 2001, offers several possibilities for a world history course. It could be used as a possible introduction and/or conclusion to a world history course, since it sets up the connections between what began to happen in the 15th century (where many regular high school courses begin) and issues in our own 21st century. The readings in Part I, "Through the Looking Glass," and Part II, "Echoes and Resonances," in the resource guide are a helpful accompaniment for teachers and students. Both video and guide are available from The American Forum for Global Education at globaled.org.

Encounters between Cultures—at the beginning of the course

Goal: Students will be able to explain three different perspectives on Calicut, India in the 15th century.

Procedures: To begin this lesson, tell students the story of the blind men and the elephant (it is described in the video) that makes the point about multiple perspectives. The parable describes six blind men who go to see the elephant and, depending on whether they are feeling the elephant's side, its tusk, its trunk, its knee, its ear, or its tail, decide the elephant is like a wall, a spear, a snake, a tree, a fan, or a rope. The parable concludes:

And so these men of Indostan
Disputed loud and long,
Each in his own opinion
Exceeding stiff and strong.
Though each was partly in the right
They all were in the wrong.

Explain to students that they will be doing reading and research on different peoples and their encounters with and views of each other. Ask them to watch in the video for connections between the past and present, for example material woven in India in the 15th century and jeans today, between selling pepper in India then and now, and between shipbuilding in China in the 15th century and today. Tell students that at the end of the course, they will be looking at many issues born in the 15th century.

Start the video several minutes in as the on-camera narrator introduces Calicut, India in the 15th century and its visitors, Zheng He from China, followed by the Muslims and Portuguese. Show about the first 20 minutes of the first video, then perhaps skip the 10 minutes of detailed description of the Ming Empire and more recent Chinese history to the (about) 20 minutes on the Muslim traders (and the Ottoman Empire) and the Portuguese (specifically Vasco da Gama and Pedro Cabral).

Assign the students to groups to accomplish the following tasks:

Group 1: The Indians in Calicut—This group can watch the video excerpt a second time, focusing on what they observe. They will have to invent their story from the video since there are no readings from their perspective.

Groups 2, 3, and 4: Students should divide up readings according to their interest/ability/reading speed. After reading, they should discuss what they have learned and what they think is most important to emphasize as they represent their group.

Group 2: Chinese: Prologue: Phantoms in Silk, The Chinese Reconnaissance, Poem Commemorating the Journey, Down to the Western Ocean, Zheng He's Notes, and The Country Ku-Li.

Group 3: Muslims: The Baburnama, Notes of a Muslim Traveler, Samarqandi, A Different Viewpoint: Indo-Portuguese Conflict, ca. 1578.

Group 4: Portuguese: Vasco Da Gama Reaches India, Vasco Da Gama in Calicut, How the Captain Went to the King of Calicut in the Year 1500.

Group 5: Reporters: The number of reporters can vary, but there should be at least one to interview each group. Reporters should probably be fast readers so they can skim readings and design questions for the group they are assigned to interview.

Group 6: Cartographers: Several students can design a world map with Calicut in the middle and the voyages of discovery marked.

Coming back together, cartographers should show maps, pointing out Calicut and voyages, and reporters should interview each of the four groups. For a culminating discussion and/or writing assignment, students should respond to the following questions: What were the results of the encounter between Calicut and each of the three groups of visitors? How was Calicut affected? What role did curiosity, trade, power, and religion each play? What are the links between the history of the 15th century and today?

Researching Echoes and Proposing Solutions— at the end of the course

Goal: Students will research echoes of encounters since the 15th century and present the results, and, after listening to historians answer the question about issues and solutions, they will write a letter on the topic "Toward a Better World."

Procedure: Show the excerpt toward the end of the second video on "echoes" of our encounters since the 15th century, such as adoption or adaptation of food products and architectural styles. Students can work alone or in pairs or small groups to research and present a poster, powerpoint, or skit on an "echo" of their choice.

Then show the finale of the second video during which the on-camera narrator asks the big question: "As we enter the 21st century, where and how are we to find the creative and original solutions to the issues we have addressed, issues born 500 years ago, surfacing with renewed passion today: migration of peoples, spread of disease, economic and cultural imperialism, the deep and enduring problem of racism?"

The narrator is followed by historians who offer their answers: Gutierrez: change distribution of wealth; Knight: concern for human rights; Kennedy: enlightened political leadership, raising the status of women, and education/wisdom; Dawson: sustainability; and Tsin: rearranging power relationships to be more just and equitable. (Teacher should list answers on overhead so students can see them after they have heard them.)

After discussion of the historians' solutions, ask students to write letters on the topic "Toward a Better World," explaining their preferred and original solutions. The letters could be addressed to the school or community newspaper, the President, or the Secretary General of the United Nations.

We revel in the contributions of especially creative people and appreciate the art of Matisse and Picasso and the artists of Benin. But we are also interested in more ordinary people and want to know about their lives. Yes, we want to know about named people, like Anne Frank, but also about other people, unnamed in history. A box of items from my great-uncle who served in World War I serves as an inquiry project for my teacher education students and is always at the top of memorable lessons when they evaluate the course. They dig in eagerly to look at the scrapbook of photos, the postcards, the engineering maps, the official papers, the letters home—and then ask questions.

Angene Wilson

The activities that illustrate the dry national standards for world history in *Bringing History Alive!* include a number of ideas for teaching about people. The following, selected from Era 8, the first half of the 20th century, focus on "important" individuals, but others ask students to assume the role of a Russian worker in 1905 or a peasant supporting the Mexican or Chinese revolution.

- Research the life of a leading European conservative, liberal, or socialist at the beginning of the century such as Stanley Baldwin, Ramsay MacDonald, Emmeline Pankhurst, Jean Jaures, Raymond Poincaré, Peter Stolypin, Alfred Krupp, or Rosa Luxemburg. How did the selected individual influence political or social policy in pre-war Europe?
- Research the life of Tsar Nicholas II. What beliefs or principles motivated his actions? How did he react to the revolution of 1905? What personal steps did he take? What political actions did he take?
- Research the career of Abd al-Krim, the Moroccan resistance leader of the 1920s. Why did he challenge Spanish rule in northern Morocco? What tactic did his fighting forces use? Why was he finally defeated? Was he a nationalist leader?
- Investigate the life of a scientist or inventor such as Thomas Edison, Marie Curie, Albert Einstein, or Guglielmo Marconi. How did the work of the person you selected change society?[25]

People show up in other curriculum materials, too. For instance, the National Center for History in Schools' units include "Wang Mang: Confucian Success or Failure," "Mansa Musa: African King of Gold," "Crowning the Cathedral of Florence: Brunelleschi Builds His Dome," "Trajan's Rome: The Man, the City, the Empire," "Mao and Gandhi: Alternate Paths to National Independence and Social Change," and "Emperor Ashoka of India: What Makes a Ruler Legitimate?"[26]

The topic "Liberator-Hero and Western Revolutions" in the primary source reader *Discovering the Past* focuses on George Washington, Jean-Paul Marat, and Toussaint L'Ouverture, looking at their eulogies and portraits. The Feminism and the Peace Movement topic in the same reader includes writings by Olive Schreiner, Maude Royden, Jane Addams, Huda Sha'rawi, Miyado Shinohara, Dagmar Wilson, Madeline Duckles, Coretta Scott King, Tamar Swade, Ann Snitow, and Leonie Caldecott.[27]

This proverb from Ghana, where gold and kente cloth are crucial to the Akan culture, is an appropriate conclusion to remembering people: "It is the human being that counts. I call gold; it does not answer. I call cloth; it does not answer. It is the human being that counts."[28]

Relating Past to Present

Linking the past and the present or comparing across time makes both the past and the present more understandable, and of course, we can often learn from history.

As John Lewis Gaddis writes in *The Landscape of History*: "If we can draw upon the experiences of others who've had to confront comparable situations in the past, then—although there are no guarantees—our chance of acting wisely should increase proportionately.[29] Gerda Lerner asserts in *Why History Matters*: "We act individually and collectively in a process over time which builds the human enterprise and tries to give it meaning. Being human means thinking and feeling; it means reflecting on the past and visioning into the future."[30]

The guide *Building A World History Curriculum* cautions that relating past to present should not lead us to ignore the context of the time and place being studied. Hence, a question that students should often hear is: "Could students in the future form a true and fair picture of you and their society by applying only their own attitudes and values, and not bothering with yours?"[31]

Two recent books that offer particular interpretations of

Teaching Idea 30
Around the World in 1688, using *1688, A Global History*[32]

Goal: Students will research a person of the world of 1688 and, after presenting speeches as historical persons, will consider connections around the world and connections to the present.

Procedures: Begin with the author's definition of "baroque" as the "formal interweaving of uncannily individual voices," a word to describe the world of 1688, maybe even playing in the background some of Purcell's music (The last chapter tells the story of "Blessed are they that fear the Lord"). Explain that the class will learn about individuals all over the world of 1688 and sometimes their connections. Beforehand, create a large outline map of the world on one wall on which students can mark the location of their assigned persons. (There is such a map in the book.)

Let students draw an individual's name out of a hat—maybe a hat from some place else! Give each student a copy of the few pages from the book about their individual. Students can do further research if they wish to prepare a 5-minute speech given as if they are their historical persons. Possible individuals (and there are more) from the book include: Coronelli, Sor Juana, Chino/Kino, Dom Joao Manoel Grilho, Jean l'Archevêque, Father Vieira, William Dampier, Klaas, Rumphius, Phaulkon, Wang Fu Zhi, Shitao, Shi Lang, Gerbillon, Wu Li, Saikaku, Basho, Madame de Maintenon, William of Orange, the Duke of Albemarle, Increase Mather, William Penn, Pierre Bayle, Valvasor, Cornelia van Nijenroode, Aphra Behn, Newton, Locke, Leibniz, Osman Agha, Aurangzeb, Glikl bas Judah Leib, Purcell.

The teacher's job after the speeches is to help students see connections across space and time, across the globe (for example, noting Liebniz' reading of Confucian texts or asking students to trace Cornelia van Nijenroode's travels from Japan to Batavia, Indonesia to the Netherlands) and with the present (for instance, Klass's imprisonment on the same Robben Island as Nelson Mandela).

periods of history, one of which we always teach and one of which we rarely teach, suggest how scholars can help us reflect on the past and vision into the future. *14-18 Understanding the Great War*, translated from French in 2002, is a fascinating book because it goes beyond causes and battles and looks at what we don't usually study in world history: not only the violence of battle, but also the experience of civilians and the internment of civilians and military prisoners; the nationalistic, crusader, racist mentality that developed so quickly; and the collective and personal mourning. In all three aspects of the conflict that the two women authors studied, there is room for relating to the present, for going beyond pretending to be soldiers writing letters home in the often used trench warfare simulation. In dealing with the second aspect, for example, they write about the role of religion and its linkage with patriotism—"God is with us, Dieu est de notre côté, Gott ist mit uns."[33] We might ask: How is religion linked with patriotism and with war today?

We are not as likely to teach about medieval Spain, but *The Ornament of the World: How Muslims, Jews and Christians Created a Culture of Tolerance in Medieval Spain* suggests we might. The Abbasids are part of the AP course, but the Umayyad prince who set up a caliphate in Cordoba is not. However, the story of an Islamic polity in medieval Europe is fascinating because Menocal lets us see Cordoba with running water and a library of 400,000 volumes, and introduces us to people like the poet Samuel the Nagid and to Judah Halevi. The picture of the tomb of Ferdinand III in Seville in 1252 with its inscriptions in Arabic, Latin, Hebrew, and Castilian is perhaps the ultimate example of the culture of tolerance. In her epilogue, Menocal tries to explain how the culture of tolerance fell apart. We know "the determinedly crusading forces from Latin Christendom and the equally religious Berber Almohads" met at Las Navas de Tolosa in 1212 and the Almohads lost. Are the "strains of ferocity" within the monotheistic religions winning again? Menocal explains that Ferdinand and Isabella chose to go down "the modern path, the one defined by an ethic of unity and harmony, and which is largely intolerant of contradiction. The watershed at hand was certainly the rise of single-language and single-religion nations, a transformation that conventionally stands at the beginning of the modern period and leads directly to our own." However, Menocal writes, "it was no easy task to eradicate many of the deep-seated attitudes that they themselves had seemed to personify, from the love of Arab baths and clothes to the reliance on Jewish physicians." The questions

The Rich and the Poor: in China Then, in the World Now

Goal: As students learn about the T'ang dynasty in China, they will analyze a poem to look at the relationship between rich and poor. They will then look at the rich/poor gap in the world today and consider policies of rich countries that help or hurt poor countries.

Procedures: After reading the following poem, students should discuss how China is described in the eighth and ninth centuries and what they know about the great achievements of the T'ang dynasty. Then ask: Are there any "frivolous rich" today? Is there a rich/poor gap in the United States? Is there a rich/poor gap in the world? Why might it be in the interests of the rich to be concerned about the poor? What might rich countries do to help solve world poverty—in terms of trade, aid, and other policies?

Further Ideas and Resources: Students can individually or in pairs look at and report on the rankings of 21 rich countries in the Commitment to Development Index, which ranks those countries on how their policies on aid, trade, migration, investment, security, technology, and the environment help or hurt poor countries. The indexes for 2003 and 2004, calculated a little differently and published in *Foreign Policy*, can be found at foreignpolicy.com as Ranking the Rich. The website of the Center for Global Development at cgdev.org is also a source. For 2004, Denmark and Netherlands were at the top, U.S. at seventh, and Japan last. The 2004 report also showed how government surpassed private aid in every country, including the U.S. Looking at both the 2003 and 2004 reports is instructive in seeing not only differences but how such indexes are developed.

The Frivolous Rich

With their arrogant manner, they fill up the road;
The horses they ride glisten in the dust.
"May I inquire, who might that be?"
People say that's a palace eunuch.
Those with red sashes are all high ministers;
The purple tassels might signify generals.
Haughtily they go to dine with the troops,
Their prancing horses passing like clouds.
Goblets and tankards will overflow with every wine;
Water and land have yielded every delicacy.
Fresh-picked fruits, and Tung-t'ing [Dongting] oranges;
T'ien-ch'ih [Tianchi] fish, all scaled and sliced.
After gorging themselves, their minds will be at ease;
Drunk on wine, their spirits will soar.

    This year drought devastated the South,
    And in Ch'u-chou [Chuzhou] people cannibalized
    each other.

        Po Chu-I [Bai Juyi] (772-846)[34]

at the end of epilogue reverberate today, for example: "Is the strict harmony of our cultural identities a virtue to be valued above others that may come from the accommodation of contradictions?"[35]

In relating past and present, the point is to understand that there may be connections, patterns, and similar questions at different times. Students may find the connections, patterns, and questions instructive and even interesting. *World History Best Practices* includes several lesson plans that are illustrative. In "Demographic Change on the Great Plains," students consider the availability of water as a possible reason for a decrease in a small Kansas community and compare the use of groundwater from the Ogallala Aquifer with the Libyan aquifer. In "Cowries: Money from the Sea," students make a time chart about money from before 1000 to 2000 for six different parts of the world.[36]

Christopher Ferraro, writing in the Spring 2003 *World History Association Bulletin*, explains how students in his AP class understood change over time and thus connected the past to the present. A variation of this project could certainly be used in regular classes, too. After he introduces them to the concept of linking their modern trends to historical ones and examining how trends have changed or remained the same over time, he asks students to select a trend they want to follow in media outlets for six weeks and then to write a research paper. Rupal, he explains, compared surgery performed by the Inca to medieval bloodletting and contemporary non-invasive procedures. She accurately identified the switch from religious beliefs to science in medicine and the current less-is-better approach of Western medicine. Tim tracked early uses of cavalry by the Mongols and gunpowder by the Chinese, and the development of the tank in World War I, and linked these to advanced battlefield technologies currently being employed in Afghanistan and Iraq such as laser-guided weapons and Unmanned Aerial Vehicles. He also pointed out increasing speed in combat through history and the uses of technology to save lives.[37]

Dealing with Eurocentrism

As we organize the course, remember people, and link the past and present, it is a particular challenge to deal with our Eurocentrism. Some universities still teach Western Civilization courses rather than world history courses, so future teachers are often only introduced to the rest of the world in regional courses on East Asia or Latin America or the Middle East or Africa and not in the context of a holistic human history. There are also still social studies teachers who say, speaking of their students and western civilization: "It's their culture. It's what made America. It's all they need to know."

John Willinsky points out in *Learning to Divide the World: Education at Empire's End* that "imperialism afforded lessons in how to divide the world. It taught people to read the exotic, primitive, and timeless identity of the other, whether in skin color, hair texture, or the inflections of taste and tongue. Its themes of conquering, civilizing, converting, collecting, and classifying inspired educational metaphors equally concerned with taking possession of the world—metaphors that we now have to give an account of, beginning with our own education.[38]

The old canon that privileges European and white American perspectives remains powerful. *The National Geographic Atlas of World History*[39] is a classic example with its four pages on Africa in the nineteenth century that focus only on European "explorers in unknown Africa" and the "race to claim Africa," with pictures of Stanley, Park, and Speke. Even a 2002 World History text features an artist's drawing of the Stanley/Livingstone meeting and primary sources from Livingstone and Stanley writings, although the following page places side by side the Mahdi, Sudanese national hero, and General Gordon, the British hero. If teachers follow the World History Standards sample activities, they will deal with nineteenth century resistance movements and leaders in Algeria, West Africa, Ethiopia, and South Africa. If not, teachers and their students will probably continue to associate Africa mostly with the slave trade, the explorers, the

> When I talk with teachers, a major concern they share is making their courses truly global. The AP course description states very clearly that coverage of European history should not exceed 30 percent of the whole course, and explains how that can be done. Yet, in many regular world history courses, western civilization is still privileged, sometimes by the textbook, sometimes by belief and design, and sometimes by teacher ignorance of other parts of the world.
>
> Angene Wilson

scramble, and colonialism—from a European perspective with a bit of pity for the "poor Africans." This approach will not help students understand Africa.

It is important to acknowledge the very long history of teaching western civilization as world history. For example, while the titles of two histories published in 1883 and 1896 in the United States are *A Brief History of Ancient, Medieval, and Modern Peoples* and *A Brief History of the Nations and of Their Progress in Civilization*, China and India appear only briefly at the beginning of both books, and Africa is absent entirely.[40]

However, "we are at the beginning of a paradigm shift in world history," asserts Heidi Roupp, past president of the World History Association, in the *AP World History Teacher's Guide*. She describes world history as the "big picture" or macrohistory.

It is not the study of a tree, or a forest, but a study of ecosystems. To develop this macrohistory, world historians investigate large-scale historical themes such as migrations, the human response to climatic change, the spread of religions, technological exchange, and the expansion of the market economy. In world history, 1492 is not simply the story of Columbus discovering the "New World." Instead, it is the story of human migrations, transatlantic trade, and the exchange of plants, animals, diseases, art, and technology between Africa, Europe, and the Americas. World history focuses on the historic roots of the current globalization beginning with peopling of the earth. By its very nature, it is a story told from multiple perspectives. It enables us to improve our understanding of how humans have interacted with each other and the planet to shape the present.[41]

As teacher Helen Grady writes in the same *Teacher's Guide*, "adjusting and manipulating this new, wider lens takes some practice." Her suggestions to help students "shift their idea of the world from one firmly rooted in the West" seem helpful: looking at familiar maps and asking questions and then looking at unfamiliar projections and asking the same questions. She also describes the range of documents she has used to encourage critical analysis, for example, documents that enunciate the goals of early twentieth century revolutionaries to illustrate the similarities and differences in the Chinese, Mexican, and Russian Revolutions and art that illustrates how leaders want their images to be projected, with examples from China, Byzantium, Congo, India, France, Benin, and the United States.[42]

Comparative studies, as described by Grady, is one alter-native to the usual Western story. The comparative approach also has the virtue of offering multiple perspectives on a topic, instead of just one primary source after the other from different parts of the world, sometimes boxed in a text at the side. Several collections of primary sources are exemplars. In *World History in Documents: A Comparative Reader*, there are documents from Latin America and Russia under the heading "forced labor" and issues of cultural identity in the twentieth century as written about by Chinua Achebe and Octavio Paz.[43] Another collection of primary sources, *Discovering the Past*, takes a problem approach. For example, the chapter entitled "First Encounters: The Creation of Cultural Stereotypes (1450-1650)" includes European and African accounts of Africa, European and Native American accounts of the Americas, and European and Japanese accounts of Japan.[44]

Dealing with Eurocentrism definitely means a commitment to multiple perspectives on the past and an understanding of the influence of imperialism on how we have taught history. It is a recognition that, in the Big Picture or Big Story, both the hunter and the lion get to tell their stories. As a proverb from Zimbabwe says: "Until the lion tells his side of the story, the tale of the hunt will always glorify the hunter." Global world history is not a winner take all game or an Oscars Night for the star countries. The fact that the lion (in this case, the Native American) gets to tell his side of the story in *Rethinking Columbus* from Rethinking Schools is one of the reasons that collection of materials and strategies is so powerful.

Two examples of "lion" perspectives come from people living in European colonies who fought in World War II on "our" side and whose voices are not usually heard. Kip, the sapper from India in *The English Patient*, is one. In the novel, though not in the movie, he rages against the "English" patient after hearing about the dropping of the atomic bomb. "What have I been doing these last few years? Cutting away, defusing limbs of evil. For what? For this to happen? I'll leave you the radio to swallow your history lesson... Listen to the radio and smell the celebration in it. In my country, when a father breaks justice in two, you kill the father."[45]

A second "lion" perspective comes from a World War II veteran who also fought with the British "mother country." On February 28, 1948, he participated in a protest march to hand a petition to the governor of the Gold Coast. A British police officer gave the order to fire and the leader of the marchers and two others were killed, and riots followed. Interviewed by Basil Davidson for the video series *Africa*, the veteran reflected, "It looks awkward—one fights for three good years in Burma and then comes home to die at this crossroads." Today there is a street named February 28 in Accra, Ghana's capital, because that incident is considered part of Ghana's struggle for independence.[46]

Teaching about the concept of imperialism itself is, of course, considerably more complicated than only two perspectives: hunter and lion, us and them. In *Classroom in Conflict, Teaching Controversial Subjects in a Diverse Society*, John Williams writes insightfully about trying to get students to understand that the colonizer/colonized dichotomy is too simple: some of the colonized people collaborated (to modernize and/or to keep their traditional power) and some people resisted (to become independent again or to express traditional beliefs).[47]

A particularly helpful and interesting book for teachers as they help students understand the relations between the world and the West is Philip Curtin's book of that name, *The World and the West*. Notable for its use of case studies to look at the changing relations between the world and the West, Curtin describes modernizing monarchies in Hawaii, Madagascar, and Siam; millennial movements such as the Ghost Dance and cargo cults; and paths to independence in Indonesia and Ghana. His cases illustrate Williams' point about complexity.[48]

Besides dealing with the multiple perspectives of both hunters and lions, both powerful and less powerful, teachers and students must be willing to grapple with questions like Yali's in Jared Diamond's *Guns, Germs, and Steel*. He asked Diamond: "Why is it that you white people developed so much cargo and brought it to New Guinea, but we black people had little cargo of our own?"[49] The discussion should include considering that cargo or material goods are not the only way to measure a society. (A Nigerian friend of one of the authors pointed out years ago that the U.S. was certainly a developing country in terms of race relations.) Diamond's book urges us to try to understand the role of environment in dealing with Yali's question, without becoming environmental determinists. Diamond concludes that four sets of differences seem most important in answering Yali's question over long periods of history: continental differences in the wild plant and animal species available as starting materials for domestication; rates of diffusion within continents; rates of diffusion between continents; and population size.

Diamond recently published another book, *Collapse*, which uses the same comparative method as *Guns, Germs,*

and Steel to understand societal collapses to which environmental problems contribute. Connecting past to present, teachers could begin with Diamond's question: Why do some societies make disastrous decisions? They could then use several of his historical case studies (perhaps Easter Island and Greenland) and several modern ones (perhaps Dominican Republic/Haiti and Australia) and consider how what they learn relates to their own region of the United States.

The domination of the West has certainly been a popular topic for historians in the *Journal of World History*. Besides McNeill's article on "World History and the Rise and Fall of the West" in the fall 1998 issue, a reviewer of books in the Fall 1999 issue dealt with the question: Was it pluck or luck that made the West grow rich? In the fall 2001 issue there was a review of the thesis that coal and colonies account for the "great divergence" and in the spring of 2002 an article entitled "The Role of the State in the Rise of the West." As well, "Why Europe?" an inquiry lesson based largely on Diamond's data and theories, won the World History Association 2001 Prize for world history lesson. However, Japanese colonialism in Korea was the topic for the Fall 2002 prize lesson, and there are many articles in the Journal on topics other than the West, ranging from Chinese diplomatic missions to middle India in the seventh century to the United Nations Decade for Women. The February 2004 online discussion from World History Connected, sponsored by the World History Association, focused on the topic "Africa's Discovery of Europe."[50]

One way for world history teachers to learn about parts of the world beyond the west is to take advantage of travel experiences provided by organizations such as Japan's Keizai Koho Center and the Korea Society of New York as well as the Fulbright Program. Many universities also offer study tours for credit.

Dealing with his or her own Eurocentrism and that of students is probably the most difficult job a world history teacher has. As Jean Elliott Johnson writes: "Giving up Western exceptionalism, culminating in the belief that the West is the only 'modern' civilization or the ultimate cultural achievement of all human evolution, is perhaps the most important principle, and source of major contention, behind some of the current efforts to reconceptualize world history."[51]

We should note that our specifically American exceptionalism has a long history, too. At the end of *A History of the United States*, published in 1830, the author states: "The citizens of this republic should never forget the awful responsibilities resting upon them. . . To them is committed an ex-

Goal: Students will learn about Igbo and British perspectives on religious beliefs through this excerpt from Chinua Achebe's *Things Fall Apart*, a novel that is set in colonial Nigeria in the early twentieth century and is often used in high school English classes.

Procedures: Ask students to read the dialogue aloud and then discuss similarities and differences. This excerpt is in *Through African Eyes*,[52] as "A Missionary Meets His Match," as are other appropriate and interesting readings for middle and high school students.

Further Ideas and Resources: Other possibilities for comparison in *Things Fall Apart* are how court cases are settled and how proverbs reveal values.

Whenever Mr. Brown went to that village he spent long hours with Akunna in his obi talking through an interpreter about religion. Neither of them succeeded in converting the other but they learned more about their different beliefs.

"You say that there is one supreme God who made heaven and earth," said Akunna on one of Mr. Brown's visits. "We also believe in Him and call Him Chukwu. He made all the world and the other gods."

"There are no other gods," said Mr. Brown. "Chukwu is the only God and all others are false. You carve a piece of wood—like that one" (he pointed at the rafters from which Akunna's carved Ikenga hung), "and you call it a god. But it is still a piece of wood."

"Yes," said Akunna. "it is indeed a piece of wood. The tree from which it came was made by Chukwu, as indeed all minor gods were. But he made them for His messengers so that we could approach Him through them. It is like yourself. You are the head of your church."

"No," protested Mr. Brown. "The head of my church is God Himself."

"I know," said Akunna, "but there must be a head in this world among men. Somebody like yourself must be the head here."

"The head of my church in that sense is in England."

"That is exactly what I am saying. The head of your church is in your country. He has sent you here as his messengers and servants. Or let me take another example, the District Commissioner. He is sent by your king."

"They have a queen," said the interpreter on his own account.

"Your queen sends her messenger, the District Commissioner. He finds that he cannot do the work alone and so he appoints kotma to help him. It is the same with God, or Chukwu. He appoints the smaller gods to help Him because His work is too great for one person."

"You should not think of him as a person," said Mr. Brown. "It is because you do so that you imagine He must need helpers. And the worst thing about it is that you give all the worship to the false gods you have created."

"That is not so. We make sacrifices to the little gods, but when they fail and there is no one else to turn to we go to Chukwu. It is right to do so. We approach a great man through his servants. But when his servants fail to help us, then we go to the last source of hope. We appear to pay greater attention to the little gods but that is not so. We worry them more because we are afraid to worry their Master. Our fathers knew that Chukwu was the Overlord and that is why many of them give their children the name Chukwuka 'Chukwu is Supreme.'"

"You said one interesting thing," said Mr. Brown. "You are afraid of Chukwu. In my religion Chukwu is a loving Father and need not be feared by those who do His will."

"But we must fear Him when we are not doing His will," said Akunna. "And who is to tell His will? It is too great to be known."

periment, successful hitherto, the final result of which must have a powerful influence upon the destiny of mankind. . . May they never betray their sacred trust."[53]

Clearly, none of the foregoing means that students should not be proud of what the United States stands for or not learn about the immense contributions of the West to the world. We are simply suggesting more openness, less arrogance, and what the founders of our nation called in the Declaration of Independence "a decent respect for the opinion of mankind."

Conclusion

Teaching global world history is a reality in many schools today. There is a strong cadre of teachers, at the high school and college levels, who are not only teaching world history in innovative, interesting ways but are organized through the World History Association to help each other and new teachers or teachers who are new to world history.

Many people have been active in making world history a field. Twenty years after its founding, The World History Association is a thriving organization of high school and college educators that publishes a scholarly journal and bulletin twice annually, and has just opened a new headquarters at the University of Hawaii. Three projects—"Teaching a Global Perspective," "Establishing the Teaching Field: World History for the 21st Century," and the World History Network—have been funded by the National Endowment for the Humanities and others and have offered summer institutes for teachers, initiated programs for preservice teachers, and organized the World History Network website.

We also have such important reasons for teaching world history. We want our students to become informed and active citizens in their communities and in the world, and we know that understanding history in terms of multiple voices and a global perspective will be valuable and interesting. As Steve Olson concludes in *Mapping Human History, Discovering the Past Through Our Genes*: "We are members of a single human family, the products of genetic necessity and chance, borne ceaselessly into an unknown future."[54]

Our students will make and live in that future. What a world they have to drink from!

Notes

1. Leften S. Stavrianos, ed. *Readings in World History* (Boston: Allyn and Bacon, 1962).

2. As quoted in Greg Figgs and Angene H. Wilson, *A Framework for Teaching a World Civilization Course* (Kentucky Council for the Social Studies, Kentucky Association for Teachers of History, Kentucky Humanities Council: 1984). This framework was designed in response to a state mandate to require World Civilization for entrance into Kentucky state universities; that mandate gradually developed into an expectation that all students would take world history.

3. *National Standards for History*, Revised Edition (Los Angeles, CA: National Center for History in the Schools, 1996); Ross E. Dunn and David Vigilante, *Bring History Alive: A Sourcebook for Teaching World History* (Los Angeles, CA: University of California National Center for History in the Schools: 1996); Heidi Roupp, ed., *Teaching World History, A Resource Book* (Armnot, NY: M. E. Sharpe, 1997); *Building a World History Curriculum: A Guide to Using Themes and Selecting Content* (Westlake, OH: National Council for History Education, 1997), This guide is part of the Building a History Curriculum Series: Guides for Implementing the History Curriculum, recommended by the Bradley Commission on History in Schools; *Teacher's Guide, AP World History* (New York: College Board, 2000); *AP World History Best Practices* (New York: College Board, 2002); *AP World History Course Description* (New York: College Board, May 2004-May 2005).

4. Bill Bigelow and Bob Peterson, *Rethinking Columbus: The Next 500 Years* (Milwaukee WI: Rethinking Schools, 1988).

5. Ancient World History Program, World History from 500 to 1700 Program, and Modern World History Program (Palo Alto, CA: Teachers Curriculum Institute, 1999).

6. Stanford Program on International Cross-Cultural Education (SPICE) (spice.stanford.edu); American Forum for Global Education, globaled.org; National Peace Corps Association (globalteachnet.org). Asia Society (askasia.org).

7. Ross E. Dunn, "AP World History: A Matter of Definition," in *Teacher's Guide, AP World History* (New York: College Board, 2000).

8. Ibid., 32.

9. Ibid.

10. Ibid., 31

11. AP World History Course Description

12. Ibid., 5.

13. Ibid., 7.

14. J. R. McNeill and William H. McNeill, *The Human Web: A Bird's Eye View of World History* (New York: Norton, 2003), 322.

15. Ibid., 181.

16. Ibid., 288.

17. Condensed from a syllabus by Gloria Barnes, Franklin Learning Center High School, Philadelphia, PA, in *Teachers Guide, AP World History*, 89-98.

18. Dunn and Vigilante, 41.

19. Ibid., 48, 49.

20. Robert B. Bain, "Building an Essential World History Tool: Teaching Comparative History" in Roupp, ed.

21. Heidi Roupp, "World History: Developing the Teaching Field" in *Teacher's Guide, AP World History*.

22. Lyn Reese, *I Will Not Bow My Head: Documenting Political Women in World History* (Berkeley, CA: Women in World History Curriculum, 1995).

23. "The Crucible of the Millennium" was shown on PBS. The accompanying resource guide, *Part I: Through the Looking Glass* and *Part II: Echoes and Resonances*, were published by the American Forum for Global Education.

24. This teaching idea was adapted from a lesson that appeared in *The National Peace Corps Association Global TeachNet Newsletter*, May-June 2002.

25. Dunn and Vigilante, 237-245.

26. National Center for Teaching History in the Schools.

27. Merry E. Weisner, William Bruce Wheeler, Franklin M. Doeringer, and Kenneth R. Curtis, *Discovering the Global Past, A Look at the Evidence* (New York: Houghton Mifflin, 2002).

28. Kwame Gyekye, *African Cultural Values* (Philadelphia, PA and Accra Ghana: Sankofa Press, 1996), 25.

29. John Lewis Gaddis, *The Landscape of History: How Historians Map History* (New York: Oxford University Press, 2003), 9.

30. Gerda Lerner, *Why History Matters* (New York: Oxford University Press, 1997), 21.

31. National Council for History Education, *Building a World History* (Westlake, Ohio: National Council for History Education, 1997): 19.

32. John W. Wills Jr., *1688: A Global History* (New York: W. W. Norton, 2001).

33. Stepahnie Audoin-Rouzeau and Annette Becker, *1914-18 Understanding the Great War* (New York: Hill and Wang, 2000).

34. From Charles O. Hucker, "China's Imperial Past: An Introduction to Chinese History and Culture in Imperial China," in *The Art of the Horse in Chinese History Teachers Guide* (Lexington, KY: Kentucky Horse Park, 2000). Spellings in the brackets follow the pinyin system of romanization. Teachers who would like background information on China's T'ang dynasty are encouraged to read Patricia Ebrey, *The Cambridge Illustrated History of China* (Cambridge University Press, 1999).

35. Maria Rosa Menocal, *The Ornament of the World: How Muslims, Jews, and Christians Created a Culture of Tolerance in Medieval Spain* (Boston: Little Brown, 2002), 267, 271, 277.

36. *World History Best Practices.*

37. Christopher Ferraro, "Teaching the 'Big Picture' of World History," *World History Bulletin* 19, no. 1 (Spring 2003): 10-11.

38. John Willinsky, *Learning to Divide the World: Education at Empire's End* (Minneapolis, MN: University of Minnesota Press, 1998), 13.

39. Noel Grove, *Atlas of World History* (Washington, DC: National Geographic, 1997), 288-291.

40. These books are from the library of the grandfather of one of the authors, Angene Wilson. Joe Dorman Steele and Esther Baker Steele, *A Brief History of Ancient, Medieval, and Modern Peoples* (New York, Cincinnati, Chicago: American Book Company, 1883); George Part Fisher, *A Brief History of the Nations and Their Progress in Civilization* (New York: American Book Company, 1896).

41. Roupp, *Teachers Guide, AP World History*, 23.

42. Helen Grady, "Constructing an AP World History Course" in *Teacher's Guide, AP World History*, 9.

43. Peter N. Stearns, ed. *World History in Documents, A Comparative Reader* (New York: New York University Press, 1998).

44. Weisner, Wheeler, Doeringer, and Curtis.

45. Michael Ondaatje, *The English Patient* (New York: Vintage Books, 1992), 284-85.

46. Basil Davidson, *Africa, The Story of a Continent* (London: RM Arts, 1984). Video.

47. John Williams, *Classroom in Conflict, Teaching Controversial Subjects in a Diverse Society* (Albany: State University of New York: 1994).

48. Philip D. Curtin, *The World and the West: The European Challenge and the Overseas Response in the Age of Empire* (Cambridge: Cambridge University Press, 2000).

49. Jared Diamond, *Guns, Germs and Steel* (New York: W.W. Norton, 1997), 14.

50. *The Journal of World History* is published quarterly by the University of Hawaii Press. Individual subscriptions are available and include membership in The World History Association.

51. Jean Elliott Johnson, "Patterns and Comparisons in the Human Drama," in Ross E. Dunn and David Vigilante, *Bring History Alive: A Sourcebook for Teaching World History* (Los Angeles: University of California National Center for History in the Schools, 1996), 41.

52. As excerpted in Leon Clark, ed., *Through African Eyes, Vol. 1: The Past, the Road to Independence* (New York: The Center for International Training and Education, 1988), 188-190.

53. *History of the United States, from their First Settlement as Colonies to the Close of the War with Great Britain in 1815 to which is added Questions, adapted to the Use of Schools* (New York: Collins and Hannay, 1830), 298.

54. Steve Olson, *Mapping Human History: Discovering the Past Through Our Genes* (New York: Houghton Mifflin, 2003), 238.

Websites on World History

World History Association, www.thewha.org

Become a member and receive *The Journal of World History* and get information about the annual conference.

World History Connected: The e-journal of Learning and Teaching, www.worldhistoryconnected.org

Posted by the University of Illinois Press, this site presents innovative, peer-reviewed articles to keep readers up-to-date with teaching methods and practices, and recent scholarship. It includes teaching resources and book reviews. The e-journal is free of charge and articles can be downloaded for class use.

World History Resource Center at Northeastern University, www.whc.neu.edu/recenter/

This site includes questions and answers on designing a world history course and explains differences between thematic approaches as opposed to chronological or regional approaches.

World History for Us All, www.worldhistoryforusall.sdsu.edu

This site includes Panorama Lessons for each of the big eras of history. For instance, for Big Era 5: Patterns of Interregional Exchange, 300-1500 CE, an introductory Panorama PowerPoint Slide Slow, focuses on four major factors that increased cultural exchange and helped form patterns of interregional unity. Lessons follow that deal with the spread of religions and migration of people; the rise and decline of states and empires; the expansion of trade networks and exchange of products and technologies; the development of educational institutions and the transfer of knowledge; and the trans-hemispheric transfers of crops and agriculture.

Women in World History, www.womeninworldhistory.com

This site includes biographies of women rulers, lessons, essays and reviews. Curriculum units for sale include "Women in India" and "Women in the Muslim World," among others.

National Center for History in the Schools, www.sscnet.ucla.edu/nchs

The catalogue of this Center includes *Bring History Alive! A Sourcebook for Teaching World History* and world history units on topics ranging from *The Code of Hammurabi: Law of Mesopotamia* to *Women at the Heart of War, 1930-1945*. The Center has also co-published units with the Council for Islamic Education, The Getty Educational Institute for the Arts, and the Asia Society.

CHAPTER 5

Connecting the United States to the World

America is woven of many strands; I would recognize them and let it so remain... Our fate is to become one and yet many.   RALPH ELLISON

A teacher once asked if her students could do an exhibit on the United States for our annual college International Fair. We said yes. The United States is, after all, part of the world. However, we sometimes set ourselves apart as we teach social studies. In particular, when we are teaching U.S. history or government, we often do not connect what we are teaching to the rest of the world.

In this chapter we will first offer suggestions for infusing a global perspective into U.S. history and U.S. government, including four teaching ideas for each course. Second, we will raise two other possibilities: (1) How U.S. history and government can utilize comparative studies, and (2) Why a few schools have considered combining U.S. and world history and how that might work. Each possibility will be illustrated by a teaching idea.

Infusing a Global Perspective

1. In U.S. History

For U.S. history, one way to begin to think about adding a global perspective is to make a list of events that involved the U.S. beyond its borders and then to find short primary sources that bring the world in through another perspective. For instance, a list of major wars that engaged us in the world would

include: French and Indian War, American Revolution, War of 1812, War with Mexico, Civil War, Spanish-American War, World War I, World War II, Korean War, Vietnam War, the Gulf War, and the War in Iraq. Or a teacher might begin with concepts or questions. The three "I"s included in every U.S. History course—Industrial Revolution, Immigration, and Imperialism—are all connected to the wider world. Overarching questions whose answers would be richer if connected to a global perspective include: "What were the causes and consequences of the abolition of the trans-Atlantic slave trade and slavery?" and "What were the causes and consequences of the Great Depression?"

Teaching Ideas 33-36 include primary sources that add a global perspective when teaching about the American Colonization Society and the founding of Liberia and when teaching about the Mexican War, the Spanish American War, and the Vietnam War (pp. 86-89).

TEXT CONTINUED ON PAGE 90

A particularly interesting challenge is to relate "here" (where our students are in location) to "there"—the world. About 20 years ago, working on a Kentucky Studies project, I tried to connect Kentucky to the world through primary sources from the special collections archives at our university. For example, I developed a lesson plan using a letter from Mary Breckinridge, founder of the Frontier Nursing Service in eastern Kentucky, telling about her experience in France after World War I. Another lesson used transcripts of interviews with local veterans who were on the Bataan March in the Philippines in World War II. Still another used a letter from Liberia written by a freed slave from Kentucky. The latter has proved particularly effective with high school students who are amazed to find that people from their state helped found the nation of Liberia and that one became president of the country in the nineteenth century. Teachers in other states will find their own connections with the world.

Angene Wilson

Goal: Students will read a letter from Liberia written by a freed slave who settled there and describe his situation and feelings.

Procedures: As students learn about the American Colonization Society and the founding of Liberia in American history, ask them to read a letter from Liberia and understand firsthand the importance of freedom for the enslaved as well as the motives of abolitionists and slaveowners. The following letter is one of many letters in *Slaves No More: Letters from Liberia, 1833-1869.*[1]

Further Ideas and Resources: Look at the American Colonization Society Collection at the Library of Congress website for early maps and see the timeline that includes personal stories at memory.loc.gov/ammem/gmdhtml/libhtm/liberia.html. To understand Liberia's history from founding to present order the video "Liberia: America's Stepchild" from PBS and look at the website for accompanying lesson plans on "Liberia and the U.S.," "Historic Ties and Policy Decisions and Private Profits and Public Policies." Current news of Liberia can be obtained by subscribing to a listserv sponsored by Indiana University library and Friends of Liberia (www.fol.org).

Primary Source: Letter from Liberia

Rev'd N. M. Gordon Monrovia, Liberia, July 4th, 1848

Dear Sir: I take this oppitunity of writing you a few lines the object of which is to inform you of my helth and Condition up to this date. George, Frances, and my Self are all having the aclimating fever and have all bin down but I Give thanks to allmight God that we have bin sparred and raised to our feet againe. I all So state that all of us are highly pleased with the Country and flatter our Selves that we will be able to useing industry and Good Economy to Secure to our Selves a Comphortable and honorable living. This Country I believe to be the Colored man's home. Why should we not be Contented? Please to make application to Messrs. Casady and Rainey Store in Louisville by which application you will assertain that things were left off—and a cupple of working tools and a cupple of watter buckets, one pare of shares (shears) belonging to frances and the silk handerchiefs and all. So a box containing several dozen of blacking. Give my best respects to inquiring friends particularly my Colored Friends. Tell them that we are all well Satisfied and we have grown to the full stature of men—an experience [they are?] unacquainted with and will continue to be so long as they [remain] in America. I have the honour to remain your humble servant.

Jacob Harris

(in Gordon Family Papers, University of Kentucky. Jacob Harris appears on the passenger list of the *Nehemiah Rich*, departing New Orleans January 7, 1848 as age 24 from Kentucky.)

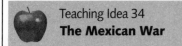

Goal: Students will read a Mexican textbook account of the war with Mexico and be able to compare that account to the one in their own textbook. The selection students will read is excerpted from a Mexican textbook on the annexation of Texas and the U.S. intervention in Mexico, as seen in a book titled *As Others See Us*.[2]

Procedures: When students learn about the Mexican War, ask them to read a Mexican perspective on the war and make a Venn diagram showing differences and similarities in the Mexican textbook and their textbook account.

Further Ideas and Resources: *Voices of the Alamo*, a children's book, offers multiple perspectives, beginning with a Payaya maiden and a Spanish conquistador and including a Tejano rancher and a Texan farmer, as well as Santa Anna and David Crockett.[3] It could be the basis for a reading or dramatization in class. Another excellent three part series of lesson plans, entitled U.S.-Mexican Relations, is available from SPICE (Stanford Program on International and Cross-Cultural Education). Part I deals with Episodes in History, Part II with contemporary issues and Part III with economic interdependence with perspectives from both sides of the border. SPICE materials are listed in Resources.

Mexican Textbook on the Annexation of Texas and the U.S. Intervention in Mexico

The territory of Texas seceded from Mexico in 1835 and then tried to be annexed to the United States, despite the protest of our [the Mexican] government, even though the treaty was rejected by the American Congress. Thereupon the annexation of the Texas territory was proposed in the U.S. House and approved on March 1, 1845. This caused our Ambassador in Washington to withdraw. The Texans, backed by the American government, claimed that its boundaries extended to the Rio Bravo del Norte [Rio Grande], whereas in fact the true limits had never passed the Nueces River. From this [boundary dispute] a long controversy developed [during which negotiations were carried on] in bad faith by the Americans.

They ordered troops to invade places within our territory, operating with the greatest treachery, and pretending that it was Mexico which had invaded their territory, making [Mexico] appear as the aggressor. What they were really seeking was to provoke a war, a war in which the southern states of the Union were greatly interested, in order to acquire new territories which they could convert into states dominated by the slavery interests. But since the majority of the people of the United States were not pro-slavery nor favorable of a war of conquest, President Polk tried to give a defensive character to his first military moves, foreseeing the opposition which he would otherwise encounter. Once he obtained a declaration of war, Polk made it appear that he wanted nothing more than peaceful possession of the annexed territory. What at the city of Mexico was captured, he made his fellow countrymen understand that they would receive no other indemnity for the expenses of war and the blood spilled than a cession of territory. Thus Polk would achieve the goal he sought from the outset. . .

The Mexican War was a brilliant move, astutely planned by the United States. The magnificent lands of Texas and California with their ports on both oceans, the gold deposits soon to be discovered in the latter state, and the increase in territory which made possible the growth of slave states compensated [the United States] many times over the cost in men and money of the unjust acquisition.

Teaching Idea 35
José Marti and the Spanish American War

Goal: Students will learn about the views and dreams of José Marti for "our America."

Procedures: As students learn about the Spanish American War, they will read the following passages, excerpted from a famous essay, "Our America," written by Marti in 1891 while he was in exile in the United States planning the insurrection against Spain. He was killed four months after the revolution began; his statue is prominent in Havana, Cuba today. These translated excerpts appear in a lesson plan in *Resistance in Paradise: Rethinking 100 Years of U.S. Involvement in the Caribbean and Pacific*.[4] Students should notice how Marti distinguishes between two different Americas and what he says about racism.

Primary Source: "Our America" by José Marti, Cuban Patriot

"What are we?" is the mutual question, and little by little they furnish answers… The youth of America are rolling up their sleeves, digging their hands in the dough, and making it rise with sweat of their brows. They realize that there is too much imitation, and that creation holds the key to salvation. "Create" is the password of this generation. The wine is made from plantain, but even if it turns sour, it is our own wine! That a country's form of government must be in keeping with its natural elements is a foregone conclusion… Freedom, to be viable, has to be sincere and complete. If a republic refuses to open its arms to all, and move ahead with all, it dies. The tiger within sneaks in through the crack; so does the tiger from without… Nations should live in an atmosphere of self-criticism because criticism is healthy, but always with one heart and one mind. Stoop to the unhappy, and lift them up in your arms! Thaw out frozen America with the fire of your hearts! Make the natural blood of the nations course vigorously through their veins. The new Americans are on their feet, saluting each other from nation to nation, the eyes of the laborers shining with joy. The natural statesman arises… He reads to apply his knowledge, not to imitate. Economists study the problems at their point of origin… Playwrights bring native characters to the stage. Academics discuss practical subjects… In the Indian republics the governors are learning Indian.

But perhaps Our America is running another risk that does not come from itself but from the difference in origins, methods, and interests between the two halves of the continent, and the time is near at hand when an enterprising and vigorous people who scorn or ignore Our America will even so approach it and demand a close relationship. And since strong nations, self-made by law and shotgun, love strong nations, and them alone;… since its good name as a republic in the eyes of the world's perceptive nations puts upon North America a restraint that cannot be taken away by childish provocations or pompous arrogance… among Our American nations, the pressing need of Our America is to show itself as it is, one in spirit and intent, swift conqueror of a suffocating past, stained only by the enriching blood drawn from hands that struggle to clear away the ruins, and from the scars left upon us by our masters. The scorn of our formidable neighbor who does not know us is Our America's greatest danger. And since the day of the visit is near, it is imperative that our neighbor know us, and soon, so that it will not scorn us. Through ignorance it might even come to lay hands on us. Once it does know us, it will remove its hands out of respect. One must have faith in the best in men and distrust the worst. One must allow the best to be shown so that it reveals and prevails over the worst. Nations should have a pillory for whoever stirs up useless hates, and another for whoever fails to tell them the truth in time.

There can be no racial animosity, because there are no races… The soul, equal and eternal, emanates from bodies of various shapes and colors. Whoever foments and spreads antagonism and hate between the races, sins against humanity… [I]n a period of internal disorder,… the rapidity with which the country's character has been accumulating [can] be turned into a serious threat for the weak and isolated neighboring counties, declared by the strong country to be inferior and perishable. The thought is father to the deed. And one must not attribute… a fatal and inborn wickedness to the continent's fairskinned nation simply because it does not speak our language, or see the world as we see it… or look charitably from its still uncertain eminence upon those less favored by history, who climb the road of republicanism by heroic stages… [T]he problem can be resolved, for the peace of centuries to come, by appropriate study, and by tacit and immediate unity in the continental spirit. With a single voice the hymn is already being sung. The present generation is… sowing the seed of the new America throughout the Latin nations of the continent and the sorrowful island of the sea!

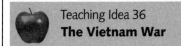

Teaching Idea 36
The Vietnam War

Goal: Students will read Vietnamese folk songs about war, as another perspective in their study of the Vietnam War.

Procedures: As students learn about the Vietnam War, they can try to understand how Vietnamese viewed the war in their land through the following folk songs by Trinh Cong Son. They were translated by Francois Sully, a *Newsweek* correspondent killed in a helicopter crash in Vietnam in 1971, and appeared in *We the Vietnamese*, edited by him.[5]

Further Ideas and Resources: David Lamb's recent *Vietnam Now: A Reporter's Return* includes stories about Vietnamese people, another Trinh Cong Son ballad, and the Vietnamese national anthem. He writes, "We claimed the history and the pain of the war as ours exclusively. The Vietnam Veterans Memorial wall in Washington became the symbol of all we had lost. . . Surely one question remained to be asked: What happened on the other side of the wall?"[6] A new interdisciplinary curriculum, *Vietnamese Americans: Lessons in American History*, is available for free downloaded at teachingtolerance.org.

Primary Sources: Vietnamese Folk Songs

I Had a Lover

I had a lover. He died on the battlefield of Pleime
I had a lover. He died on the battlefield of Dong Xoai.
I had a lover. He died in Hanoi. He died in War Zone D.
He died on the frontier.
I had a lover. He died on the battlefield of Chu Prong.
I had a lover. His body lies in a river, in a rice field, in the woods.
He died. His body became cold and was burned to ashes.

I want to love you. Love Vietnam.
The day when the wind is strong, I wander
With my lips whispering your name, the name of
Vietnam
And we are so close, of the same voice and yellow race
I want to love you. Love Vietnam.
I have just grown up and my ears are already familiar
      With the sound of bullets.

Useless are my arms.
Useless are my lips.
From now on, I shall forget your voice.
I had a lover. He died on the battlefield of A Shau.
I had a lover. He died in some valley. His body broken.
He died under a bridge, naked and voiceless.
I had a lover. He died on the battlefield of Ba Gia.
I had a lover. He died only yesterday, suddenly without hate.
He died as a dreamer.

Mother's Heritage

A thousand years dominated by the Chinese
A hundred years enslaved by the French.
Then twenty years of destructive fratricidal war, day after day.
Mother! What heritage have you left to your children?
Mother! Your heritage is Vietnam in sorrow.

A thousand years dominated by the Chinese
A hundred years enslaved by the French.
Then twenty years of destructive fratricidal war, day after day.
Mother! Your heritage is a forest of dry bones.
Mother! Your heritage is an immense graveyard.

Children! Learn from me the voice of truth.
I hope you will never forget the color of your skin.
The color of Vietnam is old.
I hope you will be home soon.
Oh children faraway! Oh children of the same father1
I am looking forward to seeing you; forget your hates.

A thousand years dominated by the Chinese
A hundred years enslaved by the French.
Then twenty years of destructive fratricidal war, day after day.
Mother! Your heritage is parched rice fields.
Mother! Your heritage is rows of homes in flames.

A thousand years dominated by the Chinese
A hundred years enslaved by the French.
Then twenty years of destructive fratricidal war, day after day.
Mother! Your heritage is a horde of rootless people.
Mother! Your heritage is a horde of traitors.

2. In U.S. Government

For government and civics classes, infusion should be fairly easy because of the *National Standards for Civics and Government*.[7] Several are particularly relevant. First we make brief suggestions that link to the standards' questions. Second, we offer teaching ideas with primary sources for studying such topics as "what is government?" and "what are the nature and purposes of constitutions?" and for learning about people and agencies (Peace Corps and the State Department) involved in our foreign policy.

What are Civic Life, Politics, and Government?

1. What is civic life? What is politics? What is government? Why are government and politics necessary? What purposes should government serve?
   Link with students outside the United States and hold an online discussion about the purposes of government.
2. What are the essential characteristics of limited and unlimited government?
   Invite a speaker who has lived in a country with a totalitarian system.
3. What are the nature and purposes of constitutions?
   Compare the U.S. Constitution with constitutions of several other countries in terms of rights of citizens.
4. What are alternative ways of organizing constitutional governments?
   Watch the British Parliament on television and compare to our Congress.

What is the Relationship of the United States to Other Nations and to World Affairs?

1. How is the world organized politically?
   Do a mock meeting of the members of the Antarctica Treaty Consultative Parties meeting. Look at antarctica.ac.uk for more information.
2. How do the domestic politics and constitutional principles of the United States affect its relations with the world?
   Read Latin American views of our policies toward Latin America. Look online for newspapers of the world (with those key words) and particularly of Latin America.
3. How has the United States influenced other nations, and how have other other nations influenced American politics and society?
   Role play a variety of nations' views of the World Trade Organization.

The following Teaching Ideas (37-40) present the concept of leadership held by a fourteenth-century Muslim scholar, a comparison of constitutional principles in Canada and the U.S., and two lessons that could be useful in studying U.S. foreign policy—one based on the letters of a Peace Corps volunteer in Afghanistan in the 1960s, and the other on a trip to the Czech Republic by Secretary of State Madeleine Albright (pp. 91-96 below).

TEXT CONTINUED ON PAGE 97

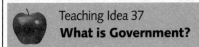

Teaching Idea 37
What is Government?

Goal: Students will consider a Muslim scholar's view of leadership, particularly the importance of "mildness."

Procedures: As students hypothesize about the attributes of good political leadership, they can use Ibn Khaldun's views as one source. Ibn Khaldun (1332-1406 CE) was a statesman, jurist, historian, and scholar, born in Tunis. The following is excerpted from The Muqaddimah or Prolegomena, an introduction to a universal history, and is found with several other political writings in *Beyond a Thousand and One Nights, A Sampler of Literature from Muslim Civilization*.[8]

Further Ideas and Resources: The Council on Islamic Education has other excellent resources, for instance, *The Emergence of Renaissance, Cultural Interaction Between Europeans and Muslims*. They have also published a handbook for educators, *Teaching about Islam and Muslims in the Public School Classroom*. Their website is cie.org.

Primary Source: Ibn Khaldun on Good Rulership

Good rulership is equivalent to mildness. If the ruler uses force and is ready to mete out punishment and eager to expose the faults of people and to count their sins, (his subjects) become fearful and depressed and seek to protect themselves against him through lies, ruses, and deceit. This becomes a character trait of theirs. Their mind and character become corrupted. They often abandon (the ruler) on the battlefield and (fail to support his) defensive enterprises. The decay of (sincere) intentions causes the decay of (military) protection. The subjects often conspire to kill the ruler. Thus, the dynasty decays, and the fence (that protects it) lies in ruin. If the ruler continues to keep a forceful grip on his subjects, group feeling will be destroyed. If the ruler is mild and overlooks the bad sides of his subjects, they will trust him and take refuge with him. They love him heartily and are willing to die for him in battle against his enemies. Everything is then in order in the state.

The concomitants of good rulership are kindness to, and protections of, one's subjects. The true meaning of royal authority is realized when the ruler defends his subjects. To be kind and beneficent toward them is part of being mild to them and showing an interest in the way they live. These things are important for the ruler in gaining the love of his subjects.

An alert and very shrewd person rarely has the habit of mildness. Mildness is usually found in careless and unconcerned persons. The least (of the many drawbacks) of alertness (in a ruler) is that he imposes tasks upon his subjects that are beyond their ability, because he is aware of things they do not perceive, and through his genius, foresees the outcome of things at the start. (The ruler's excessive demands) may lead to his subjects' ruin. Muhammad said: "Follow the pace of the weakest among you."

Muhammad therefore made it a condition that the ruler should not be too shrewd. For this quality is accompanied by tyrannical and bad rulership and by a tendency to make the people do things that are not in their nature to do.

Teaching Idea 38
Alternative Ways of Organizing Constitutional Governments

Primary Source: The Canadian Constitution (online)

Goal: Students will understand another way of organizing a constitutional government and specifically compare parts of Canada's Constitution to the U.S. Constitution.

Procedures: Students will have to access several websites to learn about Canada's Constitution, which is complicated because it has a central core of written codified instruments and a surrounding sphere of unwritten rules, called conventions. The written parts of the Constitution are two "Constitution Acts": the 1867 Constitution Act (formerly the British North America Act) that outlined the division of powers between the provincial governments and federal government; and the Constitution Act of 1982 that entrenched the Canadian Charter of Rights and Freedoms. Students should begin by reading the introductory "What is the Canadian Constitution?" on the website uni.ca/what_is_const.html. Then students can study the Canadian Charter of Rights and Freedoms and compare them to our constitution, including our Bill of Rights.

Further Ideas and Resources: To understand how the Canadian government has changed over time, in contrast to our sharp break with Britain after the American Revolution followed by our written Constitution, students should look at the timeline of constitutional documents, available at solon.org/Constitutions/Canada/English. Another website, polisci.nelson.com/constitution.html, includes documents such as Indian Treaties and constitutional amendments on language and education rights, plus links to aboriginal issues, Quebec and national unity and federalism.

Excerpts from The Canadian Constitution Act

Part I: Canadian Charter of Rights and Freedoms
Everyone has the following fundamental freedoms:
(a) freedom of conscience and religion
(b) freedom of thought, belief, opinion and expression, including freedom of the press and other means of communication.
(c) freedom of peaceful assembly; and
(d) freedom of association.

Democratic Rights
Every citizen of Canada has the right to vote in an election of members of the House of Commons.

Mobility Rights
Every citizen of Canada has the right to enter, remain in, and leave Canada.

Legal Rights
- Everyone has the right to life, liberty and security of the person and the right not to be deprived thereof except in accordance with the principles of fundamental justice.
- Everyone has the right to be secure against unreasonable search or seizure.
- Everyone has the right not to be arbitrarily detained or imprisoned.
- Everyone has the right on arrest or detention
(a) to be informed promptly of the reason therefore;
(b) to retain and instruct counsel without delay and to be informed of that right; and
(c) to have the validity of the detention determined by way of habeas corpus and to be released if the detention is not lawful.

Equality Rights
Every individual is equal before and under the law and has the right to the equal protection and equal benefit of the law without discrimination based on race, national or ethnic origin, colour, religion, sex, age, or mental or physical disability.

Official Languages of Canada
English and French are the official languages of Canada and have equal rights and privileges as to their use in all institutions of the Parliament and government of Canada.

Excerpts from The Bill of Rights (Amendments I -X of The Constitution of the United States)

Amendment I. Congress shall make no law respecting an establishment of religion, or prohibiting the free exercise thereof; or abridging the freedom of speech, or of the press; or the right of the people peaceably to assemble, and to petition the government for a redress of grievances.

Amendment II. A well regulated militia, being necessary to the security of a free state, the right of the people to keep and bear arms, shall not be infringed.

Amendment III. No soldier shall, in time of peace be quartered in any house, without the consent of the owner, nor in time of war, but in a manner to be prescribed by law.

Amendment IV. The right of the people to be secure in their persons, houses, papers, and effects, against unreasonable searches and seizures, shall not be violated, and no warrants shall issue, but upon probable cause ...

Amendment V. No person shall be held to answer for a capital, or otherwise infamous crime, unless on a presentment or indictment of a grand jury, except in cases arising in the land or naval forces, or in the militia, when in actual service in time of war or public danger; nor shall any person be subject for the same offense to be twice put in jeopardy of life or limb; nor shall be compelled in any criminal case to be a witness against himself, nor be deprived of life, liberty, or property, without due process of law; nor shall private property be taken for public use, without just compensation.

Amendment VI. In all criminal prosecutions, the accused shall enjoy the right to a speedy and public trial, by an impartial jury of the state and district wherein the crime shall have been committed, which district shall have been previously ascertained by law, and to be informed of the nature and cause of the accusation; to be confronted with the witnesses against him; to have compulsory process for obtaining witnesses in his favor, and to have the assistance of counsel for his defense.

Amendment VI. ... the right of trial by jury shall be preserved, and no fact tried by a jury, shall be otherwise reexamined in any court of the United States, than according to the rules of the common law.

Amendment VIII. Excessive bail shall not be required, nor excessive fines imposed, nor cruel and unusual punishments inflicted.

Amendment IX. The enumeration in the Constitution, of certain rights, shall not be construed to deny or disparage others retained by the people.

Amendment X. The powers not delegated to the United States by the Constitution, nor prohibited by it to the states, are reserved to the states respectively, or to the people.

How Has the United States Influenced Other Nations, and How Have Nations Influenced American Politics and Society?

Goal: Students will read excerpts from letters sent home by a Peace Corps Volunteer in Afghanistan between 1964 and 1967 and understand her work and life in Afghanistan and what she learned.

Procedures: This lesson could be used in a civics/government class that is studying foreign policy (particularly our policy toward Afghanistan) or when teaching about the development of the Peace Corps in 1961 in U.S. History. Ask students to read the letters and be able to describe the Volunteer's job and experiences over the two years. Ask them to speculate about how returned volunteers might influence foreign policy.

Further Ideas and Resources: If the students want to know more about Afghanistan, they can go to worldviewmagazine.org, click on "talk about issues" and find a lesson plan and articles from an issue devoted to Afghanistan. Helpful websites to learn about Afghanistan today are afghansforcivilsociety.org (school links through iEARN), eurasia.net for current events and commentary, and iwpr.net, Institute for War and Peace Reporting. To learn more about the Peace Corps today, go to peacecorps.gov.

Primary Source: Letters from a Peace Corps Volunteer in Afghanistan[9]
Fran Irwin

July 20, 1964: There were at least ten PCT's (Peace Corps Trainees) on that flight (to Keene, NH). . . We're supposed to have 320 hours of language training before we leave so we started with four today and will have six a day after this week.

Nov. 7, 1964: It is Saturday night but that now has a different meaning. . .it is really Monday of a six-day week at work. . .The first day (at the *Kabul Times*) was really great. . . we plan to move into our house Monday night via taxi if the PC delivers our 56 bags of sawdust tomorrow.

Dec. 26, 1964: (New Year's Letter to friends and relatives.) I am one of the 55 members of Afghan IV, which is the fourth Peace Corps contingent to come to Afghanistan. Half of our group is teaching in the provinces and the other half is teaching, nursing, or working in various ministries in Kabul as secretaries, mechanics, or irrigators. (Afghanistan) is an Islamic country about the size of Texas. . . Perhaps 350,000 of its thirteen million people live in the capital city Kabul (equal stress on each syllable) which is situated at 6700 feet, several hundred kilometers west of the Khyber Pass and within sight of the snow-covered ranges of the Hindu Kush to the North. More specifically, I live in a six-room mud house enclosed by a ten foot compound wall, and along with two fellow PCVs. My job is working on *The Kabul Times*, a four page daily (except Friday) English language newspaper sponsored by the government. I work with an all Afghan staff. . . editing wire service stories from Reuters, AP, Tass, and New China News Agency. . . A new constitution has just been written and under it a new press law will allow some freedom of the press by next year. Political parties may be formed; more women may come out of chadri. It is an exciting time to be getting to know the people who are rediscovering the East and West and trying to emerge with a synthesis of their own.

Feb. 20, 1965: I am always starved at supper since I am afraid I don't find my lunch of plain rice and turnips very enticing. . . I am addicted to nan (bread), apricot jam, orangeade, kebabs, and good kabuli (rice with carrots and raisins) . . . The sawdust stove is burning hot tonight rather than long apparently because the sawdust is loosely packed. . .We have had no trouble with exploding stoves yet. They just make pleasant popping sounds. . .

Aug. 17, 1965 (on reporting trip around the country): . . . we are off at 6 tomorrow morning to roam Afghanistan and see how Allah has conceived creation here. . . It is strange to be leaving Kabul for such a long time for it is like leaving home. . . there are now lots of people I care about here.

Aug. 25, 1965: I am sitting under a mulberry tree on my sleeping bag on a mat on a rug about 100 feet above the green, fast-flowing Kokcha River. This morning I woke up about six to the sound of camel bells; three caravans totaling about 150 camels passed by in the next hour about 15 feet in front of me through a row of poplars. Faizabad is the capital of Badakhshan, the northeastern province. The numerous warnings that we could not get through were given meaning by the dust storm, landslide, and flash flood we went through in the two days it took us to get here from Khanabad. In the six days since we left Kabul we have seen at least 4000 camels, one bridal caravan, thousands of goats, sheep, and donkeys. We have also seen part of six different *Jeshan* (independence) celebrations.

Occasionally we remember we are supposed to be working. . . We took off over an apparently barren hill and found a beautiful valley—the Willian—and talked to three different families on the way through about schools, hospitals, water, and machinery. At the first house there were three brothers who raised melons, one of whom had been sick for four years. (My colleague) gave him a note to a doctor in Kabul. One of the boys there did go to school. Down the hill we sat on the roots of a mulberry tree and talked to a man threshing wheat by driving five cattle round and round. He noted that they probably did that by machine where I came from which was interesting because he had not been to school or further than Faizabad. Then we crossed the river and saw how an Uzbeki had made water power run a fan for his summer house. . . Our next major stop was Baghlan where we had numerous good interviews. The governor stressed the importance of changing attitudes of building monuments to one's term in office. . . I talked to the principal of the only coed school in the country and also the agricultural school principal and the education director. We usually write our stories at night in the dark and retype them in the morning in the light.

June 20, 1966: I asked our new (Peace Corps) director. . . this afternoon if I could still extend for a year. The justification, of course, is my job. . . I can write the stylebook, fix up a headline chart, organise and put to use the reference books and magazines, make a datebook for the year. . .

July 4, 1967: I just had what I trust will not be my last farsi lesson ever but only for awhile. We spent it reading through a picture book with lovely frogs, turtles and porcupines (known in farsi as green skin, stone skin and thorn skin respectively) which I hope Miatta (her niece) will enjoy. It is printed in Moscow so the farsi is really tajiki and a little different from the Kabul variety.

July 12, 1967: Although it was a hectic week of trying to terminate . . . I have also been working about three-quarters time. Somehow, everything that goes on here still interests me. . . A green-bound stylebook sits on the table and has at least been looked at occasionally. It joins the blue-bound headline chart and the red-bound yearbook.

Goal: Students will learn about the role of the Secretary of State from an autobiographical description of one event.

Procedures: As students are learning how foreign policy works, ask them to read the following description of Madeleine Albright's first trip to the Czech Republic as Secretary of State.[10] The excerpt puts a human face on foreign policy, in this case the expansion of NATO.

Further Ideas and Resources: Students can go to state.gov for general information about the U.S. State Department. The website includes information about careers in the foreign service and a student page, future.state.gov. Excellent materials for teaching about U.S. foreign policy come from the Choices Program, choices.edu, including units on such topics as global environmental problems, U.S. trade policy, and foreign aid. Historical units deal with such foreign policy events as the Cuban Missile Crisis and wars, such as the Vietnam War. Their lesson plan on the U.S. Role in a Changing World appeared in the January/February 2004 *Social Education*. For an historical view of American foreign policy and a thought-provoking framework, teachers can read *Special Providence, American Foreign Policy and How It Changed the World* by Walter Russell Mead (New York: Routledge, 2002).

Primary Source: Madam Secretary in the Czech Republic in 1997

Since first arriving in America [Albright was born in Prague in 1937 and left in 1948], I had been back to Czechoslovakia, or the Czech Republic, as a tourist, goodwill ambassador, pollster, promoter of democracy, and UN permanent representative. Now President Clinton brought word of NATO's invitation to Poland; Defense Secretary Cohen had gone to Budapest; my assignment was Prague. It was, to understate the case, a somewhat emotional trip, beginning with my visit to Pinkas Synagogue [she had recently learned that her grandparents were Jewish and three of them and other family members had died in Nazi concentration camps], followed by [President Vaclav] Havel's presentation to me of the Order of the White Lion. As he placed a red and white sash over my head, I was reminded of the lampshade party dress I had worn way back in Denver.

My official focus, however, was the speech I was to deliver in Smetana Hall of the Municipal House, where the first Czechoslovak Republic was announced in 1918, in parallel with Tomas Masaryk's declaration in America. The structure was designed by the art nouveau master Alphonse Mucha, with the intent of countering German influence by celebrating Slav culture. Each room is different and dedicated to a place where Slavs live. I had never been inside because the building had long been in the process of being restored. Every light fixture, mural, sculpture and stained glass window had been returned to its original beauty.'

On the stage where I would speak were the Czech and American flags. I walked down the aisle with Foreign Minister Josef Zieleniec, then on stage to wait for the presidential fanfare. Finally Havel arrived and the gathering was complete.

Zielneiec gave me an eloquent introduction, and I got up to speak. Before me were rows of familiar faces—with my cousin Dasa in the first. After four and a half years in public office, I had delivered many speeches, but never one in which the personal and the professional were so intertwined. My words were evidence of the pride I felt in the people of my native land.

"The Communist authorities kept from you the truth and still you spoke the truth," I said, thinking of Prague Spring and Charter 77. "They fed you a vacuous culture and still you gave us works of art that fill our lives with intelligence, humor, and warmth. They tried to smother your allegiances, your faith, and your initiative, and still you taught the world the meaning of solidarity and civil society. They banished your finest leaders, and still you gave us Vaclav Havel."

Prime Minister Vaclav Klaus told me later that no Czech leader could have given such a speech, because it was so optimistic and so American. After I finished, I had to deal once more with the emotions of hearing the Czech and American national anthems played in sequence. Much later I walked along the streets, tears in my eyes, waving at little old Czech ladies with tears in their eyes, seeing in each the reflection of my mother.

3. Comparative Studies

We have already noted that the United States can be included in world history. A unit on Revolution would clearly be incomplete if the American Revolution was not considered. There are many examples of the inclusion of U.S. history in world history that could also be used to relate the world to United States history. For comparative studies to be successful, teachers of world history and of American history must talk with each other and decide in which course a particular comparative study fits best.

U.S. history teachers should consider borrowing from world history primary source readers. One previously mentioned example compares George Washington, Jean-Paul Marat, and Toussaint L'Ouverture.[11] Another comparison, entitled "The Industrial Crisis and the Centralization of Government (1924-1939)," includes speeches from British, American, German, and Japanese leaders and a number of tables.[12] In another comparative reader, one section includes the United States in presenting French, U.S. and Indian views of women in the nineteenth century, and deals with Russian peasants after emancipation and African Americans after slavery in "The Emancipations and Their Consequences."[13]

Sample student activities in *Bring History Alive!* offer comparative examples, too. For the twentieth century, students: (1) examine art works and photographs depicting hunger and poverty (during the Great Depression) such as those by German artist Kathe Kollwitz, Mexican muralist Jose Clemente Orozco, and American photographer Dorothea Lange and (2) conduct a roundtable discussion on the theme: "What human progress means to me" with participants such as Karl Barth, Mussolini, Trotsky, Mao Zedong, Ataturk, Pope Leo XIII, John Maynard Keynes, and Franklin Roosevelt.[14]

The standards on civics and government listed earlier expect students to be able to describe historical and contemporary instances of how constitutions have been disregarded or used to promote the interests of a particular group and to be able to explain how constitutions in several countries have been vehicles for change and resolving social issues. The students should be able to compare presidential and parliamentary systems. They are expected to explain economic, technological, and cultural effects the U.S. has had on the rest of the world and the effects of developments in other nations on their own lives.

The Democratic Process: Promises and Challenges, a resource guide produced for the Democracy Education Exchange Project (DEEP),[15] includes a number of appropriate comparative lessons. For example, a Historical Timelines lesson compares the Czech Republic and the USA in the development of democracy. Several lessons use descriptions of imaginary countries to analyze whether the country possesses a democratic culture or the challenges of developing one. A lesson on voter turnout includes a chart with data of voter turnout in four other nations, as well as the U.S. In still another lesson, entitled "Each One Teach One," students share and discuss facts about democracy in the U.S. and Russia, Central Asia, and Eastern Europe, such as "The U.S. is one of the few countries to still allow the death penalty. Countries that belong to the European Union may not sentence a person to death. Therefore, any Eastern European country applying to become a member of the European Union must not have a death penalty" and "Freedom of speech in the U.S., although not without limitations, does allow hate speech to be heard. Some countries have outlawed speech that advocates hate, such as speech preaching a superior race." Finally, in the lesson "Values and a Society: A Democratic Experiment," students are asked to examine how important democracy and free markets are in creating a desirable society. One part of the lesson is doing Internet research on a country to discover such factors as infant mortality and educational enrollment ratio (male/female), and income per capita.

A model comparative course is *Emerging Civil Societies*, developed as a tenth grade civics course by Caryn Stedman for the Metropolitan Learning Center Interdistrict Magnet School in Bloomfield, Connecticut. This course includes units on the nature of politics and government, the foundations of representative government (including a review of the French, Haitian and American revolutions), constitutions (comparing the U.S., British, Japanese and Indian constitutions), the balance of power in the U.S. and elsewhere (legislative, executive, judicial), rights, international organizations, and civic participation (how can we make a difference in local and global decisions?).

Teaching Idea 41, and the accompanying handout, introduce students to comparative information on the proportion of women serving in legislatures in different countries (p. 98).

A Woman's Place is in the House and the Senate: Democratic Governance and Women in Politics[16]

Material for this lesson comes from the United Nations Development Program's Human Development Report 2002[17]

Goal: Students will construct graphs showing the percentage of women serving in the national legislatures of different countries, learn about various ways in which other countries have tried to increase the percentage of women in their legislatures, and create a plan to increase the percentage in the U.S. Congress.

Procedures: The teacher can begin by noting that one of the Report's characteristics of democratic governance is "Women are equal partners with men in private and public spheres of life and decision-making." Then the teacher can ask, "How does the U.S. compare to other countries in terms of women serving in legislatures?" (This is one of the indicators the Report uses to rank countries in terms of democracy.)

Students should be given the task of illustrating the following list by developing a bar graph or a map to show the selected countries and percentages.

Argentina	31.3
Canada	23.6
France	10.9
Germany	31
Japan	10.9
Mexico	15.9
Mozambique	30
Netherlands	32.9
New Zealand	30.8
Russia	6.4
South Africa	29.8
Tanzania	22.3
Turkmenistan	26
United Kingdom	17.1
United States	13.8

After completing the graphs or maps, teacher can ask how nations have tried to increase the number of women serving in their legislatures. Information on the following handout should prompt discussion about whether any of these ideas would work in the United States. As an assessment, pairs of students could research what efforts are being made to increase female participation in the U.S. Congress and design their own plans for increasing participation.

Legislated quotas in legislatures

In India, one-third of the seats in local governments have been reserved for women since 1993. Local parties and interest groups have had to seek out female candidates to represent them and win their support. In 1998, women won as many as 40% of seats in local government.

In France, a 1999 constitutional amendment required that at least half the candidates for municipal elections be women. As a result, women won 48% of elections in 2001, up from 22% in 1995. In national elections, where there is no such requirement, the share of women elected increased from 7% in 1998 to about 10% in 2001.

Voluntary quotas in political parties

In 1994 South Africa's African National Congress introduced a one-third quota for women, triggering impressive gains. With 120 women in the 400 member National Assembly, the country now ranks 8th in the number of women in national parliaments, up from 141st in 1994.

In the United Kingdom, the Labour Party introduced all-women shortlists for open seats from 1993 until the 1997 general election. In 2000 the British House of Commons had 131 female members, nearly twice as many as in 1995.

Other help

In the Philippines the Center for Legislative Development provides training in such areas as legislative agenda setting, proposal development, advocacy and participation in committee and floor deliberations. This training has helped female legislators in three provinces pass gender-related ordinances, such as the creation of crisis centers for women, and promoted gender responsive policy decisions on issues such as violence against women.

In Trinidad and Tobago a network called "Working to Get the Balance Right" trained 300 women to run in local government elections in 1999. The goal was to sensitize the women to gender-specific concerns and to how these concerns can be addressed through their participation as advocates of public officials. The number of female candidates nominated to run was 91, an almost 100% increase over 1996. And 28 won seats—a 50% increase.

Combining U.S. and World History

In the 19th century hour of the CNN Millennium video series, it was disappointing that the narrative dealing with imperialism stopped its consideration of Africa after simply mentioning the scramble for colonies. However, the video then turned to the conquering of the American West and Native Americans and brought together overseas and overland imperialism—and the world and the United States.

Over the last ten years one of the authors has worked with two small groups of teachers who have grappled with the possibility of joining World History and U.S. History and teaching the courses over a two-year period. The idea was that putting U.S. expansion in a worldwide context would be valuable, and the groups recognized a perennial problem in teaching the 20th century. Students are sometimes taught the world wars twice in some depth (perhaps in world history as a sophomore and then in American history as a junior) and the courses then often cruise quickly through the last third of the 20th century. The materials and topics also seem to focus more on the U.S. in both courses.

One proposal, in a five high school Kentucky school system, would have begun in ninth grade with a semester of world history to about 1900, then a semester of U.S. history through the nineteenth century, then a semester of Twentieth Century U.S. and World History together, followed by a semester of Global Issues. That proposal assumed world history to 1500 would be taught in middle school. The plan died, partly because of the arrival of site-based decision making at high schools and partly because combining is not easy. A group of teachers in Evansville, Indiana is currently working on a similar idea, combining all U.S. and World History in a chronological way from the beginning to the present over two years. They are including literature and the arts as well.

Many questions arise. Does it make sense to teach at least the twentieth century by looking at the United States and the world together? There are certainly good reasons to teach American history separately. Then should we teach it before world history or after? Americans live in the world and have a great deal to do with what happens or doesn't happen in the world, and yet the goal of preparing students to be citizens of the world makes some uncomfortable.

What about broadening our ideas of civic education, including both history and government? The teaching resource bulletin, *Globalization and Border Crossings: Examining Issues of National Identity, Citizenship, and Civic Education,* offers a strong rationale for joining global education and civic education in a globally grounded civic education. As the bulletin asserts, we now live in a world where, more than ever, people are on the move, crossing borders. Every day 500,000 people cross national boundaries on airplanes. In the United States, about 10 percent of our population were born in another country. It is also worthwhile talking about to whom we are teaching U.S. history and government and what difference that makes. For instance, how do we respond to the children of ranchero families in Chicago who affirm their traditional Mexican identity in the middle of a transnational existence? They cheer for the Chicago Bulls and send money back to their Mexican community for new houses there. The bulletin also draws on Carole Hahn's research. In her review of the status of civic education in the United States, Hahn found that students of all backgrounds "recited a common narrative that captured the chronological political history and 'waves of immigration' story that is presented in textbooks," even when they were not represented. They did learn about the contributions of individuals from diverse cultures, "but what they learned appeared to be episodic. That is, students seemed to associate Native Americans with the pre-encounter period and 'the Westward movement,' African Americans with slavery and the Civil Rights movement, and East European immigrants with the 1880s and 1920s, rather than seeing a continuous process of border crossings and constant on-going multicultural interaction within a society." Hahn also notes: "I have not yet heard teachers describe how they are consciously connecting to the diverse civic cultures from which students' families come."[18]

So how would combining work? The topic of immigration or migration is one place to begin, and offers a way for teachers to connect to the diverse cultures from which students' families come. As Ellison said, we are one and yet many.

Teaching Idea 42 offers suggestions for the study of migration, and immigration.

Teaching Idea 42
Border Crossings: Comparative Maps and Timelines

Goal: Students will construct maps and timelines that show migration of people into and out of our nation and other parts of the world.

Procedures: Ask students to read aloud several of the many poems and songs in Ronald Takaki's *Strangers from a Different Shore: A History of Asian Americans* or *A Different Mirror, A History of Multicultural America*.[19] Students should analyze the themes of the poems and songs, such as high hopes, homesickness, plans for return, prejudice, and hard work; or use the essay by Colin Powell on page 102 as a way to begin a discussion about migration and immigration.

Then students in the class whose parents or grandparents were immigrants or who themselves came from another country should be encouraged to talk about similar themes in their lives and their families' lives.

Next the students should be challenged to do research that will result in comparative maps and timelines that show what push and pull factors influenced migration both ways. For instance, while freed slaves went to found Liberia in the nineteenth century, a 14-year civil war in Liberia has recently pushed Liberians to come to the United States as refugees. Today we hear more about Mexicans coming to the U.S. for work, but U.S. citizens also go to Mexico to retire.

Further Ideas and Resources: An immigration project that includes history and is described in *Reading, Writing and Rising Up* would be an appropriate connection with an English class.[20] For a visual resource, teachers should consider *The New Americans*, a seven hour series of programs on PBS in spring 2004, focusing on Nigerian refugees, a Palestinian woman marrying an Arab American, Dominican baseball players, a Mexican family, and an Indian engineer. Additional resources and teaching ideas are on their website, www.pbs.org. See the description of the Choices Program in the Resources; one of their topics is U.S. immigration policy.

The America I Believe In
Colin Powell

(A essay broadcast on the National Public Radio program "Morning Edition" on April 11, 2005)

I believe in America and I believe in our people.

Later this month, I will be participating in a ceremony at Ellis Island where I will receive copies of the ship manifest and the immigration documents that record the arrival in America of my mother, Maud Ariel McKoy, from Jamaica aboard the motor ship Turialba in 1923. My father, Luther Powell, had arrived three years earlier at the Port of Philadelphia.

They met in New York City, married, became Americans and raised a family. By their hard work and their love for this country, they enriched this nation and helped it grow and thrive. They instilled in their children and grandchildren that same love of country and a spirit of optimism.

My family's story is a common one that has been told by millions of Americans. We are a land of immigrants: A nation that has been touched by every nation and we, in turn, touch every nation. And we are touched not just by immigrants but by the visitors who come to America and return home to tell of their experiences.

I believe that our greatest strength in dealing with the world is the openness of our society and the welcoming nature of our people. A good stay in our country is the best public diplomacy tool we have.

After 9/11 we realized that our country's openness was also its vulnerability. We needed to protect ourselves by knowing who was coming into the country, for what purpose and to know when they left. This was entirely appropriate and reasonable. Unfortunately, to many foreigners we gave the impression that we were no longer a welcoming nation. They started to go to schools and hospitals in other countries, and frankly, they started to take their business elsewhere. We can't allow that to happen. Our attitude has to be, we are glad you are here. We must be careful, but we must not be afraid.

As I traveled the world as secretary of state, I encountered anti-American sentiment. But I also encountered an underlying respect and affection for America. People still want to come here. Refugees who have no home at all know that America is their land of dreams. Even with added scrutiny, people line up at our embassies to apply to come here.

You see, I believe that the America of 2005 is the same America that brought Maud Ariel McKoy and Luther Powell to these shores, and so many millions of others. An America that each day gives new immigrants the same gift that my parents received. An America that lives by a Constitution that inspires freedom and democracy around the world. An America with a big, open, charitable heart that reaches out to people in need around the world. An America that sometimes seems confused and is always noisy. That noise has a name, it's called democracy and we use it to work through our confusion.

An America that is still the beacon of light to the darkest corner of the world.

Last year I met with a group of Brazilian exchange students who had spent a few weeks in America. I asked them to tell me about their experience here. One young girl told me about the night the 12 students went to a fast food restaurant in Chicago. They ate and then realized they did not have enough money to pay the bill. They were way short. Frightened, they finally told the waitress of their problem. She went away and she came back in a little while saying, "I talked to the manager and he said, 'It's ok.'" The students were still concerned because they thought the waitress might have to pay for it out of her salary. She smiled and she said, "No, the manager said he is glad you are here in the United States. He hopes you are having a good time, he hopes you are learning all about us. He said it's on him."

It is a story that those young Brazilian kids have told over and over about America. That's the America I believe in, that's the America the world wants to believe in.

Colin Powell spent 35 years in the military, rising from ROTC in college to become a four-star general and chairman of the Joint Chiefs of Staff during the 1991 Gulf War. He has worked in the administrations of six presidents including serving as secretary of state from 2001 to 2005. This essay is available at www.npr.org/templates/ story/story.php?storyId=4583249

Notes

1. Bell I. Wiley, ed. *Slaves no More: Letters from Liberia, 1833-1869* (Lexington, KY: The University Press of Kentucky, 1980), 261; Alan Huffman, *Mississippi in Africa: The Saga of the Slaves of Prospect Hill Plantation and Their Legacy in Liberia Today* (New York: Gotham, 2004), This saga is a journalist's quest to find descendants of slaves who were freed in Mississippi in the first half of the 19th century to go to Liberia.

2. Excerpt from the curriculum *Many Faces of Mexico* by Octavio Ruiz, Amy Sanders, and Meredith Sommers (Minneapolis: Resource Center of the Americas, 1998), 139. The curriculum includes other interesting sources and lessons on such topics as Aztec life, colonialism, the Mexican Revolution, the 1968 student movement, the uprising in Chiapas, and mutually beneficial tourism.

3. Sherry Garland, *Voices of the Alamo* (New York: Scholastic Press, 2000).

4. *Resistance in Paradise: Rethinking 100 Years of U.S. Involvement in the Caribbean and Pacific* (Philadelphia, PA: American Friends Service Committee, 1998), 41-43.

5. Francois Sully, *We the Vietnamese: Voices from Vietnam* (New York: Praeger, 1971), 260-262.

6. David Lamb, *Vietnam Now: A Reporter's Return* (New York: Public Affairs, 2002), 5.

7. *National Standards for Civics and Government* (Calabasas, CA: Center for Civic Education, 1994).

8. Susan L. Douglass, *Beyond a Thousand and One Nights: A Sampler of Literature from Muslim Civilization* (Fountain Valley, CA: Council on Islamic Education, 2000), 84-85.

9. Letter excerpts are used with the permission of the author, Fran Irwin.

10. Madeleine Albright, *Madam Secretary: A Memoir* (New York: Miramax Books, 2003), 261.

11. Merry E. Weisner, William Bruce Wheeler, Franklin M. Doeringer, Kenneth R. Curtis, *Discovering the Global Past: A Look at the Evidence* (New York: Houghton Mifflin, 2002).

12. Ibid.

13. Peter N. Stearns, ed., *World History in Documents: A Comparative Reader* (New York: New York University Press, 1998).

14. Ross E. Dunn and David Vigilante, *Bring History Alive! A Sourcebook for Teaching World History* (Los Angeles: University of California National Center for History in the Schools, 1996).

15. *The Democratic Process: Promises and Challenges* (New York: The American Forum for Global Education, 2003).

16. This teaching idea appeared in the National Peace Corps Association's *Global TeachNet* newsletter, January-February 2003.

17. *Human Development Report 2002, Deepening Democracy in a Fragmented World* (New York and Oxford: Oxford University Press, 2002), 226, 70.

18. Charlotte C. Anderson and James H. Landman, *Globalization and Border Crossings: Examining Issues of National Identity, Citizenship, and Civic Education* (Chicago, IL: American Bar Association Division for Public Education, 2003), 34.

19. Ronald Takaki, *Strangers from a Different Shore: A History of Asian Americans* (New York: Penguin, 1989); *A Different Mirror: A History of Multicultural America* (Boston, MA: Little, Brown, 1993).

20. Linda Christiansen, *Reading, Writing, and Rising Up: Teaching about Social Justice and the Power of the Written Word* (Milwaukee, WI: Rethinking Schools, 2000).

Resources

The Choices Program, Watson Institute for International Studies, Brown University, choices.edu

U.S. History and Global Studies lessons link the U.S. to the world. Examples in U.S. History are *Challenges to the New Republic: Prelude to the War of 1812* and *Reluctant Colossus: America Enters the Age of Imperialism.* Examples in Global Studies, also appropriate for U.S. government courses, are *U.S. Immigration Policy in an Unsettled World* and *U.S. Trade Policy: Competing in a Global Economy.* (The Choices Program is highlighted in Chapter 6.)

SPICE (Stanford Program on International and Cross-Cultural Education), Institute for International Studies, Stanford University, spice.stanford.edu

Curricula that link the U.S. to the world include: The three part U.S.-Mexico Relations *(Part I: Episodes in the History of U.S.-Mexico Relations; Part II: Contemporary Issues in U.S.-Mexico Relations*; and *Part III: U.S.-Mexico Economic Interdependence: Perspectives from Both Sides of the Border, Contemporary Issues in U.S.-Mexico Relations)*, Episodes in the History of U.S.-Japan Relations: *Case Studies of Conflict, Conflict Management and Resolution.* The Media in U.S.-Japan Relations: *A Look at Stereotypes.* (SPICE is highlighted in Chapter 6.)

BOOKS

The Democratic Process: Promises and Challenges. New York: The American Forum for Global Education, 2003. A resource guide of lessons produced for the Democracy Education Exchange Project (DEEP)

National Standards for Civics and Government. Calabasas, CA: Center for Civic Education, 1994. Specific content standards for K-12.

CHAPTER 6

Teaching Global Issues

We hope the world won't narrow into a neighborhood until it has broadened into a brotherhood. LYNDON B. JOHNSON

How, we ask, do we teach about issues such as terrorism, war, nation-building and natural disasters in a world that has some attributes of a neighborhood but often not the attributes of a brotherhood? First, we need to answer the following questions:

- What are global issues that are important for our students to understand?
- Where in the curriculum can these global issues be taught?
- What is the context for teaching about these issues?

The first section of this chapter deals with what issues and where in the curriculum. The second describes a rationale for teaching global issues in the context of globalization. We then deal with pedagogy for teaching issues and discuss the disadvantages of looking at issues only as problems. We suggest trying to connect problems with progress and making sure students understand that issues are complex. Finally, we include ideas for encouraging students to make choices and take action and to engage in international service learning.

What Issues and Where in the Curriculum?

One list of potential issues comes from Kenneth Tye's cross-national study of global education that elicited responses from 52 countries. In responding to the question of what issues young people need to understand, the following were most frequently cited:

- Ecology and the environment
- Development issues

- Intercultural relations
- Peace and conflict
- Technology
- Human rights
- Social justice

Other topics mentioned include: democracy, population, HIV/AIDS, international organizations, racism, sexism, and global citizenship.[1]

Another longer list of issues appears on the World Bank website: AIDS, climate change, corruption, education, energy, food and agriculture, gender, health, information and communications, international trade, natural resources, pollution, population, poverty, private sector development, sustainable development, urbanization, water and sanitation, and youth. The "Do You Know?" quiz on their website (click on Resources for Kids and Schools) could be a pretest on the issues.[2]

A free curriculum developed by the American Federation of Teachers, *Down the Street, Around the World*, chooses seven issues—education, environment, health, human rights, labor, migration, and security—for student briefing books which include website resources. Students are expected to map out their information, identify similarities and differences about how their topic affects the U.S. and other parts of the world, understand various positions, use newspapers, interview various persons in the community to make connections, and finally make and present a plan to their classmates. The teacher's guide also contains a Test Your Global IQ, an

My Chinese colleague told me to turn on the radio as she came by my office on the morning of September 11, 2001. She and I and my colleague/doctoral student from Ghana, who had just defended his dissertation the week before and was planning to fly home that weekend, sat in shock listening to reports of the first and then the second plane crashing into the World Trade Center. Later, in spring 2003, my Chinese colleague was scheduled to lead a faculty trip to China, but the SARS epidemic forced its cancellation. In the next year, 2004, we witnessed the continuation of the war in Iraq that started in 2003, an election in Afghanistan, a humanitarian crisis and the ongoing civil war in the Sudan, and the horrific natural disaster of the tsunami in Asia at the year's end.

Angene Wilson

article on economic globalization by International Monetary Fund staff, and a Human Bingo game.[3]

The following questions offer one set of guidelines for teachers as they decide what issues to teach.

- Is the issue relevant to students' lives and real world conditions and events?
- Does the issue prompt reflective and informed thinking?
- Will the critical and systematic analysis of the issue at hand produce action?
- Are values conflicts at the core of the controversy regarding moral and critical decision making?
- Are resource materials available?
- Is it appropriate for the students' development level?[4]

The second question "Where in the curriculum do we deal with these topics?" inspires further questions. Should Global Issues be a separate course? Or should issues be dealt with at the beginning of the year in world history to entice students into understanding why they need to learn about the history of the world? Or do global issues belong in an international relations section of civics/government? Or should global issues simply be infused when they arise as current events, the subject of the next chapter?

Clearly, and perhaps especially at the secondary level where history and the social science disciplines often rule, global issues need a home and probably homes. As we offer teaching ideas in this chapter, we have purposefully not tried to designate issues as appropriate for one course or another. Global issues do not divide conveniently into government/ civics or economics or geography—and culture and history may be relevant, too. So teachers will have to decide both what issues are most important to teach and where in the curriculum to include them.

The Context of Globalization

Thomas Friedman's *The Lexus and the Olive Tree* popularized the notion that a new globalization with many exciting possibilities has overtaken the world. We know from world history that there have been global encounters for centuries (how did we begin to drink coffee and tea, how did disease spread?), but today's connections seem unprecedented. Friedman explains that he looks at the world through the multiple lenses of politics, culture, national security, financial markets, technology, and environmentalism. He defines globalization as the integration of markets, nation-states and technologies with a democratization of technology, finance,

and information. The Lexus represents "the drive for sustenance, improvement, prosperity, and modernization" while the olive tree "represents everything that roots us, anchors us, identifies us and locates us in this world."[5]

To encourage our students to develop a global perspective, we may ask them: How does globalization look to someone who does not even own a car, much less a Lexus? Is it only the olive tree or the home/ethnic culture that opposes the onslaught of globalization? Or is poverty an equally important barrier when the richest 5% of the world's people have incomes 114 times those of the poorest 5%. Can poor people invent businesses that will thrust them into what Friedman calls the "fast world?" Or will the cell phone or the television only keep them in touch with but not part of globalization— Liberians in war-torn Monrovia calling relatives in the United States? Do the poor see globalization as Americanization or as neo-colonialism being shoved across the ocean? Or do they see what Chandra Muzaffar, the president of a Malaysian human rights organization, told Friedman: "As a result of globalization, there are elements of culture from dominated peoples that are now penetrating the north. . . There are opportunities now for others to state their case through the Internet. . . In Malaysia, Mahathir now gets some coverage through CNN... To argue that it is a one-way street is not right and we should recognize its complexity."[6]

Another view of globalization is offered in Saskia Sassen's *Globalization and its Discontents*. She is especially concerned about the concentration of the management and finance of the transnational system in global cities and points out that the rich/poor gap exists not only between countries, but also within cities. Sassen believes the global city is a "strategic site for disempowered actors because it enables them to gain presence, to emerge as subjects, even when they do not gain direct power."[7] She notes the incorporation of Third World women into wage labor and their resulting growth in autonomy and independence. She makes interesting connections, too, that students could explore: the sugar price support provision for U.S. producers in the early 1980s resulted in a loss of 400,000 jobs in the Caribbean Basin from 1982 to 1988, which was also an era of large increases in immigration from the region.[8]

Still another view of globalization comes from Amy Chua in *World on Fire*. Her thesis is contained in the subtitle of her book: *How Exporting Free Market Democracy Breeds Ethnic Hatred and Global Instability*. She explains how free markets have often concentrated disproportionate wealth in the hands of an ethnic minority, for example the Chinese in Southeast Asia (her family is part of the Chinese minority in the Philippines), the Lebanese in West Africa, or the Jews in post-Communist Russia. Chua then applies the concept of wealthy minority to the United States in its relation to the rest of the world because it has been the major beneficiary of globalization. Students could debate her solution, which she calls "a more honorable way." Her solution is voluntary generosity by market-dominant minorities, in the case of the United States meaning an increase in our foreign aid, which is paltry (compared to other OECD countries), targeted (Israel $3 billion and Egypt $2 billion a year), and conditioned (use American consultants who fly American airlines and order American products).[9]

Friedman recognizes the problems of globalization, too: that it may just be too hard in some countries, may connect us too much, may be too intrusive, too unfair for too many people, and too dehumanizing. He proposes a safety net. Jared Diamond, whom Chua quotes, makes very specific proposals about "providing health care, supporting family planning, and addressing chronic environmental problems." Diamond writes, "When people can't solve their own problems, they strike out irrationally, seeking foreign scapegoats, or collapsing in civil war over limited resources. By bettering conditions overseas, we can reduce chronic future threats to ourselves."[10]

Students might consider Diamond's proposals and the challenges of balancing between the Lexus and the olive tree as introduced in the following teaching idea.

Teaching Idea 43
Tensions of Globalization

Goal: Students will be able to define globalization and understand the tensions or dilemmas of globalization.

Procedures: First ask students to work in small groups with newspapers and magazines to make collages, placing half the articles under the heading "Lexus—A Better Life" and the other half of the articles under heading "Olive Tree—Our Home." Explain this tension is one of the issues of globalization. Suggest as one definition of globalization: "the acceleration and intensification of interaction and integration among the people, companies, and governments of different nations." Have students read and discuss handouts with the Friedman, McNeill, and Annan quotes on page 108.

As one alternative, ask students to look at the Globalization Index in *Foreign Policy* (May/June 2005), available at foreignpolicy.com. After understanding the economic, technological connectivity, personal contact and political engagement indicators, each could choose one of the 62 ranked countries to report on.

Or ask students to read "The Three Tensions of Globalization" by Laurence Rothenberg at globaled.org (site requires registration). Then, small groups could look at the three tensions (between individual and societal choices, between free market and government intervention, between local authority and supra-local authority) and come up with examples.

Teaching Materials
Rethinking Globalization

Rethinking Globalization: Teaching for Justice in an Unjust World, edited by Bill Bigelow and Bob Peterson and published by Rethinking Schools Press in 2002, is curriculum with an "attitude" and a goal. As the authors explain, this is partisan teaching that invites a diversity of opinion but has as its aims alerting students to global injustice, helping them find explanations, and encouraging activism. Initiated to deal particularly with sweatshops and child labor, the curriculum grew to include resources and teaching ideas on the topics of the legacy of inequality and its colonial roots, the global economy (especially but not exclusively sweatshops and child labor), and then sections on "Just Food?" and "Culture, Consumption, and the Environment." The book sometimes includes multiple perspectives, for instance, "Ten Benefits of the WTO System" and "Ten Arguments Against the World Trade Organization." A Transnational Capital Auction and a role play on "Oil, Rainforests, and Indigenous Cultures" are examples of activities. The poetry choices are especially powerful, and there is also a bibliography of "Songs with a Global Conscience." Finally, the book includes articles and ideas related to activism.

Thinking about Working for a Global Future

Secretary-General of the United Nations Kofi Annan challenges us to think about the role of international organization as community:

> Faced with the potential good of globalization as well as its risks, faced with the persistence of deadly conflicts in which civilians are the targets, and faced with the pervasiveness of poverty and injustice, we must identify areas where collective action is needed—and then take that action to safeguard the common, global interest.[a]

William McNeill writes about the shape of the future in *The Human Web*.

> Perhaps the most critical question for the human future is how cell-like primary communities can survive and flourish within the global cosmopolitan flows that sustain our present numbers, wealth, and power, without being disrupted by those flows and without disrupting them. . . to preserve what we have, we and our successors must change our ways by learning to live simultaneously in a cosmopolitan web and in various and diverse primary communities.[b]

Thomas Friedman's *The Lexus and the Olive Tree* popularized the notion that a new globalization with many exciting possibilities has overtaken the world:

> The challenge in this era of globalization—for countries and for individuals—is to find a healthy balance between preserving a sense of identity, home, and community and doing what it takes to survive within the globalization system. Any society that wants to thrive economically today must constantly be trying to build a better Lexus and driving it out into the world. But no one should have any illusions that merely participating in the global economy will make a society healthy. If that participation comes at the price of a country's identity, if individuals feel their olive tree roots crushed, or washed out, by this global system, those olive tree roots will rebel. They will rise up and strangle the process.[c]

Sources

(a)   Kofi Annan, "Problems without Passport," *Foreign Policy*. September/October 2003, 30-31.
(b)   Thomas L. Friedman, *The Lexus and the Olive Tree: Understanding Globalization* (New York: Farrar Straus Giroux, 1999), 27.
(c)   J. R. McNeill and William H. McNeill, *The Human Web, A Bird's Eye View of World History* (New York: Norton, 2003), 326-327.

Connecting Problems and Progress

Teaching about issues or problems has a long and well-known history in social studies. Long ago John Dewey suggested that a problem or a doubt was the natural beginning of reflective thinking. The National Council for the Social Studies publication, *Handbook on Teaching Social Issues*, offers several models for issues-based teaching. For instance, the Engle-Ochoa model sets out seven phases: orientation to a problem area, identify and define one problem, engage students by the use of probing questions, identify value assumptions, identify alternatives and predict consequences, reach and justify a decision, and proclaim the results and reflect upon the process. The Massialas and Cox model begins with an orientation phase, then moves to hypothesis, definition, exploration, evidencing, and generalization.[11]

However, there are limitations in using only problem-based approaches to teach about the world, even when value assumptions are included. Two ways of teaching can mitigate the negative features of focusing on problems so, for instance, Africa becomes in students' minds mostly hunger or AIDS or civil wars. One way is to balance problems with progress. So, for example, the SPICE (Stanford Program on International and Cross-Cultural Education) unit, "Examining Human Rights in a Global Context," deals with both accomplishments and challenges in the 20th century. A second way is to show how problems faced by other countries are also faced by the United States, so that they can be seen as global issues that we in the United States face in common with other countries. A SPICE unit that connects us with the problem, "A Global Investigation of Child Labor: Case Studies from India, Uganda, and the United States," is described in more detail later in this chapter (p. 118). Another SPICE unit on "Comparative Health Care: The United States and Japan" includes a lesson on bioethics that introduces students to the ethical considerations surrounding the issues of brain death and organ transplantation in the U.S. and Japan, as well as lessons on aging and health care financing and delivery.

One way to begin teaching about problems and progress and to connect both to the United States is to look at excerpts from the United Nations Human Development Report 2002 balance sheet. Focusing on the progress may also help us understand how problems can be solved. A teacher could give each pair of students one example from the Human Development balance sheet and ask them to hypothesize why each happened, and then consider how the progress could be continued, and how U.S. involvement through non-governmental organizations and our government would contribute.

A second exercise would ask pairs of students to read the "Good News for Some Poor Countries" and then each choose one poor country of low medium development and one of medium human development (according to the Human Development Report charts). Their task would be to check national statistics in the most recent report to see how their countries measure up against the first six Millennium Development goals (See p. 111). Students should also look under "countries" on the World Bank website. On the Ghana section, for instance, there is a heading on Millennium Development goals.

The "Cows and Cotton Receive More Aid than Poor Countries" figures are meant to be a discussion starter that relates to the seventh Millennium Development goal: develop a global partnership for development. The teacher could ask questions such as: Why do rich countries pay subsidies to domestic food producers? How could the elimination of such subsidies, as agreed upon at the 2001 World Trade Organization conference in Doha, Qatar, help poor countries? What are other steps rich countries could take to help change trading patterns and thereby help poor countries? How do tariffs on agricultural goods and simple manufactures, such as processed textiles, affect poor countries? Is trade as important as aid? How would your perspective on these issues differ, depending on whether you are an EU or Japanese dairy farmer or a U.S. cotton farmer or an African farmer or a consumer anywhere?

Teaching Ideas 44-46 offer additional activities to help students evaluate progress in providing greater access to HIV/AIDS medicines, understand the elements of environmental governance, and investigate the concept of individual liberty in different countries (pp. 112-117 below).

Human Development Balance Sheet: Excerpts from 2002 Report[12]

GLOBAL PROGRESS	GLOBAL FRAGMENTATION
Democracy and Participation	
140 countries of the world's nearly 200 countries now hold multiparty elections, more than any time in history.	Only 82 countries, with 57% of the the world's people, are fully democratized
125 countries, with 62% of the world population, have a free or partly free press.	In 2001, 37 journalists died in the line of duty, 118 were imprisoned and more than 600 were physically attacked or intimidated.
Only 6 vetoes were cast in the UN Security Council between 1996 and 2001, compared with 243 between 1946 and 1995.	The World Trade Organization operates on a one-country, one-vote basis but most key decisions are made by the leading economic powers in "green room" meetings.
Economic Justice	
The proportion of the world's people living in extreme poverty fell from 29% in 1990 to 23% in 1999.	The richest 5% of the world's people have incomes 114 times those of the poorest 5%.
The more than 500 million Internet users today are expected to grow to nearly 1 billion by 2005.	72% of Internet users live in high-income OECD countries, with 14% of the world's population. 164 million reside in the United States.
Health and Education	
Since 1990, 800 million people have gained access to improved water supplies, and 750 million to improved sanitation.	Child immunization rates in Sub-Saharan Africa have fallen below 50%.
57 countries, with half of the world's people, have halved hunger or are on track to do so by 2015.	At the current rate it would take more than 130 years to rid the world of hunger.
Between 1970 and 2000 the under-five mortality rate worldwide fell from 96 to 56 per 1,000 live births.	Every day more than 30,000 children around the world die of preventable diseases.
Worldwide, primary school enrollments rose from 80% in 1990 to 84% in 1998.	93 countries, with 39% of the world's people, do not have data on trends in primary enrollment.
90 countries, with more than 60% of the world's people, have achieved or are on track to achieve gender equality in primary education by 2015—and more than 80 in secondary education.	Of the world's estimated 854 million illiterate adults, 544 million are women.
Peace and Personal Security	
38 peacekeeping operations have been set up since 1990—compared to just 16 between 1946 and 1989.	Genocide occurred in Europe and Africa, with 200,000 killed in Bosnia in 1993-1995 and 500,000 killed in Rwanda in 1994.
Reflecting pressure from some 1,400 civil society groups in 90 countries, the 1997 Mine Ban Treaty has been ratified by 123 states.	Major countries such as China, the Russian Federation, and the United States have not signed the Mine Ban Treaty

Good News for Some Poor Countries during the 1990s from Human Development Report 2003[13]

- Ghana reduced its hunger rate from 35% to 12%.

- Benin increased its primary enrolment rate from 49% to 70%.

- Mauritania increased the ratio of girls to boys in primary and secondary education from 67% to 93% between 1990 and 1996.

- Bangladesh reduced under-five deaths from around 14% to 8%.

- Uganda reduced HIV/AIDS rates for eight consecutive years.

Millennium Development Goals: to be achieved by 2015[14]

- Eradicate extreme poverty and hunger
- Achieve universal primary education
- Promote gender equality and empower women

- Reduce child mortality
- Improve maternal health
- Combat HIV/AIDS, malaria and other diseases
- Develop a global partnership for development

Cows and Cotton Receive More Aid than People: 2000 statistics in 2003 Human Development Report[15]

- Annual dairy subsidy of the European Union—$913 per cow
- Average income in Sub-Saharan Africa—$490 per capita
- Annual aid to Sub-Saharan Africa from the European Union—$8 per African person

- Annual dairy subsidy in Japan—$2700 per cow
- Average income in Sub-Saharan Africa—$490 per capita
- Average aid to Sub-Saharan Africa from Japan—$1.47 per African person

- U.S. domestic subsidy for cotton—$10.7 million per day
- U.S. aid to Sub-Saharan Africa—$3.1 million per day

Access to Essential HIV/AIDS Medicines: What Made the Campaign Successful?

Goal: Students will learn about a successful campaign for access to medicine for HIV/AIDS in South Africa and discover what has happened since.

Procedures: Begin by asking students to read Maphophi's Story from Lesotho and Sylvia's story from Kenya on the Global Cafe (www.pbs.org/newshour/extra/globalcafe). Ask what are Maphophi's and Sylvia's experiences and feelings about HIV/AIDS.

Then ask students to share what they know about HIV/AIDS in their own community, in the U.S., and in the rest of the world. Next ask eight students to each share one point from the following list of "What Made the Campaign Successful," adapted from the Human Development Report 2002. They can stand in front of the class and make a kind of timeline. Be sure students understand all the various organizations and terms. Ask about the role of media; ask what they have learned from the media—had they heard about this issue? Ask why malaria does not seem as important to Americans as AIDS. (Include information about the contribution of the Bill and Melinda Gates Foundation to malaria research aimed at developing a vaccine, improving existing medicines used to treat malaria, and finding new ones.) Ask why the United States' position was so important. Then challenge students to find out what has happened since the success of the campaign, for instance, researching the recent commitment to AIDS in Africa from the Bush administration.

Further idea: ask students to read about Peace Corps volunteer Justine Treadwell and her co-worker Joseph Zamawa who are trying to make an impact on AIDS in Malawi in "Virus on the Lake, a health worker learns about fishing, AIDS and orphans." The three-page article is in the March-May 2004 *WorldView* magazine and is also available at rpcv.org.

What Made the Campaign Successful[16]

The campaign worked closely with governments.

Non-governmental organizations helped developing countries frame policies and initiatives while also lobbying policy-makers in the European Union and the United States where major pharmaceutical companies are based. For example, activists advised South Africa's government on its Medicines Act. In February 1999 U.S. campaign members proposed adding a provision to African trade legislation to cut off funding to agencies that pressed African countries to adopt intellectual property laws exceeding the requirements of the World Trade Organization Agreement on Trade-Related Intellectual Property Rights.

Developing country negotiators were expert and well-briefed.

Non-governmental organizations worked closely with Southern African countries, which considered a new essential medicines strategy to counter U.S. and EU trade pressures on patent issues. Dr. Olive Shisana, the key negotiator for African countries, was tough and well-informed.

Local NGOs played an important role.

Thai NGOs organized the first demonstration demanding compulsory licenses for HIV drugs and Thai regulators permitted competition for fluconazole so that in nine months its price fell from 200 baht to 4.5 baht.

Industrial country activists were mobilized.

AIDS activists learned about patent and trade issues. Few were aware of compulsory licensing or U.S. trade pressures on South Africa, Thailand and other countries.

Generics manufacturers made the difference.

Pharmaceutical companies in developing countries played a critical role in the process. India's CIPLA offered generic substitutes of HIV drugs for $350 a year per treatment, a small fraction of the price charged by Western firms that held patents on the drugs.

The U.S. government changed its position.

President Bill Clinton announced that U.S. health care and trade policies would ensure access to needed medicines for people in developing countries at the 1999 World Trade Organization meeting in Seattle, Washington. The new trade negotiator in the Bush Administration declared that the Clinton executive order would not be overturned and that public health matters would continue to be considered when trade and intellectual property rights were an issue.

The European Commission played a constructive role.

In 2000 the European Commission launched an extensive review of its trade policy on access to medicines and consulted NGOs and drug companies. These discussions fostered the environment that in 2001 led to the World Trade Organization's supportive declaration on public health, essential drugs and the Trade-Related Intellectual Property Rights agreement.

Adverse publicity forced drug companies to withdraw their case.

In March 2001 the court case pitting U.S. and EU drug companies against the South African government began with massive global publicity. Médecins Sans Frontières' Internet petition asking the companies to drop the suit received about 250,000 signatures—about the same number of South Africans who died of AIDS the previous year.

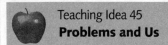

Who Governs Nature? How Do We Make Decisions for the Earth?[17]

Goal: Students will learn about seven elements of environmental governance and study five cases to learn how to answer the questions: Who governs nature? How do we make decisions for the earth?

Procedures: The teacher should first introduce students to the Seven Elements of Environmental Governance on the Handout on the next page. The teacher should use a natural resource in the local area as an example while introducing the elements. The class can then be divided into five groups, each reading and analyzing a case study using at least three of the elements of environmental governance.[17]

After the analysis, each group should prepare to present a description of the case, including locating it on a world map, and their analysis. Groups should be encouraged to come up with creative ways to present their case and encouraged to use visuals. For instance, in the first case from South Africa, students might role play various people involved in the co-management, both park officials and Sokhulu residents. Or students might show pictures of the destruction from the Ok Tedi Mine.

The cases, which show the variety of situations that challenge environmental governance, are

- Mind over Mussels: Rethinking Mapelane Reserve (Sokhulu, South Africa)
- The New Iran: Toward Environmental Democracy (Lazoor, Iran)
- Ok Tedi Mine: Unearthing Controversy (Papua New Guinea)
- Women, Water, and Work: The Success of the Self-Employed Women's Association (Gujerat, India)
- Earth Charter: Charting a Course for the Future (Global)

A real life assessment might be to educate the local community about the Earth Charter and then propose to the local government that global education be adopted as it has been in cities such as Burlington, Vermont and Toronto, Canada, where it is being used to measure city programs against the Charter principles.

Seven Elements of Environmental Governance

1. Institutions and Laws: Who makes and enforces the rules for using natural resources? What are the rules and the penalties for breaking them? Who resolves disputes?

2. Participation Rights and Representation: How can the public influence or contest the rules over natural resources? Who represents those who use or depend on natural resources when decisions on these resources are made?

3. Authority Level: At what level or scale—local, regional, nation, international—does the authority over resources reside?

4. Accountability and Transparency: How do those who control and manage natural resources answer for their decisions and to whom? How open to scrutiny is the decision-making process?

5. Property Rights and Tenure: Who owns a natural resource or has the legal right to control it?

6. Markets and Financial Flows: How do financial practices, economic policies, and market behavior influence authority over natural resources?

7. Science and Risk: How are ecology and social science incorporated into decisions on natural resources to reduce risks to people and ecosystems and identify new opportunities?

Source
Decisions for the Earth: Balance, Voice, and Power (Washington, DC: World Resources Institute, 2002-2004), www.wri.org.

Discussing Complex Issues

Issues are complex in several ways. First, they do not conveniently divide into disciplines. For example, it is rare to find an issue that relates only to geography, or only to economics. Second, issues may spill across oceans and float across national boundaries. So studying population as an issue might involve public policy, job opportunities, migration patterns, gender roles, and more.

One way to teach students how to understand and discuss complex issues is to be certain that multiple perspectives are heard. Although pro/con debates are popular with teachers and students, such debates are often not the best way to become educated about an issue. For example, to be for or against globalization isn't very helpful. The real question might be stated as "How do we manage globalization so that it becomes fairer for everyone?" A follow-up question could be: "What are four or five ways to think about managing globalization?"

Teaching Materials
Choices

One model for going beyond the pro/con debate is illustrated in the Choices materials from Brown University. Designed to stimulate public policy debate in the classroom, the Choices for the 21st Century Education Project, a program of the Thomas J. Watson Jr. Institute for International Studies, offers units in Global Studies, World History and Area Studies, and United States History. Their units usually present three or four options to be discussed, usually in a simulation format, and then encourage students to develop their own options as well. For example, in the unit entitled "Responding to Terrorism: Challenges for Democracy," the four options are: Direct an expanded assault on terrorism, support UN leadership to fight terrorism, defend our homeland, and address the underlying causes of terrorism. In the unit entitled Global Environmental Problems: Implications for U.S. Policy the four options are: put the economy first, take the lead in the green economy, promote sustainable development, and protect mother earth. Each unit asks students to recognize relationships between history and current issues, to analyze and evaluate multiple perspectives on an issue, to understand the internal logic of a viewpoint, to identify and weigh the conflicting values, to reflect on personal values, to develop original viewpoints, to communicate in written and oral presentations, and to collaborate with peers.

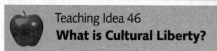

Teaching Idea 46
What is Cultural Liberty?

Goal: Students will learn a definition of cultural liberty and consider a number of examples of cultural liberty in countries around the world.

Materials: 2004 Human Development Report, available online, or in hard copy from Oxford University Press.

Procedures: Begin by asking students to draw the outline of a person on a big sheet of paper and then to draw and/or use magazine picture/text cut-outs to make a collage that illustrates various aspects of their identity. Give the following example from the Report: A person may have an identity of citizenship (for example, being French), gender (being a woman), race (being of Chinese origin), regional ancestry (having come from Thailand), language (being fluent in Thai, Chinese and English, in addition to French), politics (having left-wing views), religion (being a Buddhist), profession (being a lawyer), location (being a resident of Paris), sports affiliation (being a badminton player and a golf fanatic) musical taste (loving jazz and hi-hop), literary preference (enjoying detective stories), food habits (being a vegetarian), and so on.

After students share themselves, give them a definition of cultural liberty—the ability of people to choose their identity and to live and be what they choose; the ability to choose what priority to give one membership or identity or another in a particular context. Tell students about the 2004 Human Development Report which advocates that cultural liberty is both a human right and an important aspect of human development.

Then divide students in pairs or trios and ask each to consider one of the following quotes from the Report's Overview "Cultural liberty in today's diverse world" and to answer the question: "How does this example illustrate or relate to the concept of cultural liberty?"

- Mexican Americans may cheer for the Mexican soccer team but serve in the U.S. army.
- In Belgium citizens overwhelmingly replied when asked that they felt both Belgian and Flemish or Walloon and in Spain, that they felt Spanish as well as Catalan or Basque.
- Although underlying inequalities in South Africa were at the root of the Soweto riots in 1976, they were triggered by attempts to impose the Afrikaans language on black schools.
- Malaysia, with 62% of its people Malays and other indigenous groups, 30% Chinese and 8% Indian, was the world's 10th fastest growing economy during 1970-1990, years when it also implemented affirmative action policies.
- Electoral reforms addressed the chronic underrepresentation of Maoris in New Zealand. With the introduction of proportional representation in place of the winner-takes-all formula, Maori representation rose from 3% in 1993 to 16% in the 2002 elections, in line with their share of the population.
- India officially celebrates five Hindu holidays but also four Muslim, two Christian, one Buddhist, one Jain and one Sikh holiday in recognition of a diverse population. France celebrates eleven national holidays, five of which are non-denominational. Of the six religious holidays, all celebrate events in the Christian calendar, though 7% of the population is Muslim and 1% Jewish.
- Some indigenous people, such as the Inuits in Canada, have negotiated self-governing territories.
- India has practiced a three-language formula for decades; children are taught in the official language of their state (Bengali in West Bengal, for example) and also taught the two official languages of the country, Hindi and English.
- When the Islamic Salvation Front won the first round of elections in 1991 in Algeria, the military intervened and banned the party. The result—a civil war that cost more than 100,000 lives and spurred the growth of intolerant and violent groups. Allowing the extreme right party, the Justice and Development Party, in Morocco to contest in elections forced them to moderate their position.
- Countries are expanding the rights of civic participation to non-citizenship—"denizenship" (Belgium, Sweden). And more than 30 countries now accept dual citizenship.

- Hungary diverts 6% of television receipts to promote domestic films and Egypt uses public-private partnerships to finance the infrastructure for film making.

As students report, the teacher might ask further questions, spurring the students to do their own research about, for instance, the origin of U.S. holidays or what countries accept dual citizenship or what country's films are most watched around the world. The teacher should remind students that cultural identities are heterogeneous and are evolving and dynamic processes and also that assuring cultural liberty is complex, because of cultural exclusion and movements for cultural domination, topics discussed in the Report.

Finally, the teacher can ask students to look for evidence about whether there is a culture, noted in the Report, called "global teens, a single pop culture world, soaking up the same videos and music and providing a huge market for designer running shoes, t-shirts and jeans"?

Further Ideas: Ask students to read the special contribution of John Hume on page 82 of the Report. Hume is a member of the European Parliament and winner of the 1998 Nobel Peace Prize; his short essay is entitled "Difference is not a threat but a source of strength" and focuses on "Northern Ireland and the European Union as strong examples of how the existence of more than one culture can prove to be positive in the building and development of society through a process of conflict resolution." Then ask students to write a one page essay with the same title, focusing on the United States or their own community or school.

Another way to discuss an issue more profoundly is to help students try not to think of issues in terms of absolutes. That is often difficult for us Americans. In *The Ayatollah in the Cathedral*, Moorhead Kennedy, a hostage during the crisis in Iran in 1980, identified one of the barriers to our international understanding as our moralistic stance, "a judgmental attitude of believing one's standards to be superior to those of others, of criticizing others on the basis of standards that may not be appropriate to them." Kennedy distinguishes between "moral" as implying responsible living and the ideals that guide it and "moralistic" as conveying a judgmental and superior attitude.[18]

How does a teacher deal with a rush to judgment? He or she can raise questions and ask: What do you mean when you say that is right or wrong? What does evil mean? What does "doing good" mean? We are arguing here for a willingness to let people from a place, a nation, a culture speak for and usually decide for themselves. There are clearly universal human rights, but sometimes even those are contested and need to be carefully and thoughtfully discussed.

Encouraging Choices and Action

An advantage of teaching about global issues, whether in a separate course or as part of another course, is that students can be asked to choose issues they are interested in and to choose actions they would like to take. Here we describe a sequence of teaching ideas for getting students involved in thinking about choices and engaging in action.

To set up an expectation for choices and action, the teacher might begin by introducing students to people who have made a difference. Learning about the Nobel Laureates who won the Peace Prize is one possibility. Quotations from eight recipients are in the sidebar on page 119. Coming from *The Moral Architecture of World Peace* by Helena Cobban, based on a dialogue among eight recipients at the University of Virginia in 1998, they could provide one starting point for learning from others about action.[19] Brief student reports on the eight recipients, including a picture and focus on why each received the prize and what they have done since, could be an introduction to reading the quotations. In interpreting each quotation, the same questions could be asked: How does a person's view come out of his or her experience? What does what each person says mean for us as citizens of the world? What can we do?

Nobel Laureates

Who is going to explain to the Indonesian people the hundreds of millions of dollars wasted in weapons purchase instead of channeling them to education, health care, clean water, housing for their people?

José Ramos-Horta of East Timor

I believe that each of us has a specialty in our own areas, in our own convictions that work in favor of peace. When we struggle individually, we sometimes give it an accent—more Maya, more woman, more radical, less radical, but we're all working toward the same goal.

Rigoberta Menchu of Guatemala

Non-violence means positive action. You have to work for whatever you want. You don't just sit there doing nothing and hope to get what you want. It just means that the methods you use are not violent ones. Some people think that non-violence is passive-ness. It's not so.

Aung San Suu Kyi of Burma (She was not present but represented)

So the spirit of reconciliation [is important]: fully respect others' views, and others' rights, and develop a sense of genuine concern about others' welfare and others' right. And then, compromise. Only compromise.

The Dalai Lama of Tibet

When Voltaire wrote *Candide* over two hundred years ago, he was acutely aware of the moral obligations created by an integrating world. In this book, Candide meets a slave from the Americas who is missing both a hand and a leg. The slave's hand was cut off by dangerous machinery in a sugar cane mill, his leg was cut off by cruel masters to prevent him from escaping. As Candide looks on, the miserable slave tells him: "this is the true price of the sugar you eat in Europe." If ethics required global thinking in Voltaire's time, think of how relevant this powerful anecdote is in the age of globalization.

Oscar Arias of Costa Rica

We didn't set out to change the world. We were ordinary people who saw a problem [and] believed we could do something to make We, the children of the world, assert our inalienable right to be heard, and to have a political voice at the United Nations and the highest levels of government world-wide.

(from declaration of summit, Mothers of the Earth for World Peace) Betty Williams of Northern Ireland and the United States

The God that I worship is a strange God, because it is a God who is omnipotent, all powerful, but He's also a God who is weak. An extraordinary paradox, that it is God, a God of justice, who wants to see justice in the world, but because God has such a deep reverence for our freedoms all over the place, God will not intervene like, I mean sending a lightning bolt to dispatch all despots! God waits for God's partners—we!

Archbishop Desmond Tutu of South Africa

We saw a problem (the landmine issue), knew it had to be resolved, we came together to do it... Don't sit back and wait for the other guy to make it better. Join in, and help make it better yourself.

Jody Williams of the United States

After learning about the lives and projects of the Nobel Laureates, students can choose issues they want to study as a class and/or individually or in small groups. As part of their study, students can construct a survey on global issues for adults in the community and announce results in an article in the local newspaper, in the exhibit case in the front hall of the school, and on the school website.[20]

One way to encourage students to act on what they have learned is to require an international community service project. The project description included in this chapter inspired such projects as researching and making an after school presentation entitled "Free Tibet," developing and delivering curriculum for a sister's Girl Scout troop to complete the international badge, organizing a lawn-mowing marathon to raise money for Doctors Without Borders, volunteering at the International Book Project, and helping prepare welcome packets for new international students at the local university.[21]

International Community Service Project

Community Service Requirement: four hours of service to an organization or cause that will either benefit someone outside the United States or educate people here about an issue, place or culture outside the United States.

Documentation Requirement: create a brochure to document your experience. Your brochure should be attractive, colorful, and professional looking and attempt to attract future volunteers to your cause or organization. The brochure should include the following components, for 50 points each:

- Information about the organization, cause, or issue
- Information about the activities you completed during your hours of community service
- Information about how others could volunteer in the future, including contact information for people in charge of the organization or a website
- Reflective comments on your own experience and how you feel community service impacts global citizenship

You may work as an individual or volunteer with other students. However, each person must turn in his or her own brochure independently of other students. We will be creating a bulletin board using a global map to track our service projects. You will be expected to briefly tell the class about your project and brochure as we create the bulletin board throughout the semester. There is a flexible due date but I will accept projects earlier. It will be more exciting if we complete our map in stages.

Conclusion

Global issues in this age of globalization have the power to move us and involve us. Although the issues are complex, many of us want to understand, to act, and to see the world not only as problems to solve, but as people working together—toward brotherhood and sisterhood.

Musician and philanthropist Bono writes in the 2002 Human Development Report:

> Many things about the 21st century are bizarre. That people listen to rock stars talking about politics. That if your daughter is born in Malawi, chances are she may not reach her 5th birthday—but if she is born in the United States, she'll probably still be around at 80. The facts that shock us must also anger us and inspire us to be bold. If everybody, whether born in Accra or Albuquerque, is to be able to achieve their full potential, the immense structural inequalities that define our world need to be broken down.... Too much is at stake for silence to be anybody's option.[22]

In *Crossing the Divide: Dialogue Among Civilizations*, a book created by a group of eminent persons selected by Kofi Annan after September 11, the last words are from the Sufi mystic, Rumi. They seem appropriate for the last words of a chapter on global issues as well:

> Out beyond ideas of wrongdoing and rightdoing, there is a field. I'll meet you there.[23]

Notes

1. Charlotte C. Anderson and James H. Landman, *Globalization and Border Crossings; Examining Issues of National Identity: Citizenship, and Civic Education* (Chicago: American Bar Association Division for Public Education, 2003).
2. World Bank, worldbank.org.
3. *Down the Street, Around the World* (Washington, DC: American Federation of Teachers International Affairs Department, 2002), aft.org.
4. Changwoo Jeong and Ronald L. VanSickle, "Moral Education in the Context of Globalization and Multiculturalism," *The International Social Studies Forum* 3, no. 1 (2003), 233-243.
5. Thomas L. Friedman, *The Lexus and the Olive Tree: Understanding Globalization* (New York: Farrar Straus Giroux, 1999), 27.
6. Ibid., 291, 292.
7. Saskia Sassen, *Globalization and Its Discontents* (New York: The New Press, 1998), xvi.
8. Ibid., 33.
9. Amy Chua, *World on Fire* (New York: Ballantine Books, 1995).
10. Ibid., 286.
11. Ronald W. Evans and David Warren Saxe, *Handbook on Teaching Social Issues* (Washington DC: National Council for the Social Studies, 1996).

12. United Nations Development Programme, *Human Development Report 2002: Deepening Democracy in a Fragmented World* (New York: Oxford University Press, 2002), 10-11.

13. United Nations Development Programme, *Human Development Report 2003: Millennium Development Goals: A Compact Among Nations to End Human Poverty* (New York: Oxford University Press, 2003), 45-46.

14. Ibid., 1-3.

15. Ibid., 155.

16. *Human Development Report 2002*, 106.

17. *Decisions for the Earth: Balance, Voice, and Power* (Washington, DC: World Resources Institute, 2002-2004). This teaching idea appeared in the National Peace Corps Association Global TeachNet newsletter, March-April 2004.

18. Moorhead Kennedy, *The Ayatollah in the Cathedral: Reflections of a Hostage* (New York: Hill and Wang, 1986), 197.

19. Helena Cobban, *The Moral Architecture of World Peace: Nobel Laureates Discuss Our Global Future* (Charlottesville, VA: The University of Virginia Press, 2000). Another possibility would be to use David Bornstein's *How to Change the World: Social Entrepreneurs and the Power of New Ideas* (New York: Oxford University Press, 2004). It includes fascinating biographies of people from around the world with new ideas, such as Jeroo Billimoria, who started Childline in India, Fabio Rosa, who worked on rural electrification in Brazil, and an American, J.B. Schramm, who created College Access.

20. This idea comes from Susan Carey who teaches social studies, including Global Issues, at Woodford County High School in Kentucky.

21. This international community service project description comes from Ashley Barbour who teaches social studies, including ninth grade government, at Henry Clay High School in Lexington, Kentucky.

22. *Human Development Report 2002*, 104.

23. Giandomenico Picco, A. Kamal Aboulmagd, et al., *Crossing the Divide: Dialogue Among Civilizations* (South Orange, NJ: Seton Hall University, 2001), 215.

Resources

Amnesty International, www.amnestyusa.org/education

Besides lesson plans on a variety of topics from the death penalty to slavery, this site includes information on human rights issues such as "conflict diamonds" (illicit diamond smuggling that fuels groups engaged in violent conflict) and refugees.

The Christian Science Monitor, www.csmonitor.com

This newspaper (published five days a week) always has world news on the front page and often has articles that can be used in the classroom.

Cyberschoolbus, www.cyberschoolbus.un.org

This website includes such items as an introduction to the United Nations, a gallery of art made by students from around the world, ask an ambassador, a country at a glance, flag tag, and lessons on topics such as peace and cities.

Foreign Policy, www.foreignpolicy.com

This bimonthly magazine is devoted to global politics, economics, and ideas. Besides always being provocative and including multiple perspectives, the main articles conclude with a "want to know more" section of resources.

Foreign Policy Association, www.fpa.org

FPA is a national nonprofit, nonpartisan, nongovernmental educational organization that educates Americans about significant international issues. Its Great Decisions Global Affairs Education Program includes a teacher's guide and classroom packets. Topics range from world regions to globalization and trade and migration and refugees and the United Nations and the U.S. role in the world.

Human Development Reports, hdr.undp.org/reports/global/2003/

These reports are issued annually by the United Nations Development Programme. Besides country statistics in the second half of the report, the articles and boxes are sources for teachers and students. They are available from the United Nations and from Oxford University Press. The title for the 2004 report is *Cultural Liberty in Today's Diverse World*.

World Bank, www.worldbank.org

Under Resources for Kids and Schools, teachers and students can find information under Exploring Countries and Regions and Tackling the Issues. Under the Sustainable Development issue are learning modules associated with the Development Education Program. Under "Data" are the world development indicators and country tables.

CHAPTER 7

Teaching Current Events from a Global Perspective

What's more important anyway? Understanding why their fathers are being sent to Saudi Arabia or teaching world cultures as though nothing is happening in the Middle East? If this war has a silver lining, it is that now they really want to look at maps of the Middle East, learn about Arabs, and find out why Saddam Hussein invaded Kuwait.   A SOCIAL STUDIES TEACHER IN COLUMBUS, OHIO, OCTOBER, 1990

Powerful world events happen every school year that change the course of history. It seems that only yesterday we watched the pro-democracy protesters face tanks in Tiananmen Square, the Berlin Wall come down, and the Soviet Union fall apart. Mandela walked out of prison and soon we watched Black South Africans stand in line to vote for the first time. The terrorist attacks of September 11, 2001, were not only history in the making, they were defining moments for today's students, who will always remember where they were that morning. In this chapter we discuss how teachers can respond to current events and use news stories to strengthen worldmindedness.

Social studies teachers who want their students to understand current events face many constraints they know all too well: curriculum mandates that leave no room for new content, the need to find reliable resources on unfamiliar issues or parts of the world, and the sensitive nature of many events and issues in the news. Since current events are not going to be on high stakes tests, teachers must justify their inclusion, especially in schools where No Child Left Behind and other mandates have punitive consequences for low test scores.

In this chapter, we identify strategies from teachers' practice that can inform the social studies. Then we outline a number of methods for using current events and news stories to infuse global perspectives into ongoing social studies courses. We discuss the issue of balance and look at ways teachers can deal with sensitive issues. Finally we provide an overview of resources that can provide access to reliable information and primary sources on events in the news.

Enhancing Worldmindedness Through Global Events and Media

Current events from around the world often can make social studies truly world-centered. Global perspectives on events in our community, state, or nation help students recognize their connections to people around the world who may share similar situations or have different reactions. Global events often highlight underlying global economic or environmental systems and provide case studies of how the local community is affected by and, in turn, influences people around the world.

Current events are also used to teach skills in research, higher-level thinking, and perspective consciousness. Documentaries, editorials, and articles in newspapers, magazines or television can add insights to students' knowledge of world cultures and help them develop skills in perspective consciousness. The activity on page 127, "I Am Not An African Woman," developed when a teacher read an op ed piece in a newspaper and recognized how it could be used to help her students see Americans through the eyes of "The Other." (See Teaching Idea 47.) A 2004 PBS series on immigrants was adapted by another teacher for similar reasons.

Here are seven approaches to bringing news and media into social studies classrooms that teachers have used in the last few months:

1. News stories and media visuals can add depth and complexity. A teacher recently taped a television story on suicide bombers in order to take students into the homes of average Israelis and Palestinians who have been affected by these attacks. The news clip allowed students to see and hear individuals and recognize that Israelis and Palestinians have many lifestyles and political positions.[1]

Responding to Current Events: A Case Study from the Gulf War

During the 1990-1991 school year I worked with 12 teachers in three school districts in Columbus, Ohio to answer the question, "How do teachers make instructional decisions as they teach about the world?" I and Ann Ratliff, a Columbus Public School teacher on sabbatical with me as she pursued her Ph.D., spent our days observing 12 elementary, middle and high school teachers who had been identified by their districts as exemplary in teaching about the world. Their courses ranged from world cultures and cultural geography to world history, global studies, and world environmental studies. Their schools were as different in class and ethnicity as is possible in Central Ohio. They included a highly diverse international magnet school, two schools in high poverty areas, an elementary school serving a neighborhood undergoing gentrification, a school with a high ESL population, and quite different schools in two of Columbus's more affluent suburban districts.[2]

As we observed them teach and talked to the teachers about their instructional decisions each week, we found ourselves recording their decision-making on how to deal with the conflict that was building in the Persian Gulf as Saddam Hussein invaded Kuwait and the United States and its allies responded with Operation Desert Shield and Storm. Week by week many issues arose that all social studies teachers face when significant events happen that capture the attention of Americans.

- What should I teach about unfolding events as they happen?
- Can I ignore the mandated curriculum for a time if events are profoundly affecting my students, our city, nation, or world?
- What resources can I trust since these events are not in my curriculum materials? How do I find reliable information?
- How should I teach about the perspectives of people in that region of the world?
- What do I do when the events are in a part of the world I know little about?
- How should I handle emotional or sensitive issues that may make students angry, afraid, or upset?
- How can the news be used to teach important knowledge and skills in my courses?
- Do I assess their learning about current events?

Although the teachers responded differently in many ways to current events, 10 of the 12 made substantive changes in their courses to teach students to understand events in the Gulf across the school year.[3] The most common ways that teachers responded to the Gulf crisis from September 1990 to May 1991 were by:

1. Providing background knowledge which, to some degree, was selected both to address course goals and to respond to student questions and interests. Topics considered most essential regardless of grade level were: the geography of the Persian Gulf and relevant countries, Islam and Muslims, Arab culture, American foreign policy with some references to other U.S. interventions, and the politics of Iraq, Iran, Kuwait, Saudi Arabia, which were often linked to the Arab-Israeli conflict.
2. Linking content in their courses to current events. One world history teacher had her students compare the military tactics of the Roman army to those of the Iraqis. Another teacher linked his environmental unit on pollution to the realities of pollution from

2. News stories can illustrate global connections within the local community. A teacher made copies of two news stories on refugees settling in the local community to help students see local connections to a civil war in another part of the world they are studying. Students mapped the journey these people have made and examined websites on the refugee camps they lived in.

3. Media resources can teach critical thinking skills. A teacher gathered together several editorials from local, national, and international newspapers (see the resource section for online newspapers at the end of this chapter) to kick off a class discussion about how people interpret events in Iraq.

4. Online media allow students to access news stories that are important in another country or world region but are underreported here. Without access to news reports in other countries, students cannot understand events that are happening across the planet. In 2004 these events might include Putin's consolidation of power in Russia; security problems in Kosovo; détente between Libya, on one hand, and the U.S. and Britain on the other; the effects of the Israeli security wall; economic and social changes in China; and the economic disaster of land and agricultural policies in Zimbabwe.

burning oil wells and environmental terrorism in the Gulf. The teachers made conscious connections between their social studies content and topics coming out of the Gulf War throughout the school year.

3. Involving students in some way with people in the Gulf or people in the community with connections there. In one school a social studies teacher in the National Guard was called up and he provided a connection for students to send letters and goodies to the troops. Several teachers developed writing projects with people from their community who were stationed in Saudi Arabia or Kuwait. Most of the teachers had guest speakers from Arab countries come and talk to their students. One elementary classroom had a student from Kuwait whose family came to the school several times to teach the children about their culture and country.

4. Addressing the affective outcomes of events and issues. There were many discussions to defuse fears and confusion as some children were afraid the Scud missiles or Iraqis were going to come here. Some students suffered from anxiety over their family members in the Gulf. Others expressed the attitude of "nuke 'em." Teachers used role-playing, journaling, poetry, and other activities to give students a chance to talk about war and the vivid images they saw on television, and put events into a larger historical context.

It is important to note that although these commonalities existed, there were also significant differences as each teacher had a unique way of deciding when and how to bring current events into the classroom. We learned that that many contextual factors shaped the teachers' decisions—their curriculum, the school climate, the local community, their own education, and their international experiences as a result of travel or living in another country (one teacher spent several years in France as a child).

All the teachers were also influenced by their students, their backgrounds, questions, and, to some degree, their interests. When teachers had students who were immigrants or refugees, their questions often had a larger impact. A fourth grade teacher in a suburban school had a Palestinian student whose questions led her to take two days to help the class look at how the Israeli-Palestinian conflict was related to the Gulf War and American foreign policy. As with other teachers in the study, she explained that she had not taught that content before and probably would not have done so in 1990-1991 if that particular student had not been in her class.

The differences in homogeneous, as compared to heterogeneous, schools were especially dramatic when comparing two teachers at a economically diverse high school with large numbers of ESL students with two teachers in an affluent suburban high school that was 99% white. The teachers in the first school had a mix of whites, African Americans, and students from China, Vietnam, Somalia, Mexico, Jordan or other countries in every class. When we compared the transcripts of student questions and teachers' responses between that school and the homogeneous suburban school we could see instructional differences in content, perspectives and resources. Students growing up in poverty and students from other countries ask different questions than do white middle class students. When teachers respond to meet their students' needs, what is learned reflects to some degree who is in that classroom.

Merry Merryfield

5. *News stories can make the study of history, politics, economics, sociology, and global studies relevant to students' lives.* When news stories poured out of Afghanistan following September 11, it was a teachable moment for students in world history courses as no one could say, "why do we have to learn this?" when the teacher connected the history of resistance to colonialism in South Asia to understanding Afghanistan today. Students were fascinated to learn how many empires and nation-states have tried to conquer and rule Afghanistan and how Afghans have worked to resist foreign occupiers. In geography courses students suddenly saw how geographic knowledge has practical value in explaining cultural divisions and why terrorists in Afghanistan are hard to capture.

6. *News stories, editorials, and editorial cartoons can teach students perspective consciousness and provide raw materials for teaching multiple perspectives.* Undoubtedly many students assume that people around the world think like they do and will behave like they do given similar circumstances. If students are to understand global issues and world conflicts, they need to develop perspective consciousness and recognize that people across the planet have many ways of viewing an event or issue and they will not necessarily respond as Americans would.

Teaching Idea 47
I Am Not an African Woman

Goal: Students examine the effects of stereotypes and simplifications of people's cultures on cultural understanding.

Procedures: After initial work on African stereotypes, place students in small groups to read "I Am Not an African Woman," an article written by Bunmi Fatoye-Mat for *The Christian Science Monitor*. Provide each group with large sheets of paper. Then ask ⅓ of the groups to make a list of the reasons why she objects to being called an African woman. Another ⅓ of the groups list characteristics and experiences she uses to describe who she is. The last third of the groups write up what the author thinks Americans should know about Africa.

Have them post their group papers on one wall and have the class examine each. As you debrief the class, ask questions such as: what knowledge do Americans often lack about people from Africa? Why does it matter if we speak of her as being African or Nigerian or Yoruba or Christian? Do we have similar problems in understanding people from other world regions?

Teaching Idea 48
Front Page News

Goal: To help students develop a global perspective on world events.

Procedures: Following an event that is considered very newsworthy by American media, students work in groups to go online to the Newseum (www.newseum.org/todays frontpages). Each group examines the front pages of 5-6 newspapers in a world region. They make note of the stories making headlines and look to see if they can find any news on the front page of these newspapers about a story that is getting so much attention in the American press. They also compare what kinds of stories make headlines across the world—are they political, military, economic, social, environmental or another topic? What kinds of local or national news stories are important?

7. Events can be used as symptoms or catalysts of important change. If students develop habits of mind that make them conscious of current events, they can learn to evaluate small developments that may lead to major trends or alter world systems. In an economics course, students are monitoring news stories and statistics on changes in Egypt, Ireland, India, Chile, Taiwan, Russia, and the United States. As economic "detectives," they check newspapers and websites for trends in different sectors of the economy, investment by employers, loans, unemployment, markets, debt servicing and other criteria that are indicators of economic change. They note news related to political stability and the influence of political agreements and policies. By the end of the semester, they will have learned a great deal about how to fit together the pieces of the puzzle of economic trends and changes.

Many social studies teachers keep their students and courses in the back of their minds as they read newspapers, peruse news magazines, go online or watch news specials on television. How many of us have clipped news stories or taped televised reports to use in our classes in the last six months?

Yet all current events are not the same. Teachers must make decisions as to what news stories and media coverage are appropriate for their grade level and how these best fit into the ongoing curriculum. And those decisions often have to be made very quickly. Teaching Ideas 48 (on this page) and 49 (p. 129 below) suggest ways in which teachers can help students to learn about major world events.

Preparation and Balance

As we write this book, Iraq is in the news everyday. Much controversy has raged about how teachers should or should not teach about September 11 and subsequent events in Afghanistan and Iraq. In the last three years many organizations, including National Council for the Social Studies, have produced materials and articles to help teachers teach about terrorism and events in the Middle East. Teaching about the news from Iraq is, as one teacher told us, "like walking on thin ice. You never know when you might fall through because there are so many sensitive issues. How am I supposed to explain to them why weapons of mass destruction haven't been found? They see that our troops continue to die and the threat of more terrorism is real and scary. My students asked me just last week, can we really build democracy there? This is hard."

So how should teachers address news that is sensitive or controversial? When should the news enter social studies classrooms? How can teachers prepare for the news stories to

I Am Not Just an African Woman

by Bunmi Fatoye-Mat

Printed in the *Christian Science Monitor* Monday July 1, 1996, p.16.

Before my emigration to the United States five years ago, I was known as a Nigerian of the Yoruba ethnic group. I was also a Western-educated woman with certain privileges and high expectations.

Since coming here, though, my identity has changed. I am now an "African woman." My culture, attitude, and experience are presumed to reflect all of Africa, a continent of 55 countries, 400 million people, and thousands of ethnic and linguistic groups. By definition, I am supposed to be poor, uneducated, and ridden with disease.

My first jolt came one evening in 1991, when I was a new immigrant. I was watching a public-television documentary about little children's first day at school in such countries as Japan, the United Kingdom, the United States, and, of course, "Africa."

"Africa is not a country," was my first thought. But what followed was even more distressing. While parents in other countries were shown engaging in different rituals of sending children to school, in "Africa," children were seen climbing trees in the forest. This, the narrator said, is something they learn from older children. I could not believe my eyes.

I grew up in a rural town in Nigeria. We had five primary schools and a high school. There was a post office and a small clinic. All these facilities have since expanded as Nigeria grew rich from its oil.

I remember my first day at school. My father took me, and I was so proud to be wearing a school uniform, carrying my black slate and chalk. I recall the elegance of my teacher: I wanted to dress and walk just like her. I persuaded my father to buy hair ornaments for me, even though my hair was closely cropped, as is the hair of all little children.

My primary school, run by the Anglican mission, had many flower gardens that were carefully cultivated and tended by the pupils under the supervision of the teachers.

In high school, we studied Shakespeare, George Eliot, Jonathan Swift, the Bronte sisters, and Charles Dickens. Under British colonial rule, generations of Nigerians studied such writers to the exclusion of African authors.

My teenage idol was Nancy Drew, an American teenage detective I discovered in my father's library one vacation. I read the books many times over.

The TV documentary didn't show any of this. I can understand such misconceptions from the average person. But in December 1993, Sen. Ernest Hollings (D) of South Carolina, returning from trade talks in Switzerland, jokingly implied that African leaders were cannibals.

I was shocked to read this, not only because of the insult, but also because of what it implied about the great ignorance of the realities of our lives.

Some of the worst riots in Nigeria have their roots in the disparity between the opulent lifestyles of the elite—the privileged diplomats who traveled to Geneva—and the austere lives forced on the rest of the population by the government. While a large percentage of the population is suffering, the elites are driving BMWs, Mercedes-Benzes, and Alfa Romeos. Their opulent houses are built with tall fences and staffed with servants, guards, and dogs.

Since the supply of electricity and water is erratic, the elites have generators and water pumps. Their children go to schools and colleges abroad. Their conspicuous consumption generates so much anger and resentment among the underprivileged that they sometimes take to the streets to vent their anger.

These rulers were the same ones characterized as starving cannibals. This could be said with impunity, because this is what being an African seems to mean in America.

It does not matter that some of these "cannibals" are products of the world's best universities; neither does it seem to matter that they belong to the class that controls and distributes the resources of their countries.

I am beginning to understand the differences between the myth of the African that I am in America and the Nigerian I consider myself to be. I spoke to my first Kenyan and tasted my first dish from Sierra Leone in this country. It was at a dinner given by an American friend who worried all evening that she had not prepared it in the authentic way. I doubt I convinced her that I wouldn't know an authentic Sierra Leonean dish from her version. Both were as foreign to my palate as pizza.

Even as I become accustomed to what Americans expect from me—do I know their friend in Mombasa, Kenya? Or perhaps an acquaintance in Ghana?—their stereotype of the silent and voiceless African woman remains alien to me. The women I grew up with were anything but silent.

Yoruba women of southwestern Nigeria have a long history of organization and prosperity. Many of our grandmothers put our parents through college. Many own real estate and farms. They employ workers and commute home in luxury cars after they've closed their shops. In fact, women dominate the retail segment in southern Nigeria.

And in 1939, the disturbances known later as the Aba riots began when women in southeastern Nigeria organized a peaceful protest against taxes levied by the British rulers. Women were killed as the demonstrations were violently put down. That was many decades before the current tide of Western feminism. This is a part of my history.

To become an African woman is to struggle against the myths and misconceptions of African womanhood. Yes, I am an African, but I am a Nigerian first. That is the only honest claim I can make. I cannot speak for a continent.

Call me Nigerian, and I won't tell you any tall African tales.

come? We suggest five points for consideration. Social studies educators can:

1. Educate ourselves daily from multiple sources. All social studies educators need to stay up on the news from a variety of sources. It is critical to hear how world events are perceived by different groups of people within our own country and other countries. Reading a favorite newspaper or watching network news is easy but limiting as one source, no matter how good, rarely offers a global perspective. With the availability of online newspapers from around the world and British and Canadian stations on cable television, teachers find it relatively easy to keep up with the news from different points of view.

2. Learn sources of reliable resources. In the aftermath of September 11, many teachers turned to the Middle East Centers of different universities for resources, speakers for their classes and videos and books. Others went online to global education organizations such as the American Forum and the Choices Project at Brown University as they had used their materials for other issues and areas of the world (see global education organizations at the end of Chapter 1). Many teachers visited the NCSS website to find resources. It is important to know about university-based centers and other organizations that produce instructional materials, make resources available on their websites, and provide speakers and professional development opportunities.

3. Begin with curricular connections. No matter what we teach, there are news stories every year that will breathe relevancy into the topic. Good teachers seem to make these connections easily and are constantly on the lookout for an editorial cartoon, a documentary, a news story that will enhance what they are teaching and demonstrate its worth in the world today. Discussions with colleagues and online networks can improve one's own ideas and ensure reflection. It is important to think about alternatives and weigh what is lost if time is given to current events.

4. Develop criteria for including current events. There will be times when it is difficult to connect important events to topics under study. Yet profound events that shake the world cannot be ignored. It is important that teachers work together to plan ways to respond to such events so that those decisions are not made in the midst of a crisis. During the 1990-1991 school year, a social studies department decided that all its students needed to understand the events and issues arising from the conflict in the Persian Gulf. The teachers worked together to identify materials, bring in speakers, and develop a Gulf War timeline and maps to be posted in the lunchroom. Teachers shared the resources they wanted to use and exchanged ideas on how to integrate content into their courses. The shared planning had some unintended effects. Some teachers who did not initially feel comfortable teaching the Middle East content grew in confidence as they acquired knowledge about the region and found that they enjoyed integrating the news from Saudi Arabia and Kuwait into their U.S. Government and psychology courses. The group of teachers who most wanted to spend time on the events in the Middle East discovered that they had less need to do so because of planning that included the whole school. The shared planning ameliorated teachers' individual responses and undoubtedly improved the whole school's education about the war.

5. Aim for balance. It is critical that teachers provide balance in the study of news events and issues. Balance is provided by student access to different kinds of information and points of view so that they can see all sides of an issue. For example, one recent news story focused on high tech companies out-sourcing jobs to India. The story could be relevant to teaching about the global economy in an economics course, a geography unit on South Asia, or even a unit on industrialization within a world history course. When the story broke, it was easy to find articles that detailed the number of jobs that left the U.S. and editorials decrying lost of American jobs. However, if students are to understand the issue of outsourcing from a balanced approach, they also need information on why and how the companies chose outsourcing, what the company and its stockholders gained and lost, and how the change affected workers and communities in India well as the United States.

Seeing the Middle East through Global Perspectives

Goal: Students analyze news stories about the Middle East from newspapers around the world to identify how the world's media, not only media in the US or the Middle East, perceive underlying themes and issues.

Procedures: This lesson could be developed following some special event (elections, acts of violence, etc.) or simply be a day chosen at random. I have collected materials for today, April 14, 2004, for the example below. Teachers can use several online newspapers that present different points of view (see resources at the end of the chapter) or choose a website that provides a digest of news stories from around the world.

The site www.arabworldnews.com links to news stories about the Arab world that are printed in newspapers from all world regions. The excerpt below has articles from the United States, China, the Philippines, South Africa, Australia and England.

Comparing News Stories
from www.arabworldnews.com, April 14, 2004

Mubarak offers aid
By Joseph Curl and David W. Jones - *THE WASHINGTON TIMES* - HOUSTON — Egyptian President Hosni Mubarak said yesterday that his nation is prepared to train [Iraqi] policemen ... (photo: WN) *The Washington Times*

Philippines considers withdrawing troops from Iraq
MANILA - President Gloria Macapagal Arroyo said on Wednesday that mounting violence in Iraq had prompted her government to study whether to withdraw its 100 troops from t... (photo: Malacanang) *Khaleej Times*

Bush ready to send more troops to Iraq
United States President George Bush on Wednesday night declared he was ready to send more US troops to Iraq "to finish the work of the fallen" in accomplishing the transi... (photo: US Army) *Mail Guardian* South Africa

Your history of folly in our region
During the Iraq war the western media showed, in a sentimental and at times theatrical fashion, the kindness of the occupying forces toward the civilian population. Child... (photo: US DoD file) *The Guardian*

France worried by situation in Iraq, urges citizens to leave
French Prime Minister Jean-Pierre Raffarin told parliament Tuesday that the government was "extremely worried" by the current situation in Iraq. French Prime Minister Jean-Pierre Raffarin told parli... (photo: CCI) *People's Daily*

Ashcroft barred terror briefings, ex-official says
WASHINGTON—The former acting director of the FBI testified Tuesday that Attorney General John D. Ashcroft rejected any further briefings on terrorist threats in the we... (photo: WN) *Pittsburgh Tribune Review*

IAEA chief renews Iraq inspections call
The head of the International Atomic Energy Agency (IAEA) has reiterated a call for arms inspectors to return to Iraq, saying he has asked the UN Security Council for a... (photo: IAEA file) Australian Broadcasting Corporation

Accessing Resources

What will be the next hot spot? What issues, countries, or people will be in the news next year?

How many of us turned to a map to find Kosovo when fighting broke out there? Or did some background reading about Afghanistan and Pakistan so we could answer student questions as the Taliban captured the media spotlight?

The reality is that the world is a very large and complicated place, and in our initial training for a degree in education none of us learns everything we will need to teach. The key to teaching current events is access to organizations, centers, and other data sources that can provide us with resources when we need them. If we want our students to develop global perspectives, we have to get beyond American sources. For no matter how good our local and national news sources are, they do not provide the perspectives and knowledge of 96% of the people on the planet.

In the resources listed below, we are relying heavily upon recommendations of the Title VI area studies centers, the federally-funded resource centers that have a mandate for outreach with K-12 schools and teachers. Websites are listed for centers that we have found to be very useful for their on-line resources, summer institutes, or workshops for teachers.

The site www.teachglobaled.net is the product of collaboration of Ohio State's Graduate Program in Social Studies and Global Education with OSU's five area studies centers and the Center for the Study of Global Change at Indiana University. All the websites listed below, plus about 5000 other resources related to world regions and global issues can be found there.

General Resources

BBC News, news.bbc.co.uk
> Links to all world regions.

Christian Science Monitor, www.csmonitor.com

Foreign Policy, www.foreignpolicy.com
> See sections on hot topics, breaking global news, regional media

Global Edge, globaledge.msu.edu/ibrd/GR_GlobalNews.asp
> Access to global news stories, plus regional sections.

Newspapers Online, www.newspapers.com
> Access to hundreds of online newspapers across the world

Newseum, www.newseum.org/todaysfrontpages
> Front pages of newspapers across the world

Newspapers on the World Wide Web, www.gt.kth.se/publishing/news.html

The New York Times, www.nytimes.com/pages/world/

The Washington Post, www.washingtonpost.com

World Radio Network, www.wrn.org/listeners/stations

U.S. Department of Education, www.ed.gov/programs/iegpsnrc/awards.html
> List of federally funded Ttile VI area studies centers by region.

Online media and centers by region

Africa

Africa Action, www.africaaction.org

Africa Online, www.africaonline.com/site/africa/index.jsp

Africa Point, www.africapoint.com/afrinews
    Sites by African regions

Africa-related Magazines & Newspapers on the Internet, www.isp.msu.edu/AfricanStudies/Afr_Ezines.htm

Africa World Press Guide, www.igc.org/worldviews/awpguide

Daily Mail and Guardian, South Africa, www.mg.co.za/mg

Kidon Media, www.kidon.com/media-link/africa.shtml
    Newspapers across Africa

The Nation (Kenya), www.nationaudio.com/News/DailyNation/Today/

Africa South of the Sahara, Stanford University, www-sul.stanford.edu/depts/ssrg/africa/guide.html

Boston University's African Studies Center's Outreach Program, www.bu.edu/africa/outreach/

University of Pennsylvania's African Studies Center, www.sas.upenn.edu/African_Studies/

Exploring Africa! Michigan State University, exploringafrica.matrix.msu.edu

H-AfrTeach LISTSERV for teachers interested in Africa, African history, h-net.msu.edu/~afrteach

Asia

Asia Observer, asiaobserver.com

Asia Educational Media Service, www.aems.uiuc.edu

Central Asia Caucasus Analyst, www.cacianalyst.org

China Daily, www.chinadaily.com.cn/en/home/

Finding News About China, chinanews.bfn.org

Herald Sun (Australia), www.heraldsun.news.com.au

The Korea Times, times.hankooki.com

Kyodo News (Japan), home.kyodo.co.jp

Japan Times, www.japantimes.co.jp

South China Morning Post (Hong Kong), www.scmp.com

Times of India, www.timesofindia.com

Voices from Asia, www.shaps.hawaii.edu/editorials.html
    Editorials and opinions from Asian Newspapers.

Ask Asia, www.askasia.org

Asia in The Schools, www.asiaintheschools.org/Resources/resources1.htm

Asian Governments on the WWW, www.gksoft.com/govt/en/asia.html

Asia Society, asiasociety.org

The National Consortium for Teaching about Asia, www.ucis.pitt.edu/asp/NCTA_PGH_SITE/ncta_pgh_site.html

Columbia University East Asian Institute, www.columbia.edu/cu/sipa/regional/EAI/

Cornell University East Asia Program, www.einaudi.cornell.edu/eastasia/

National Clearinghouse for U.S.-Japan Studies, www.indiana.edu/~japan/

Europe

BBC News: Europe, news.bbc.co.uk/hi/english/world/europe/

Budapest Sun, www.budapestsun.com

The CDI Russia Weekly, www.cdi.org/russia/

Czech Republic: Radio Prague, www.radio.cz/en/

The Guardian (England), www.guardianunlimited.co.uk/guardian/

Frankfurt Allgemeine (Germany), www.faz.com

Hungary: Radio Budapest, wwrn.org/ondemand/hungary.html

International Herald Tribune (England and France), www.iht.com

The Irish Post, www.irishpost.co.uk

Kiev Post (Ukraine), www.thepost.kiev.ua

Le Monde (France), www.lemonde.fr

The Moscow Times, www.moscowtimes.ru

Pravda (Russia), english.pravda.ru

The Prague Post (Czech Republic), www.praguepost.cz

The Times (England), www.thetimes.co.uk

Warsaw Voice (Poland), www.warsawvoice.pl

Access Russia, www.access-russia.com

The Harvard Center for European Studies, www.ces.fas.harvard.edu

Indiana University's Russian and East European Institute, www.indiana.edu/~reeiweb/

Ohio State University's Center for Slavic and East European Studies, www.osu.edu/csees

East European Studies Centers in the United States, www.osu.edu/csees/resources.htm

UCLA Center for European and Eurasian Studies, www.isop.ucla.edu/euro/

University of Michigan Center for Russian and East European Studies, www.umich.edu/~iinet/crees/

Latin America

Bogota Daily (Columbia), www.bogotadaily.com

Caribbean Media Corporation, www.cananews.com

Granma Internacional (Cuba), www.granma.cu

Information Services Latin America, www.igc.org/isla/

Inforpress CentroAmericana, www.inforpressca.com/CAR/

Latin American Press, www.latinamericapress.org

Lima Post (Peru), www.limapost.com

The News (Mexico), www.thenewsmexico.com

Zona Latina, www.zonalatina.com/Zlpapers.htm

RETANET, ladb.unm.edu/retanet
Resources for teaching about the Americas.

LANIC: Latin America Center at the University of Texas, lanic.utexas.edu
Also lanic.utexas.edu/subject/media/, list of newspapers and media.

Tulane University Stone Center for Latin American Studies, www.tulane.edu/~clas/

University of Michigan Latin American and Caribbean Studies, www.umich.edu/~iinet/lacs/resources/outreach.htm

The Middle East

Al Bawaba: The Middle East Gateway, www.albawaba.com

Al-Jazeera, www.cursor.org/aljazeera.htm

Arab World News, www.arabworldnews.com

Avaye Zan, www.tvs.se/womensvoice/
Iranian Cultural Women's Magazine.

The Iranian, www.iranian.com

Jerusalem Post (Israel), www.jpost.com

Middle East Insight, www.mideastinsight.org

Middle East Times (Egypt), www.metimes.com

Sahafa Online, www.sahafa.com
Across the Middle East.

Tehran Times (Iran), www.tehrantimes.com

Middle East Studies Center, Columbia University, www.columbia.edu/cu/lweb/indiv/mideast/

University of Texas at Austin, Middle Eastern Network Information Center (MENIC). menic.utexas.edu/menic.html

Middle East and West Asia Chronology, campus.northpark.edu/history/WebChron/MiddleEast/MiddleEast.html

Middle East Information Network, www.mideastinfo.com

Notes

1. See also David Hicks and E. Thomas Ewing, "Bringing the World into the Classroom with Online Global Newspapers," *Social Education* 67, no.3 (2003): 134-139. A number of issues of *Social Education* in 2001, 2002, and 2003 provide resources on teaching about Islam, the Middle East, and the problem of terrorism. See www.socialstudies.org/publications.
2. Merry M. Merryfield, "Responding to the Gulf War: A Case Study of Instructional Decision-Making," *Social Education* 57, no. 1 (1993): 33-41.
3. See Ibid, 36-39, for percentages and examples.

Index

About the Authors

Merry M. Merryfield is Professor of Social Studies and Global Education at The Ohio State University. She studies how educators teach about the world and develops online cross-cultural experiential learning for teachers. Since 1991, she has worked with six school districts in Central Ohio in a Professional Development School Network in Social Studies and Global Education.

Angene Wilson is Professor Emerita of Social Studies Education at the University of Kentucky. She continues to mentor first year social studies teachers and to teach the preparatory course for student teaching overseas and a History of Africa course. She is a member of the state international education task force, and also works with local schools in global education.